THE CELTS

T. G. E. Powell

THE CELTS

WITH 149 ILLUSTRATIONS
12 IN COLOUR

THAMES AND HUDSON

Ancient Peoples and Places

GENERAL EDITOR: GLYN DANIEL

First published in the UK in 1958 by
Thames and Hudson Ltd, London
New edition 1980

New edition published in the USA in 1980 by
Thames and Hudson Inc, New York
Library of Congress Catalog card number 79-63879

Printed in Great Britain by Butler & Tanner Ltd,
Frome and London

Color illustrations separated by Cliché Lux SA, La Chaux de Fonds, Switzerland, printed in Great Britain by CTD Printers Ltd, Twickenham

Contents

Foreword

This sketch of the Celts, the first great nation north of the Alps whose name we know, is not an orthodox presentation of all the facts and surmises that have been propounded about them. It is, rather, an attempt to describe, and discuss, some of the aspects of their life and ways that might be looked for in an account of a little-known people remote in distance rather than in time.

For the Celts, we have not only an abundance of archaeological remains, but the testimony of ancient historians, native traditional literature, and the results of modern philological research. Where these exist, each is integral to any true synthesis, but the inquiry always continues, and the present volume can, at most, contribute one step to a fuller knowledge, and a clearer view, of these fascinating forerunners of the historical nations of Western and Middle Europe.

The heritage of Celtic literature, surviving from ancient times in Ireland and Wales, is the oldest in Europe next after Greek and Latin. It holds up a mirror to the modes of that archaic rural life in temperate Europe in which all our roots lie. The Celts are, therefore, a very relevant factor in the appreciation of European origins, and the 'barbarian classics', in their ancient tongues, deserve a more general recognition than they have so far received.

Some words should be said about using this book. For the general reader, I have kept the chapters free of specialist references, whether to individuals or publications. For the student, I hope the notes at the end of each chapter, and the bibliography, will help to substantiate the text. I have, however, not hesitated to include terms, and names, in the original languages where these have seemed to clarify the issues, or to reveal points not widely known.

In writing this book, I have profited greatly from the work of others, and their names are enshrined in the bibliography. The quest for photographs was necessarily far-flung, and I have been anxious to avoid, where possible, the more commonly known, and oft-reproduced, subjects. In this search, my particular thanks are due to the following for their unstinted help: Mr R. J. C. Atkinson, Prof. H. G. Bandi, Prof. Gerhard Bersu, Prof. Carl Blümel, Mr Rainbird Clarke, Col. Mário Cardozo, Prof. Wolfgang Dehn, Mlle Gabrielle Fabre, Prof. Jan Filip, Mr R. W. Hutchinson, Dr Siegfried Junghans, Dr Josef Keller, Herr Karl Keller-Tarnuzzer, Dr C. M. Kraay, Prof. Juan Maluquer de Motes, Dr J. Menzel, Dr Fr. Morton, Prof. Richard Pittioni, Col. Afonso do Paço, Dr Máire de Paor, Dr Adolf Rieth, Mlle O. Taffanel, Miss Elaine Tankard, Prof. Julio Martinez Santa-Olalla, Dr J. K. St Joseph, Mr R. B. K. Stevenson, Dr Rafael von Uslar, Monsieur André Varagnac, Mlle Angèle Vidal-Hall.

Finally, to Dr Glyn Daniel, and the publishers, I am under a special debt for inviting me to contribute to the Ancient Peoples and Places series.

T. G. E. P. 1958

Preface

The publication in 1958 of T. G. E. Powell's book, *The Celts*, provided for the first time an informed and scholarly essay on these ancient Europeans which combined archaeological and literary evidence, and was also lucidly written and well illustrated. It received an enthusiastic welcome from scholars and the general public, and today, twenty years later, though much has happened in Celtic studies, no single book has superseded it, but with the author's death an edition revised by him is not now possible. It has therefore been decided to re-issue the 1958 text intact, adapted to the new format of the Ancient Peoples and Places series but with the complement of illustrations augmented. It is a tribute to the far-reaching scope and the soundness of the scholarship of the original book that this can be done, and a new presentation of an established classic offered to another generation of readers.

STUART PIGGOTT, 1978

Archaeological

Date	Events	Culture
900	Full development of Late Bronze Age economy, and adoption of cremation rite throughout the North Alpine Zone	OLDER URNFIELD CULTURE
800	Continued expansion of North Alpine culture-province Appearance of bronze horse-gear of eastern types	YOUNGER URNFIELD CULTURE
700	First urnfields in Catalonia	
	Iron swords, and waggon graves, in Bohemia and South Germany	EARLY HALLSTATT CULTURE
	General development of iron-using economy in West-Central Europe. Hallstatt	
600	Early Greek contact with tribes in South-west Germany, Rhône route from Massilia: Vilsingen and Kappel waggon graves, Rhodian oinochoi. Heuneburg mud-brick fortifications	Phase I LATE HALLSTATT CULTURE Phase II
	Continued Greek ceramic and metal imports to expanded 'Burgundian' area. Beginning of Etruscan trade. Vix princess's tomb	
500	Beginning of native La Tène art. Etruscan imports predominant Chariot graves on Middle Rhine: Rodenbach, Klein Aspergle; and later in Champagne: Somme Bionne, La Gorge Meillet Inhumation burial rite now general	EARLY LA TÈNE CULTURE
400	Expansion of La Tène culture-province. Increasing self-reliance of La Tène art. Reinheim princess's tomb	
	Waldalgesheim tomb, dated by Campagnian bucket	
300	Beginning of British Iron Age B, and of insular 'La Tène' art style	MIDDLE LA TÈNE CULTURE
	'Dying Gaul' and related monumental statuary at Pergamon	
200	Gaulish trophies on frieze of Temple of Athene at Pergamon Roquepertuse and Entremont sculpture not later than mid-century Votive deposits at La Tène in this century Spread of cremation graves west of the Rhine: Belgae/Germani Development of large fortified settlements, 'oppida', from Gaul to Bohemia First Belgic migrations to Britain	LATE LA TÈNE CULTURE
100	Sack of Wheathampstead 'oppidum' of Cassivellaunus Alesia: siege-works and weapons Gaulish trophies on the Arc d'Orange	
BC / AD	Sack of Maiden Castle, Dorset Llyn Cerrig Bach votive deposit, Anglesey	ROMAN PROVINCES

Historical	
	900
	800
	700
'Massiliote Periplus' infers Celtic-speaking peoples in Iberian Peninsula, and mentions reports of Ierne and Albion (late seventh or early sixth century)	600
Tartessos destroyed by the Carthaginians, and cessation of Greek trade beyond Pillars of Hercules (*c.* 530)	
Hecataeus (*c.* 500) reports the Celts behind Massilia, and at Nyrax (Noricum?)	500
Herodotus (*c.* 450) reports the Celts in the Far West, and at the source of the Danube	
Celtic tribes ('The Gauls') invade Northern Italy (*c.* 400), and sack Rome (*c.* 390)	400
Gaulish mercenaries in the army of Syracuse (368)	
The Voyage of Pytheas (*c.* 325–320): Britain and Ireland called the Pretannic Islands	
	300
Galatae sack Delphi (279), and cross to Asia Minor in the next year Gaulish mercenaries in Greek service in Egypt, and widely elsewhere (274)	
Attalos I of Pergamon defeats the Galatae of Asia Minor ('The Galatians') (before 230) Roman defeat of the Cis-Alpine Gauls, and the Gaesatae, at Telamon (225)	
	200
Roman supremacy throughout Cis-Alpine Gaul (192) Roman capture of Celtiberian stronghold of Numantia (133) Roman conquest of Provence (124) Cimbri attack Noricum (113) Cimbri and Teutones defeat Romans at Orange (105) Romans finally defeat Cimbri and Teutones (102–101)	
	100
Julius Caesar begins campaign in Gaul, and defeats Ariovistus (58) Caesar's two expeditions to Britain (55–54) Gaulish rebellion under Vercingetorix, and defeat at Alesia (52)	
	BC
	AD
Roman invasion of Britain under Claudius (43)	

Archæologia Britannica,

GIVING SOME ACCOUNT

Additional to what has been hitherto Publiſh'd,

OF THE

LANGUAGES, HISTORIES and CUSTOMS

Of the Original Inhabitants

OF

GREAT BRITAIN:

From Collections and Obſervations in Travels through *Wales, Cornwal, Bas-Bretagne, Ireland* and *Scotland.*

By EDWARD LHUYD M. A. of *Jeſus College,*
Keeper of the ASHMOLEAN MUSEUM in OXFORD.

VOL. I.

GLOSSOGRAPHY.

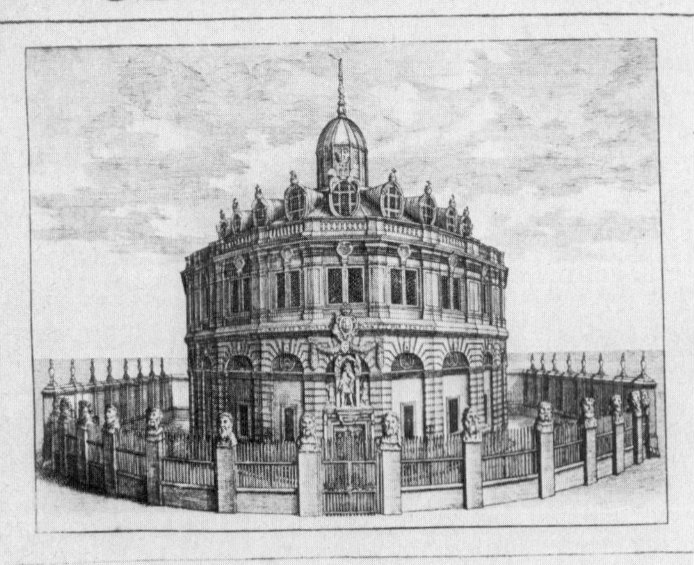

OXFORD,

Printed at the THEATER for the Author, MDCCVII.

And Sold by Mr. *Bateman* in *Pater-Noſter-Row, London*: and *Jeremiah Pepyat* Bookſeller at *Dublin.*

1
Finding the Celts

Sources and definitions

The oldest surviving references to the Celts are very brief and purely casual. Herodotus, writing in the mid-fifth century BC mentions them in connection with the whereabouts of the source of the Danube, and Hecataeus, who flourished somewhat earlier (*c.* 540–475 BC), but whose work is only known from later quotations, decribed the Greek colony of Massilia (Marseilles) as having been founded in the land of the Ligurians near the land of the Celts. Hecataeus elsewhere mentioned a Celtic town called Nyrax, and this place seems best to be identified with Noreia in the ancient region of Noricum, roughly equivalent to the modern province of Styria in Austria.

Herodotus was not primarily concerned with either the source of the Danube, or with the Celts, in his great surviving work, *The Histories*. It may be said that this was a great misfortune, for his account of peoples of whom he had first-hand knowledge, especially the Scythians, has been shown, with the aid of archaeology, to be of the highest value, and accuracy. What does seem to be important at this stage is that both he, and presumably Hecataeus, could already mention the Celts as a people not specially to be explained to Greeks.

Some further words should be said about these passing references of Herodotus to the Celts, although he explicitly states that his information on the far west of Europe was ill-founded. He states twice that the Danube rose in their territory, and that they themselves were the most westerly of the peoples of Europe except for the Cynetes who appear to have occupied Southern Portugal.

1 Title-page of Edward Lhuyd's *Archaeologia Britannica*, Vol. 1, published in 1707. Only the first volume of a projected larger work was completed by Lhuyd before his death in 1709, but it set Celtic philology on a sound footing for the first time in Europe.

In his first reference, Herodotus says that the source of the Danube was near Pyrene, a name to be connected with that of the Pyrenees, but which is known to have been a Greek trading station on the north-east Spanish coast. He comments further

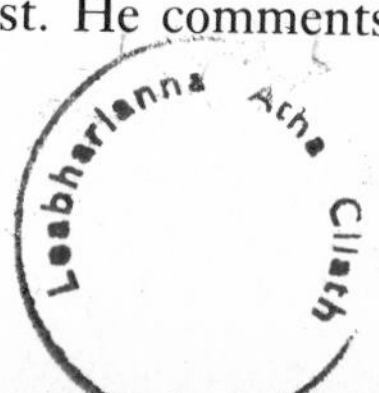

that the Celts lived beyond the Pillars of Hercules, the Straits of Gibraltar, but he can hardly have been so misled as to think that Pyrene also lay beyond them. Taken in all, the evidence Herodotus provides for Celts in the Iberian peninsula indicates that they were already widespread throughout it, and that they were recognizably the same people as inhabited the hinterland of Massilia, and very probably the region of Noricum.

It may be said here that the name *Celtici* survived in South-western Spain to Roman times, and that this appears to have been the only case where the name of this widespread people found any geographical memorial.

However misinformed Herodotus was about the location of the head waters of the Danube, his belief that it did rise in Celtic territory may not have rested only on its assumed association with Pyrene. He was much more fully informed about the Lower Danube. He knew that boats were able to penetrate far upstream, and that the river ran through inhabited land for its whole length. It seems quite likely that from this source would have come reports of Celts along the upper reaches of the river. It would not have been unreasonable to deduce that the two sources of information referred to the same location. The archaeological evidence indeed goes far to show that the region of the Upper Danube was the Celtic homeland from which some of these people had spread to Spain, as they did somewhat later into Italy and the Balkans.

Before the subsequent early historical references to the Celts are summarized, it may be worth considering why their name should appear to have been so widespread at this period. What was involved?

It seems safe to deduce that, at the time of Herodotus, the Greeks recognized the Celts to be a major barbarian people living west and north of the Western Mediterranean, and beyond the Alps. Ephorus, writing in the fourth century BC counted the Celts amongst the four great barbarian peoples of the known world – the other three were the Scythians, Persians and Libyans – and the geographer Eratosthenes, in the following century, showed them as widespread in Western and trans-Alpine Europe. Now it is clear that when Herodotus referred to other barbarian peoples, as the Scythians or Getae, he recognized them as distinctive nations or tribal confederations. He was interested in what he could learn of their political institutions, manners and customs. Languages, other than their own, were not esteemed by the Greeks, and linguistic distinctions between the barbarians would not therefore have come into his consideration. It seems reasonable to suppose that the Celts were distinguishable to Herodotus on descriptive grounds, even if he never saw any representatives, in the same way as other barbarian peoples might be identified. The term *Celts* is therefore justifiable in a proper ethnological sense, and should not necessarily be restricted to mean *Celtic-speaking* which is a concept of academic thought of quite modern times deriving from the pioneer linguistic studies of George Buchanan (1506–82), and of Edward Lhuyd (1660–1709). [1]

It is in fact clear that throughout the four centuries from Herodotus to Julius Caesar, the Celts were recognizable to their southern literate neighbours by their characteristic way of life, their political organization, and their appearance; factors which, though easily misinterpreted, have ever remained the expression of strangeness between one population group and another.

With regard to the actual name itself, the Greeks wrote it down as *Keltoi*, having received it orally from the native pronunciation. Except for the use of this name in a local tribal context in Spain, as already mentioned, it seems elsewhere to have been used in a comprehensive way to include tribes of different names, but this evidence is based on much later sources than Herodotus. The name Celt was never applied to the peoples of Britain and Ireland by ancient writers so far as is known, and there is no evidence that the natives ever used this name of themselves. This, of course, does not exclude some insular dwellers from having been Celts, but the case must rest on other kinds of evidence. In most of their modern popular applications, the words Celt and Celtic came into use as a result of the rise of the Romantic Movement from the mid-eighteenth century. These words were then borrowed from the linguistic use to which they had been put by Buchanan and Lhuyd, and of course they have been misapplied to such diverse matters as insular Christian art, physical anthropology, and all manner of things to do with 'Folk Life'.

The next point to be clarified is how it can be shown that the Celts of antiquity actually spoke tongues related to the surviving languages that in philological terminology are described as Celtic. This can be most readily demonstrated through the Classics in the names of chieftains and tribes, and particular words or terms recorded as belonging to the Celts. This body of linguistic material falls within the Celtic branch of the Indo-European language family, and in many cases the anciently recorded words can be shown to have survived into the medieval and modern languages of the Celtic group.

2 Part of the monumental inscription of the 'Achievements of the Divine Augustus' set up by the Emperor in AD 14 on the temple of Rome and Augustus at Ancyra (modern Ankara) in Asia Minor. It records the names of two British Celtic rulers who came to him as suppliants, Dumnovellaunus and Tincommius. The names can be completed from other copies of the same text elsewhere, and a coin of the first is shown in Ill. 3.

There are three other primary sources on the language of the ancient Celts. In the first place there is the existence of a large 100, 103 number of inscriptions incorporating Celtic words and names, but mainly written in Latin, or more rarely in Greek. These were inscribed on altars and other monuments in the Celtic regions incorporated within the Roman Empire, and they have been found from as far apart as Hadrian's Wall and Asia Minor, Por- 77, 97 tugal and Hungary. The second source is akin. It is numismatic, but much more restricted in space. It is particularly valuable on account of coins inscribed with names, linguistically Celtic, that can be shown on archaeological and historical grounds to have been issued by Celtic kings or tribes. The third line of evidence has to do with place-names. These are as often river or other topographical names as those of actual settlements or strongholds. A direct link can be established in many cases through the Classics in reference to the Celts, but the distributional evidence of Celtic place-names in Western and Central Europe conforms closely with the regions in which the Celts are known to have been strongest, and in which their influence lasted longest. There is a great deal of interpenetration of Celtic, Teutonic, Slavonic and other place-names, and borrowing one from the other, but this is a highly specialized philological matter, and a reliable

3 Gold coin (stater) of Dubnovellaunus (the preferred reading), a Belgic ruler of South East Britain, who preceded Cunobelinus at Camulodunum and later ruled in Kent. About twice actual size.

map of Celtic place-names in Europe has yet to be produced. All that will be ventured here is to say that apart from the British Isles, Celtic place-names have survived widely in France, Spain and Northern Italy, and more sparsely between the Danube and the Alps eastwards to Belgrade. In North-west Germany they are common to the Rhine, and extend to the Weser, perhaps even to the Elbe. It will be understood of course that place-name distribution as it survives can only give a partial picture of the original distribution, and that many factors may have contributed either to survival or to the complete oblivion of this kind of evidence.

In introducing the term *Celtic* to the study of languages, Buchanan was the first to show by means of the Classical sources that the surviving Gaelic and Welsh languages were descendants of the speech of the ancient Celts. The philological term is therefore itself based on the ethnological appreciation made by Herodotus, and followed by subsequent historians and geographers.

The far-ranging geographical factor that has emerged in all the aspects so far mentioned, makes it opportune to introduce the archaeological approach to the reality of the Celts.

Strictly speaking, archaeology is the study of the material remains of human activity in the past. It may be directed to the material culture of fully historical peoples or periods, or to periods and regions beyond the range of literate civilizations. In the latter case it is a dumb science in the sense that of itself it cannot evoke language, or elucidate the particular human contingencies reflected in the changes and chances of the anonymous material culture it reveals. The aim of modern archaeological research is to recover to the greatest possible degree, and to interpret, the life of ancient communities rather than to achieve mere classification of objects and monuments; but sometimes excessive claims are made for the feats of archaeology which of its nature it cannot fulfil. It follows, then, that in regard to the Celts, as they emerge from the kinds of evidence so far discussed, an archaeological identity must first be shown to exist for the centuries between Herodotus and Julius Caesar who stand here as the upper and lower fixed points in the historical framework. Archaeology does in fact show a great material culture province for these centuries extending over the whole area already indicated. These vestiges of barbaric civilization are firmly tied in with known Celtic tribes as in Northern Italy from the fourth century BC, in Southern France from the second, and elsewhere within the extending Roman Empire, from the first century BC.

The Celts in ancient history

The premises and source material on which an account of the Celts may be based have now been outlined, and the Classical historians must be followed again in order to make a very brief summary of the intrusion of the Celts on the literate world of the Mediterranean. Here only a chronological sketch will be attempted, as information on the Celts themselves from this source will be considered in the following chapters.

About a quarter of a century after the death of Herodotus, Northern Italy was invaded by barbarians coming through the Alpine passes. These invaders were Celts as is shown by their names and description, but the Romans called them *Galli* whence derived *Gallia Cis-* and *Trans-Alpina*. Polybius writing more than two centuries later refers to the invaders as *Galatae*, and this word was widely used by Greek writers. On the other hand, it was recognized by Diodorus Siculus, Caesar, Strabo, and Pausanias, that *Galli* and *Galatae* were equivalent names for *Keltoi/Celtae*, and Caesar makes it clear that the *Galli* of his time knew themselves by the name *Celtae*. Diodorus used these names indiscriminately, but considered that *Keltoi* was the more correct word, and Strabo says that this word was known to the Greeks because of these people living behind Massilia. Pausanias, too, gives prior antiquity to Celts rather than to Galatians or Gauls. It would probably be impossible to unravel the story of this ambiguity in names, but for the present purposes it is safe to conclude that the Celts long continued to regard themselves by this name however much other names within their nation may have come to the fore from the fifth century.

Gauls

The *Galli*, or Gauls, as is the better-known English version, settled in Italy first in the upper valley of the Po, and its tributaries. They proceeded to overthrow and overrun the Etruscans, whose civilization was already decaying, and there can be little doubt that it was signs of Etruscan weakness that brought visions of rich plunder and good lands for colonization to these trans-Alpine dwellers. That they knew of the Etruscans and had traded with them over a long period is well demonstrated in archaeology.

The later Roman historians thought that these Celtic invaders had come from the north-west, from *Gallia Transalpina* as known from the second century BC. The archaeological evidence is that the invaders had come by way of the central Alpine passes, and that their home had lain in Switzerland and Southern Germany. The names of the principal invading tribes are recorded. The Insubres are reported as the first arrivals, and they eventually established their centre at a place they called Mediolanum, the forerunner of Milan.

The Insubres were followed by at least four other tribes who settled in Lombardy. Later comers were the Boii and Lingones who had to pass through this region to find room in Emilia, and the latest migrants, the Senones, settled in less rich land along the Adriatic coast in Umbria. Not only did the Celtic invaders move as would-be settlers with their families and possessions, but fast-moving warrior bands raided far to the south. Apulia and even Sicily were reached, and Rome was a prime target from its successful sacking about 390 BC to the decisive battle of Telamon in 225 BC when a vast Gaulish army, including warriors newly brought in from beyond the Alps, was caught between two Roman forces and defeated. The end of Cisalpine Gaulish independence came only in 192 BC when the Romans defeated the Boii at their stronghold; a place that was to become the modern Bologna.

To the east, the Celts come within historical notice first in 369–368 BC, when bands of them were serving as mercenaries in the Peloponnese. This fact assumes a considerable penetration of Celtic migration into the Balkans before this date. In 335 BC, when Alexander the Great was campaigning in Bulgaria, he received deputations from all the peoples living near the Lower Danube, and amongst these was an embassy from Celts who were described as of the Adriatic. Some two generations later a horde of *Galatae* descended upon Macedonia in mid-winter. Some special misfortune must have driven them to move at this season, especially as they were accompanied by their families and waggons. They proceeded to loot, and seek places to settle. The ensuing campaign is well reported in Greek history, and the invaders were subjected to continuous guerrilla warfare. The names Bolgios and Brennus are recorded as leaders of this Celtic migration, but it is not improbable that these were the names of tribal gods rather than those of mortal chieftains. The people, allegedly under Brennus, attacked Delphi, and in so doing brought about their own destruction. The Greeks, with an eye for national differences, matched the Persian shields already hanging as trophies in the temple of Apollo at Delphi with a set of Celtic ones. Surely the earliest display in comparative ethnology.

88

Galatians

The Celts were sufficiently potent to remain in the Balkans for some time longer, but the most curious adventure in Celtic migration, recorded historically, was that undertaken by two tribes who had parted from those who had invaded Macedonia. These moved south-east to the Dardanelles, and by enlisting in local disputes, got themselves transported into Asia Minor where again great vistas were opened up for plunder and settlement. They were joined by a third tribe, the Tectosages, who had apparently won their way out of Greece after the defeat at Delphi. These three tribes enjoyed a period of almost unchecked banditry, but were finally restrained, and settled in Northern Phrygia; henceforward to be known as Galatia. These tribes possessed a common sanctuary, recorded in its Celtic name *Drunemeton*, and the Tectosages inhabited the district of modern Ankara. The Galatians, as they may now be called, retained their individuality for many centuries. Cut off from their European origins, they remained in isolation, eventually to lend their name to Christian communities, the recipients of St Paul's Epistle. Later still, the Galatians are the subject of a most interesting note by St Jerome, who, writing in the fourth century AD, reported that, in addition to speaking Greek, they had a language of their own which was akin to that of the Treveri. Now St Jerome, who had travelled in Roman Gaul, must have been acquainted with the Treveri who were a tribe settled in the district of Trier, on the Moselle. It is possible that St Jerome would have heard a purer form of Celtic amongst the Treveri than in more Latinized territory farther west into Gaul. It is difficult otherwise to account for his mentioning this particular tribe in what must be considered a scholarly comparison. A comparable survival may be instanced in the Gothic language that was spoken in the Crimea. It was implanted in the third century AD, cut off by the Slavs about a hundred years later, but did not die out completely before some of it was recorded in the seventeenth century.

121

So far the emphasis has been laid on the earliest historical documentation for the appearance of the Celts, and it has been said that by the early third century BC they were already extended in an arc from Spain to Asia Minor with a necessary, but implied, source in the European wilderness north of the Alps, a region normally beyond the range of travel to civilized Mediterraneans. The historical sources for the second and first centuries BC only extend the geographical disposition of the Celts in the sense that it became realized that the whole of Gaul (France) was occupied by them, and that by then they were a people at least partly in retreat from across the Rhine. In the first century BC Gaul, which now remained the sole continental Celtic stage, became incorporated within the Roman Empire, and thus passed into the full light of history.

Belgae

Caesar's description of native Gaul, ethnographically divisible between the Aquitani in the south-west, the Belgae in the north-east, and the Celtae elsewhere, must be considered in the light of archaeology, but here immediate interest rests on the Belgae who were his most warlike and stubborn opponents. These people inhabited the north-eastern parts of Gaul, and according to Caesar, proclaimed their pride in an untamed Germanic origin. This would seem in fact to mean no more than that they had trans-Rhenine origins for they spoke a Celtic language very similar to that spoken by the other Celts of Gaul, and their chieftains had Celtic names. The question of the early value of the name *German* is important in the present study, but for the time being it must be left aside in order to follow the historical link, provided by Caesar, that brings Britain within the Celtic world. Caesar reported that before his own time, Belgic settlements had been made in South-eastern Britain. This is the first and only record from historical sources of Celtic, or part Celtic, migration to Britain. There is a mass of other evidence to show that there had been earlier Celtic settlements, but it is as well to be clear on the exact nature of the sources. What then is the value for the present purpose, of the early references in Classical literature to Britain and Ireland?

Britain and Ireland

In the sixth century BC, and almost certainly well before the year 530, a voyage was undertaken from Massilia down the east Spanish coast, through the Pillars of Hercules, and along the Atlantic seaboard to the city of Tartessos. This was not likely to have been the first of such voyages from Massilia, but on the ship's return someone wrote an account of it giving information not only on the Spanish coasts, but on lands far to the north along the Atlantic seaways of Europe. The account of this voyage is known as the Massiliote Periplus, and it survives in fragments only, quoted in the poem *Ora Maritima* by Rufus Festus Avienus who

4

flourished in the fourth century AD. The internal evidence of the Periplus shows that it was composed before the overthrow of Tartessos by the Carthaginians, and the consequent closing of the Atlantic sea trade to the Greek colonial world.

Tartessos, which probably lay near the mouth of the Guadalquivir, had been in friendly trade relations with the Greeks since the chance voyage, beyond the Pillars of Hercules, of Colaeus of Samos about 638 BC. The Massiliote Periplus reported that the Tartessians traded as far north as the Oestrymnides, which are taken to be the islands and peninsula of Brittany. Furthermore, the Tartessians said the Oestrymnians traded with the inhabitants of two large islands, *Iernē* and *Albion*. This is the earliest reference to Ireland and Britain, and the words are Greek forms of names which survived amongst the natives speaking the Irish branch of Celtic. The Old Irish *Ériu*, and modern *Éire*, are derived from an earlier form which gave *Iernē* in Greek, and the name *Albu* was used by the Irish for Britain down to the tenth century AD. It is another matter as to whether these two names should be considered as of genuine Celtic origin, or whether they are Celtic adaptions from an older language. On the whole it seems that a case can be made out for their being Celtic, but the nature of the evidence is too slight to press an absolute decision.

Avienus, however late a source in himself, preserved a very valuable record in the Massiliote Periplus, but the names Iernē and Albion had anyway come to the general knowledge of Greek geographers, such as Eratosthenes, by the middle of the third century BC. It should perhaps be said here that although Avienus refers to the Carthaginian Himilco, an explorer of the sixth century BC, the latter does not appear to have visited the British Isles as has sometimes been alleged.

The voyage of Pytheas of Massilia, about 325–323 BC, is the next most ancient source for Ireland and Britain, but here they are referred to collectively as the *Pretanic* islands. Pytheas is again an author only known at second hand, but he is quoted, usually with disbelief, by a number of writers including Polybius, Strabo and Avienus. The name of the inhabitants would have been *Pritani* or *Priteni*, and these probably are genuine Celtic names. They survived in the native tongue to give the word *Prydain*, in Welsh, for what is now understood as Britain, and this latter name comes apparently from a Latin mispronunciation which gave rise to *Britannia*, and *Britanni*, as used by Caesar. There is no doubt from all this, and from the description given by Pytheas of his navigation, that the Pretanic islands were Iernē

4 Map showing Massilia and the sea-ways to the west and north.

and Albion. One of the later Greek geographers in fact states this to be the case.

It is very interesting that Pytheas should appear not to have used the two older names of Iernē and Albion when mentioning the Pretanic islands. It may possibly mean that the people of Massilia, who had overland trade routes with the north-west, already knew this name so that it required no explanation. But, in view of the fact that Pytheas seems only to have visited Britain, and not Ireland, it may mean that he was led to assume a general similarity between the inhabitants of the two islands. It may be said now that while an equivalent for the name *Preteni* exists in Irish literature it designates certain inhabitants of Britain, and, secondarily, settlers therefrom in Ireland. It would be tempting, of course, to suppose that the introduction of the name Pretanic to Greek usage by the fourth century BC indicated a new and predominant population in Britain (Albion); one that had not yet come about in the days of the Massiliote Periplus.

These points may perhaps prepare the way for other problems, especially connected with the Celtic languages, which must at least be stated once the archaeological evidence has been summarized.

The European prehistoric background

Herodotus and Caesar have been used as the historical landmarks in this chapter on finding the Celts; Herodotus, not only on account of his antiquity but for his stature as the father of history and anthropology; Caesar, because his campaigns brought to an end the independence of the self-named Celts. There is, of course, much useful information on the Celts, and on the British Isles, in Classical authors after Caesar, but they do not contribute greatly to setting the stage. The next task is to review the problem in archaeology.

Most archaeologists if asked what appeared to be the cultural setting for the historically known Celts, from Herodotus to Caesar, would have little difficulty in answering, especially if trained in the Continental schools, that the widespread iron-using material cultures, known by the names of Hallstatt and La Tène, substantiated, geographically and chronologically, the historical records. It would be possible to proceed immediately to give particulars in support of this statement, but it seems preferable, even at the great risk of over-simplification, to seek a more remote archaeological starting-point, and to proceed independently into the centuries and regions that are illuminated by history.

26, 74

The gradual improvement of climatic conditions at the end of the Quaternary Ice Age successively opened up new regions for human habitation from south to north across trans-Alpine Europe. By the ninth millennium BC, even that northern zone which stretched from the Pennines eastward to Denmark and the Baltic lands, had been penetrated by primitive hunters and fishers. Climatological trends in due course brought into existence the natural zone of temperate Europe, and, for millennia, the human population within it remained one of small food-seeking communities ranging widely in their particular ecological territories. In physical types, these folk would have been no less mixed than were the Upper Palaeolithic stocks from whom they were descended. Any infusion of new blood brought by possible intruders from the Eurasiatic steppes on the one hand, or from Spain, or even North-west Africa on the other, would already have removed the chance of the existence of pure races in Europe. Throughout the whole zone of temperate Europe, interchange and fusion, reflected in surviving material culture, occurred from time to time and area to area. These people may be regarded as the oldest population of the zone, and they formed a principal source from which all subsequent population groups were to a greater or lesser extent derived.

Neolithic immigrants

These Mesolithic people were probably not disturbed until the fourth millennium BC when primitive cultivators and stock raisers had begun to spread northwards from the periphery of the urban civilizations of the 'Most Ancient East'. In temperate Europe, the earliest and most important Neolithic immigrants entered from the south-east, and took possession of the rich and easily worked loess lands of the Middle Danube basin, spreading thence to the Rhine and its principal tributaries, to the confluence area of the Saale and the Elbe, and to the head waters of the Oder.

Somewhat later, Neolithic economy, brought, again in the first instance, by immigrants, spread from the Western Mediterranean along the Atlantic coasts of Europe to the British Isles, although the earliest Neolithic settlers in Britain seem to have come from a route that had struck north from the Gulf of Lions through Eastern France.

These relatively sedentary economies, with their greater paraphernalia and resources for survival, almost everywhere made a significant impact on the older Mesolithic populations. Barter seems first to have stimulated the economy and material culture of the indigenous people, but in due time, fusion in material culture seems to indicate some welding of population and consequent adjustments in economy. When, as a result of either the Danubian or Western Neolithic heritages, the whole of temperate Europe had come within the scope of primitive shifting, and highly wasteful, farming practice, the Mesolithic way of life continued only around the northern and eastern margins of the zone. By the beginning of the second millennium BC, a continuum of inter-related material cultures can be distinguished spread across Europe and showing great variety in origins, capabilities, and in degree of communication with the increasingly civilized world of the Eastern Mediterranean.

Emergence of pastoralists

At about this same date, it is possible to distinguish two divergent trends in the Neolithic economies of temperate Europe. In the riverine areas, cereal cultivation would appear to have continued, though perhaps on a somewhat diminished scale, but in upland country, and over the North European plain, pastoralism, not necessarily nomadic, was the predominant way of life. By analogy with examples in historical times, whether in Europe or elsewhere, it is reasonable to assume that such divergences in occupation and habitat imply different social groupings or political units. It is in fact not unreasonable to speak of the emergence of pastoralist and agricultural tribes, whether or not individual tribal units can always be distinguished through the media of distinctive material culture.

Early use of metals

The first half of the second millennium BC is also important for the introduction of the metal trade into Europe, and the eventual establishment of metallurgy amongst the natives. It is not altogether clear whether this came about only through trade and the diffusion of techniques, or whether immigration from Asia Minor was not also a significant factor.

The earliest copper and bronze objects, mainly ornaments and weapons, are found in Greece and the Eastern Balkans with extensions to the Middle Danube and Transylvania. These things have in the main Anatolian prototypes, but at least, in Greece and Macedonia, if not farther north, Anatolian pottery styles suggest that immigrant families, not just itinerant tradesmen, were concerned.

Matters of considerable importance for the present study arise at this stage. To begin with, it is possible, but certainly not proven, that Anatolian settlers may have brought with them an Indo-European language. This question rests largely on the further clarification of Anatolian archaeology, and the distribution and chronology of written documents. Whatever the language of the early metal workers in the Balkans, their influence was great in Central Europe, and one of the most distinctive objects that they traded or carried northward was the copper or bronze shaft-hole axe.

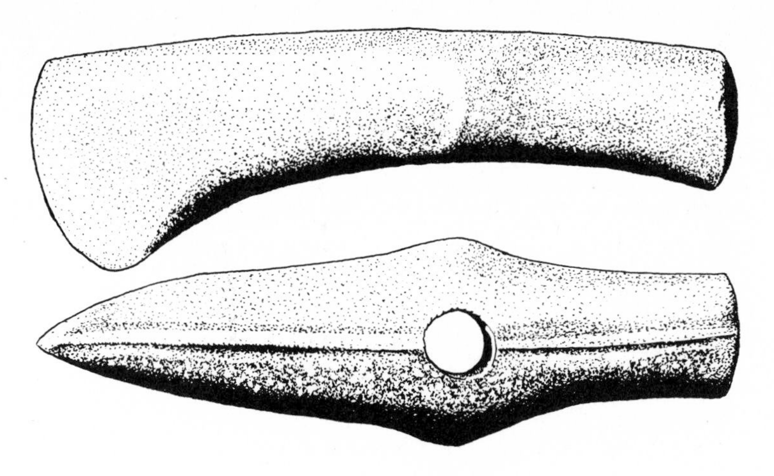

5 Stone battle-axe from Jutland copying metal prototype. Length 17.8 cm.

The Neolithic pastoralist tribes in Central and Northern Europe had already developed, from Mesolithic antler prototypes, perforated stone axes, but now a new fashion spread for which there were metal exemplars. These, like the older forms, were perforated for mounting on a wooden shaft or handle. The main regional cultures came each to possess a characteristic type, but these are not exclusive to one or two primary forms which show most clearly their derivation from metal originals. The pastoralists had, in fact, produced for themselves stone replicas in substitution for the more exotic metal axes that were too rare, and, doubtless, too expensive, to be obtained in quantity.

There was, however, another route by which knowledge of the metal shaft-hole axe may have come to European Neolithic pastoralists. This was across the Pontic steppes from the Caucasus.

From the area north of these mountains, north-westwards to the Lower Dnieper, there also ranged pastoral peoples. The comparative wealth, and grandiose pretensions, of those living around the Kuban and Terek rivers are reflected in the tombs of their chieftains. These people, in juxtaposition to the important metallurgical resources of the Caucasus, and the trading activities of the city states of Asia Minor and Upper Mesopotamia, may be said to have set the fashion for the pastoralists lying farther north and west over the grasslands.

The question of Indo-European speech arises here again with regard to the Pontic tribes; for if, as some consider, the rulers of the Hittites sprang from this kind of society, geographical contiguity might presuppose for their origin the Kuban-Terek area. Perhaps, however, Northern Anatolia had always been within the homeland zone of Indo-Europeans.

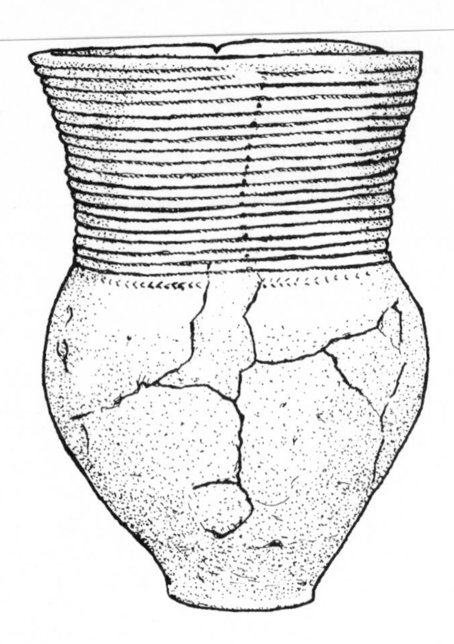

6 Corded Ware pottery vessel from Jutland, height 20 cm.

'Battle-axe' complex

In addition to the factor of metal, or stone-substitute battle-axes, the Pontic and European pastoralists held in common certain other archaeologically discernible traits. These are, in fact, probably of greater ethnological significance than an easily carried weapon however distinctive. Single-grave inhumation, often under a round tumulus, or barrow, was the principal burial rite, and, in pottery, some shapes and types of decoration, are very widespread. While all these people herded cattle and swine, there is no doubt that in some regions cultivation of cereal crops was undertaken if only on a very small scale. Perhaps the greatest interest attaches to the question as to whether these people kept horses, and in what way these animals were used. This matter again has its linguistic aspect for the documentary evidence of the mid-second millennium, in Hittite and related sources, indicates a prime relationship between horse-raising and Indo-European terminology, even with personal names that contain a 'horse' element.

Horses

Horse bones, together with those of cattle and pig, are not uncommon in graves throughout the culture-zone under discussion, but even the domestic horse might have been kept first for food and milk. On the other hand, the tarpan, the small Eurasiatic

7 Wild horses (*Equus przewalskii*) in Whipsnade Zoo. Still probably extant in Outer Mongolia, this horse is ancestral to all domesticated breeds of *Equus caballus*, and a related type, the Tarpan, existed in South Russia where it was domesticated before 3000 BC. They are small beasts, about 140 cm at the withers.

8 Engraved silver bowl from a princely grave of the middle third millennium BC at Maikop in South Russia, showing a wild horse among other animals.

9 Block-wheeled vehicle of *c.* 1500 BC from Lchashen, on Lake Sevan, Armenia SSR. This ox-drawn waggon is typical of those used from the Caucasus to central and western Europe by 2000 BC.

horse in question, is not likely to have been herded indiscriminately with cattle as a food beast, and on practical grounds it seems likely that its great value as a burden carrier must have been appreciated at a very early date. The use of the horse by pastoralists, in the third and second millennia BC, should not presuppose greater speed of movement than was conditioned by their other animals. The tarpan was probably most useful as a 'pack-pony', and riding, rather than mere sitting, was a later development due largely to selective breeding and better feeding. It seems now certain that block-wheel vehicles were coming into use in the Middle Danubian region in the early second millennium BC, but they are more likely to have been drawn by oxen than by horses.

Indo-Europeans

This complex of factors in widespread traits of material culture, in the significance of the horse, and in linguistic inferences, has been made much of in the past to create the idea of Indo-European warrior peoples irrupting, in the early second millennium BC, from Northern Europe, or, alternatively, from the Eurasiatic steppes, to dominate most of the rest of Europe, and regions even farther afield in the Near and Central East. The exclusive northern origin, or even the existence of such an expansive migration, cannot now be seriously maintained, while a total eastern origin seeks an ever more elusive homeland.

In the present writer's view the archaeological gradations discernible across the territory between the Black Sea and the Baltic reflect, for the most part, the development of common ideas and requirements amongst population groups already interrelated by virtue of their essential identity in environment and pursuits. This would have come about without any significant quantitative migration in one direction or another, but, during the early part of the second millennium BC, new stimuli in material culture, and in the use of the horse, spread from the south-east at the hands both of pastoralists and prospector craftsmen living on the periphery of the civilizations of Asia Minor. While there seem to be indications that Indo-European languages were already spoken by this date in parts of Anatolia, no more can be said for Europe than that all the grassland dwellers within the continuum may be expected to have belonged to an embracive language group.

It is only in such a general sense that, on available knowledge, the 'battle-axe' pastoralists may be claimed as Indo-European, but notice should be taken of another distinctive group more or less contemporary in the archaeological record. These are the Beaker people, so called from their fine, reddish, and very distinctive, pottery vessels designated by the older antiquaries as drinking beakers.

'Beaker' complex

In general the Beaker people also appear to have been pastoralists. Their principal weapon was the bow, with arrows mounting barbed flint heads. Sheep probably formed their main stock, and they ranged widely in Western Europe, but interpenetrated in a deep zone, roughly from Bohemia to Britain, with the Battle-Axe pastoralists. The Beaker pottery seems most probably to have developed from an Early Neolithic ceramic tradition in the Western Mediterranean region, and the 'Beaker Culture' may perhaps best be explained as a western example of that movement

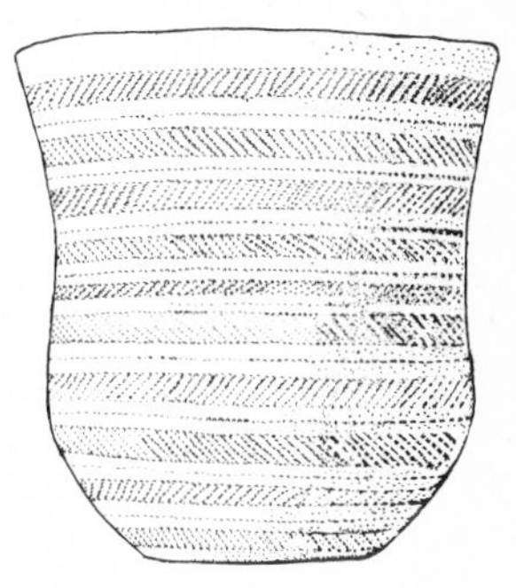

10 Pottery vessel of Bell Beaker type, decorated with comb-stamped zones, from Lérida, Spain. Height 13 cm.

towards predominantly pastoralist economy that has already been explained as a tendency widespread in Neolithic Europe.

Although of different stocks, the one Eurasiatic, the other Mediterranean, if not perhaps in some small part North African, the Battle-Axe and Archer pastoralists, respectively, can be envisaged as complementary phenomena. It is not necessary here to follow the ramifications of Beaker appearance in Spanish and French caves, or in the collective tombs of Western Neolithic agriculturalists from Portugal to Scotland. The Beaker people seem to have had an aptitude for penetrating other societies, if indeed they did not come as overlords. In isolation, they are found as practising single-grave burial, but not originally with covering barrows, and occasional metal weapons and ornaments show that they were sometimes in barter relations with copper- or bronze-working communities.

The real importance of the Beaker people for subsequent times lies in their relations with the other, Eurasiatic or Battle-Axe, group of pastoralists for, in the common zone running across Central Europe, and even in Britain, there were born various hybrid cultures from these two stems. The Battle-Axe element in these hybrids always seems to have predominated in the end. In Britain, the assumption that the Beaker people were of Indo-European stock was sometimes the basis of linguistic suppositions, whereas it is now seen that the creators of the mixed Beaker-Battle-Axe cultures may well have derived their speech from their eastern rather than their western, parent.

Fusion and continuity in the Bronze Age

Whatever views may be held about the linguistic affinities of the pastoralists, eastern or western, the developing scene in the early and middle phases of the Bronze Age in temperate Europe shows the continuation of important groups, still mainly pastoralist, who were increasingly equipped with bronze weapons, but who maintained their old environment, and tradition of single-grave barrow burial for chieftains. The warrior lord was now often adorned with gold-mounted ornaments and weapons. The battle-axe became rare and was a symbol rather than a weapon. Of these later and more clearly aristocratic societies, three may be particularly mentioned as examples: the South German Tumulus Culture, the Danish Bronze Age in its Second Period, the Wessex Culture of Southern Britain. Their optimum period may probably be placed in the fifteenth century BC.

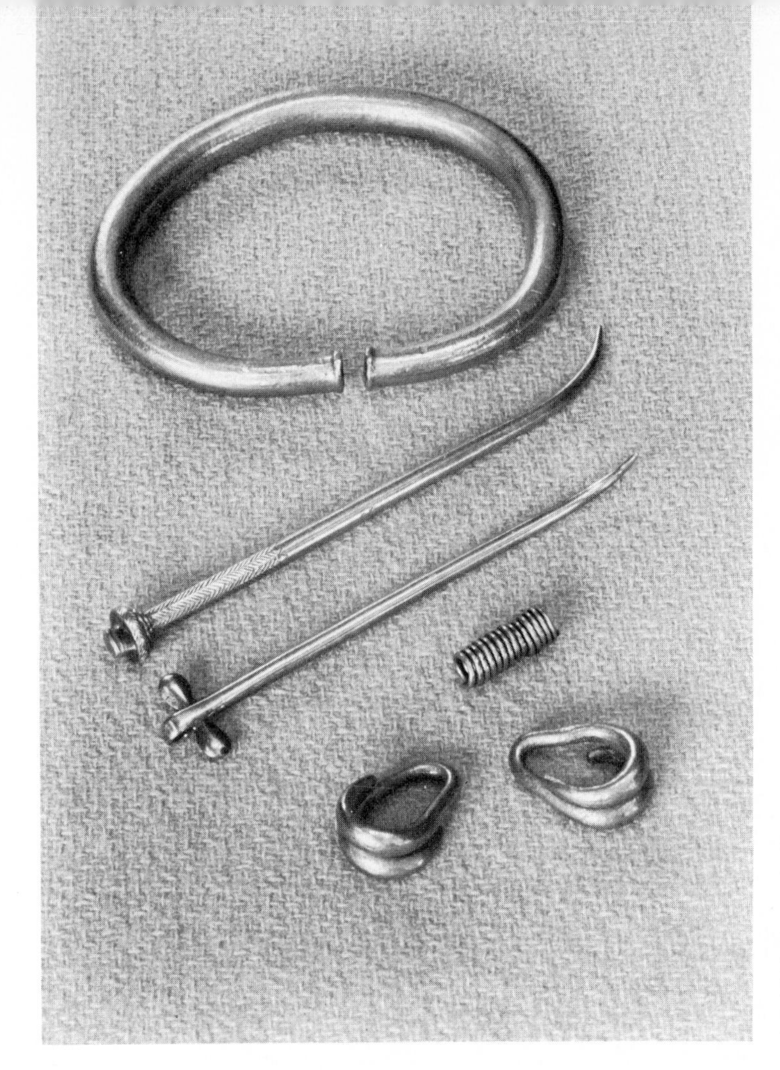

11 Gold armlet, pins, ear-rings and a bead from a chieftain's grave at Helmsdorf in the Saale valley, representative of the rich tombs of the north-west European Early Bronze Age. Armlet diameter 7.5 cm, the rest in proportion.

It will not have been forgotten meanwhile that there existed a medley of other population groups, some more predominantly agricultural, and some forming remnants of older stocks and even more primitive ways of life. In Central Europe especially, the riverine communities may well have formed an element in the over-all economy of the more dominant pastoralists, providing through vassalage, or as the object of plunder, commodities and services that were otherwise unobtainable.

The north alpine culture province

The increasing dryness of the climate in temperate Europe during the second millennium BC, which, earlier, may have been one reason for the decline in cereal cultivation, seems eventually to have reduced further the agricultural settlement. The evidence in surviving material culture and burial ritual indicates a general absorption of populations within the pastoralist tradition, and before the end of the thirteenth century BC, in that region north of the Alps, from Bohemia to the Rhine, crucial for the origin of the Celts, the stage became set for a final series of interrelated events within prehistory.

These events are discernible first in the appearance of a radically changed material culture complex, and associated burial rite, in the broad riverine lands of the Upper Danube, centred especially in Austria and Bavaria, with an important related group in South-western Bohemia. The bearers of this culture were settled farming people so that their distribution is largely different from that of the older established pastoralists. The climate can indeed hardly have become so arid that the older cultivators had abandoned the river plains for this reason only, but the newcomers certainly brought a higher standard of farming practice.

In the period following their initial appearance, these people lived in rectangular wooden houses in village or large homestead groups, usually defended by earthworks or palisades. To them can be attributed the beginnings of true sedentary mixed farming in Europe, and – at the time almost as important – the great development of the bronze industry with new working and casting techniques, new forms of weapons and tools, and the application of metal to a much wider range of uses than hitherto. The dead were generally cremated, and the broken bones placed in an urn for burial in a flat cemetery. Many of these cemeteries assumed large proportions and have been called urnfields so that the descriptive labels 'Urnfield Period' and 'Urnfield Culture' have come into use.

This rural barbaric civilization spread widely on suitable land in and around the Upper Danube. It took firm root around the Swiss lakes, in the Upper and Middle Rhine valleys, and eventually spread, as will be recounted, even farther west and north. The expansion was slow, evidently a genuine land-winning as need arose, but, in advance, went trade with the older populations; the final result was amalgamation of the old and the new cultures, the latter greatly predominating, but the former, from area to area, contributing distinctive features. It is this total population of the so-called 'North Alpine Urnfield Province', centred in Southern Germany and Switzerland, that demands special scrutiny in relation to the coming into existence of the Celts.

13

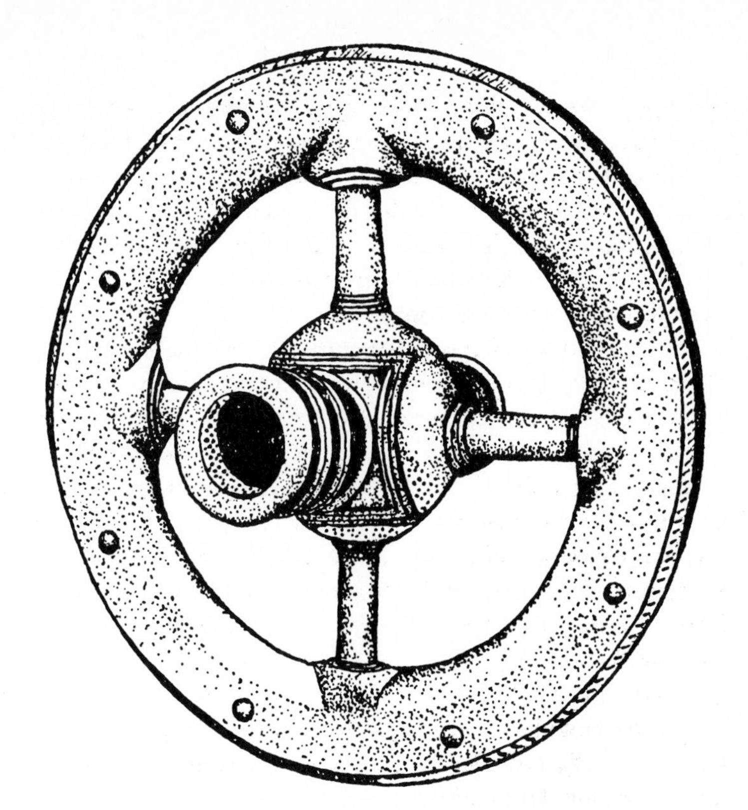

12 Reconstruction of cast-bronze wheel (Younger Urnfield Culture). Cortaillod, Switzerland. Diameter 50 cm.

The background of the older inhabitants who provided the indigenous element in the province has been sketched. It is now important to try to ascertain some of the facts and problems connected with the background of the new impulses, for large-scale invasion scarcely provides a complete explanation.

Antecedents of the 'urnfield' complex

For this purpose the south-eastern zone of Europe must again be considered. The Anatolian connections that had established copper- and bronze-working early in the second millennium BC continued to be active along the main lines of passage through the Balkans and across the Middle Danube to the auriferous tributaries of the River Tizsa, and to Transylvania where rich copper deposits were located. In all this region vigorous Bronze Age cultures came into existence, but their distribution is seemingly selective to areas of industry and trade. Information is somewhat constrained by the nature of archaeological research so far conducted in this great region, but large, and long surviving, Bronze Age communities were established at many places along the Middle Danube, including the foothills of the Slovakian mountains, as well as in Transylvania and the drainage area of the Tizsa tributaries. By the middle of the second millennium BC, the most important exotic influence at work in the region emanated from the Minoan-Mycenaean civilization of the Aegean. This may largely be attributed to the southward trading of gold and copper, and possibly other, now invisible, raw materials such as slaves.

There are three points of perhaps special significance to be borne in mind about the Middle Danubian population in their full Bronze Age. The people were settled village dwellers with an implicit agricultural food supply, their burial rite was predominantly that of urn cremation contributing to very large flat cemeteries, and their metal industry was particularly open to Mediterranean influences so that new types of weapons and tools had been most easily absorbed therefrom.

It is opportune to note here that the lords of the Mycenaean world in the mid-second millennium BC were Indo-Europeans, apparently speaking Greek as the recent decipherment of their 'Linear B' script seems to show. Cremation, however, was not practised in Greece at this time.

The cremation rite as seen first in the Hungarian Bronze Age, and later practised over so much of Europe to the west and north, provides a problem of some difficulty. Cremation had certainly been practised at times in Eastern and Central Europe by various Neolithic communities, and it probably continued into later times for occasional use; perhaps for special ritual situations. The whole nature of the urnfield rite seems nevertheless to indicate a newer concept. The most that can be said here is that there are increasing indications of the existence of a cremation-rite province in Asia Minor during the centuries in question, and that many features of the urnfield pottery in Hungary, and the area immediately to the west, show Anatolian characteristics, if not explicit derivation from ultimate oriental metal prototypes. By contrast to the Mycenaeans, the Hittite royal burial rite was cremation, as is known from contemporary written records, and a cremation cemetery has recently come to light at their capital. It may be, then, that South-eastern Europe, as far up as the Little Carpathians, should be thought of as a province within the general sphere of Anatolian culture throughout the second millennium BC, if not from a date still earlier.

A time of troubles

In the heyday of Mycenaean power, European trade had been mainly directed to that market, and had brought attendant reflexes in techniques and decorative fashions. On the gradual

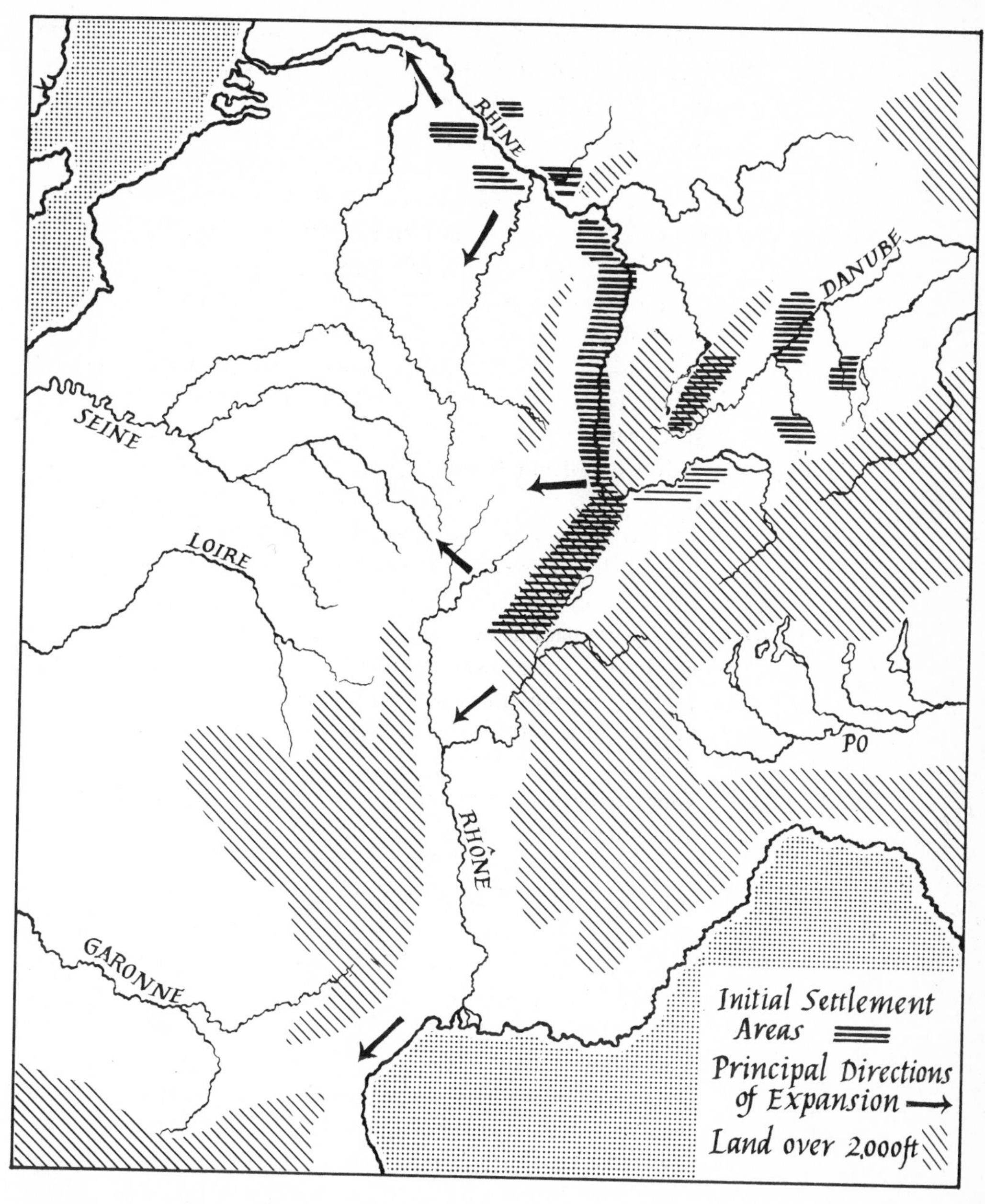

13 The North Alpine Urnfield Culture province.

decline of Mycenae, and the disruption of the Hittite Empire, beginning in the thirteenth century BC, the framework of international order, and economics, had crumbled. The evidence for this, and for widespread plundering raids, by land and sea, around the shores of the Eastern Mediterranean is well known. The supposition that the plunderers were Central Europeans is far from convincing – there were lots of barbarians nearer at

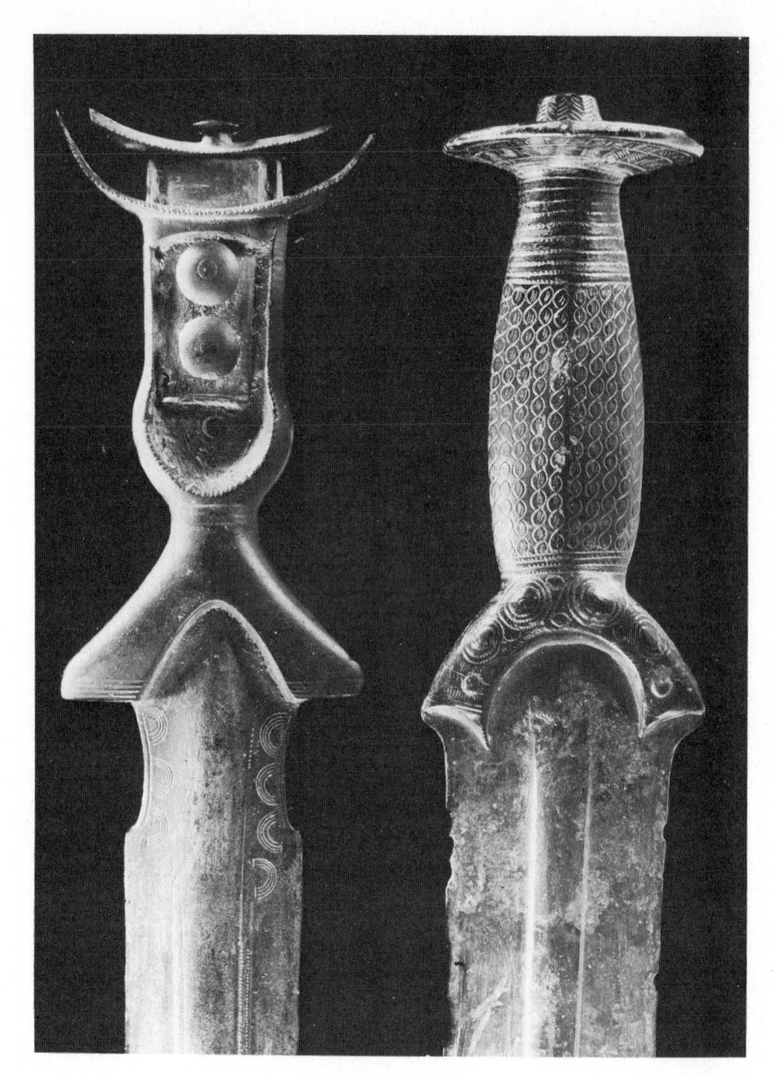

14 Types of Urnfield bronze swords *left to right*: Auvernier type from Kirschgartshausen, Kr. Mannheim; Riegsee type from Engen, Kr. Konstanz. 'Griffzungenschwert' from Hemigkofen, Kr. Friedrichshafen; Mörigen type from Gailenkirchen, Kr. Schwäbisch-Hall; Antenna sword from Schussenried, Kr. Biberach.

hand, but the effect in the Middle Danube must have been very considerable. Invasion and turmoil may well account there for the discontinuance of occupation at many village sites, together with the appearance in the Upper Danubian area of some if not many new settlers. This is but one aspect of a very large problem, for the existence of urnfields in Northern Italy, and more remotely, north of the Carpathians, in Eastern Germany and Poland, involve population groups, and cultures, lying perforce outside the immediate purpose of this sketch.

To return, therefore, to the antecedents of the intrusive element bearing the Urnfield culture to the Upper Danube, three points may especially be borne in mind. Firstly that the new pot-

tery styles are represented in at least some Middle Danubian village mounds and cremation cemeteries, in the latest phases respectively of occupation or internment. Here also is an indication of the source of improved agricultural tradition established by the Urnfielders, no less than for their burial rite, and manual crafts. Secondly, the Hungarian bronze industry had for long been the technological superior of its western contemporaries. This factor goes some way to explain the use by the Urnfielders of new metal types, especially the bronze cut-and-thrust sword, and beaten sheet-metal work. Thirdly, the development on a large scale of copper mining in the Eastern Alps should perhaps be considered in relation to the temporary decline, or unavailability, of

Transylvanian or Slovakian resources, in spite of the hypothesis that Mycenaean interests were here also at work shortly before the breakdown of that civilization's prosperity. It would appear that most of the phenomena of the Upper Danubian Urnfield cultures can be referred to conditions in the Middle Danubian basin, but the possibility of longer-distance connections, especially from the steppelands, running simultaneously with these events should not be quite ignored.

The relevance of all these considerations now comes into a clearer light because the pattern in rural settlement and economy, in material culture, and partly in burial ritual, established in the North Alpine Urnfield province, is found to be continuous, however variously enriched, into and throughout the span of the historical Celts.

Horsemen and chieftains

The foregoing pages have outlined an archaeological interpretation of the build-up of prehistoric population groups in Middle Europe down to a phase of consolidation that may be taken as achieved by the beginning of the tenth century BC. It would appear from grave furniture that there was no very great disparity in status amongst the Urnfielders, although cremation urns, when accompanied by swords, and other adjuncts, may very well represent the graves of chieftains, or heads of free families, such as might be expected in small rural societies. That there were at least occasional greater chieftains is evidenced by such graves as that found at Milaveč in Bohemia where a bronze vessel, mounted on wheels, contained the cremation, and was accompanied by a bronze sword, and other things. In Bavaria, there is the recent discovery, at Hart an-der-Alz, of a cremation grave with a fine sword, three bronze vessels, a set of high quality pottery vessels, presumably for an other-world feast, and, most interesting of all, burnt fragments of the bronze fittings for a four-wheeled waggon. This is the earliest direct evidence for the use of waggons amongst the Urnfielders.

15

The question of chieftainship is immediately important, for the remaining archaeological additions to the North Alpine province seem to have to do with overlords rather than with any supplementation of the farming population.

In considering this matter there are several factors to be taken into account. In addition to the existence of Urnfielder ruling families, on however small a scale, there is the question of a re-

15 Bronze vessel on wheels containing a cremation, from a warrior's grave at Milaveč, Bohemia. Diameter 42 cm.

emergence of some of the old pastoralist warrior stocks, and this is a high probability in view of the cultural amalgamations that took place during the course of the Urnfield expansion. There are, however, new phenomena which seem to point to new intrusions from the east. Within the eighth century BC, and therefore within the last phase of the Urnfield Late Bronze Age, there appear in Hungary, and westwards to the southern parts of the North Alpine province, bronze horse-bits, and bridle mounts, which are closely related in form to types found across the Pontic steppes in Caucasia and, even farther afield, in Iran. Considerable difficulties exist concerning the dating and priority of these objects, and, therefore, as to how this horse-gear should be interpreted. It seems on the whole that horsemen with far-flung connections over the steppes were in fact involved, but neither their number, not their linguistic importance, need have been very great. Their contribution was a stimulus in things martial and in improved horse management, and they may even have been veteran mercenaries from the armies of Assyria and Urartu. These latest Bronze Age horsemen have not been found buried with waggons, or in any very great state, but next in the archaeological sequence appear the tombs of very important warriors

16 Reconstruction of oriental-type bridle from bronze fittings found at Mindelheim, Bavaria (Early Hallstatt Culture).

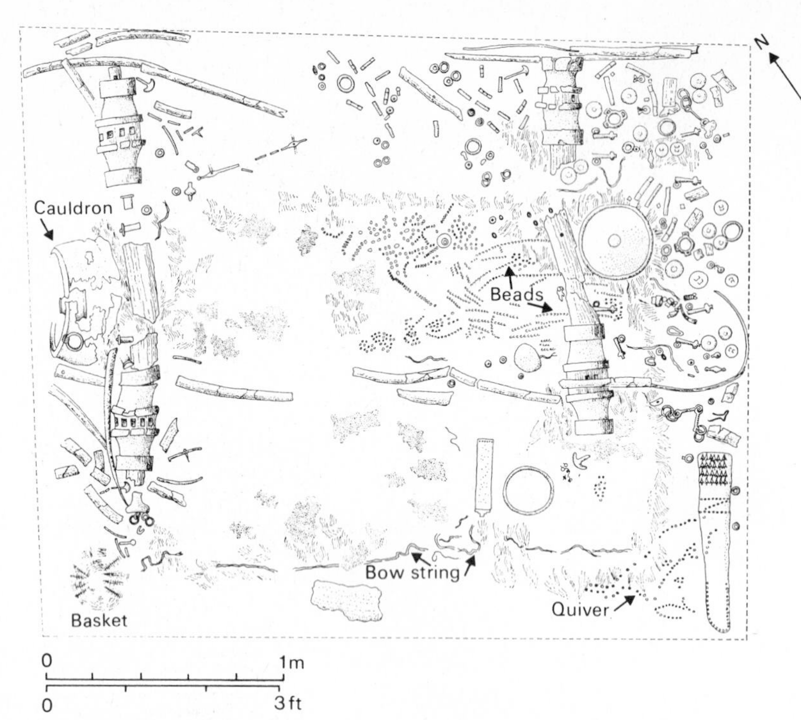

17 Plan of timber-built burial chamber with remains of metal-mounted waggon, Grave VI in the Hohmichele barrow, South Germany (Late Hallstatt Culture).

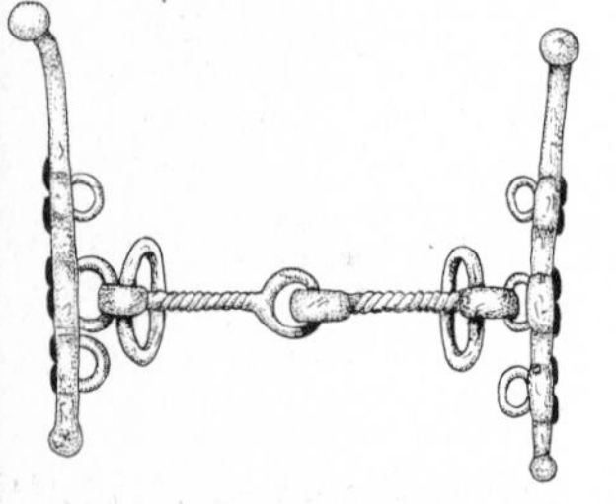

18 Bronze snaffle-bit, and cheek-bars (14 cm high). Thalmässing, Bavaria.

who must be considered as contributing a great deal to the formation of the Celts.

In these tombs the corpse was laid out unburnt on a waggon, or the dismantled parts of one, often enclosed in a wooden chamber beneath a barrow. The man was equipped with an iron sword, and spears, a plentiful supply of pottery, and joints of beef and pork. In addition to the waggon parts, there was sometimes a wooden yoke for a pair of horses, a pair of bronze bits, and a third bit presumably for a riding-horse. First of all these people appear to have been the initiators of an iron-using economy in Middle Europe, and their material culture is known by the name of *Hallstatt* from a site in Austria where it was early discovered. Secondly, and of more immediate importance, these princely tombs, the oldest of which lie in Bohemia, Upper Austria, and Bavaria, set the fashion, by inhumation with a funerary car, for a long series of rich burials which come to represent the backbone of knowledge on Celtic chieftainship, and culture, from the time of Herodotus to beyond – if only in Britain – that of Caesar.

24, 25

Who were these Hallstatt Iron Age chieftains? Their horse-gear is an elaboration of that of their predecessors from the east, but it is more divergent in form from the oriental examples. The iron swords, or bronze copies of the iron type, find their nearest

79

19* Excavated waggon grave of Early La Tène. Bell im Hunsruck, Germany. (An asterisk against a caption denotes that further information is given on pages 210–17).

20* Waggon grave at Bad Cannstatt, near Stuttgart, Germany. Late Hallstatt.

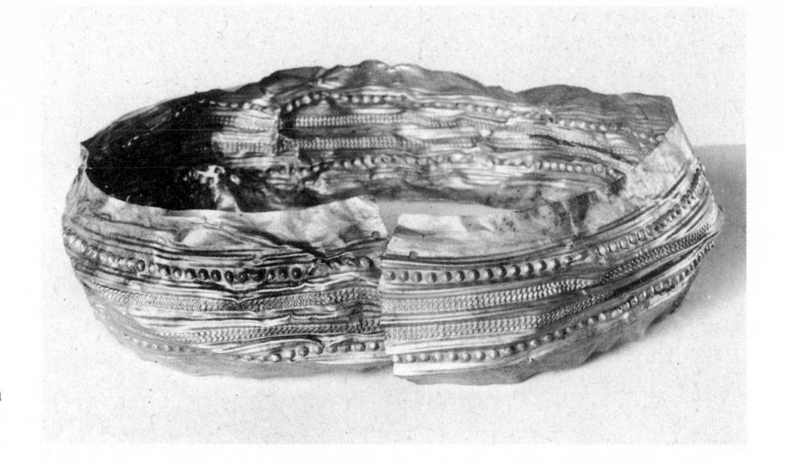

21* Gold ornament from the Bad Cannstatt grave, about 18 cm in diameter.

parallels around the Upper Adriatic, particularly in Bosnia. The wood-built burial chamber under a barrow seems to point either to an eastern source, also drawn upon by the Scythians, or to reflect influence stemming ultimately from the Etruscans whose burial pomps with funerary cars and inhumation, had reached their height at this time. The ritual use of a vehicle, real or miniature, had of course been known in Bohemia and Bavaria for some centuries previously.

In view of the preponderant Urnfield element in the early Hallstatt culture, and its continuity throughout later phases, it seems likely, on present evidence, that the first cart-grave chieftains with iron swords were natives, if only by intermarriage and a generation or two's descent. Their presence in the North Alpine zone opened the way for more intensive cultural borrowings from the Adriatic; before an apparent move westwards in the political centre of gravity encouraged the opening up of trade by the Rhône vally with Greek Massilia, and then, by Central Alpine routes, with the Etruscans.

The waggon graves from only the most remarkable of the known burials of the First Hallstatt period, but there is a special feature in their distribution as a type, from Early Hallstatt to La Tène times, suggesting that they may all belong to one particular tribe or royal family. Whereas the earlier tombs of this kind lie in Bohemia, Bavaria, and Upper Austria, the majority of those belonging to the sixth century BC are found in Württemberg, Switzerland and the Upper Rhine with outliers in Burgundy. In the early fifth century, when Etruscan trade had become direct, the funerary car became the two-wheeled chariot, and the main distribution then fell between the Middle Rhine, at Koblenz, and

23

22* Gold cup from the Bad Cannstatt grave, height 7 cm.

the Moselle. Shortly afterwards, Champagne became an important centre, and eventually Britain, in the third century, received some warriors burying in this tradition. It looks very much as if a dominant warrior society had moved, for reasons not altogether understood, across the North Alpine province in the course of some two centuries. The old areas were not completely deserted by these people, but the centre of power and wealth certainly drew westwards. It is perhaps worth mentioning here that it is only in the latest Hallstatt chieftains' tombs that gold ornaments begin to appear, and this must be related to the beginning of direct relations with the Etruscans, for it is in these tombs, and in those of the ensuing La Tène culture of the fifth century, that actual Etruscan metal imports are found. At this point the archaeological display is fully contemporary with the early Classical references to the Celts, but a return to the seventh century is first necessary in order to consider a valuable interpenetration of archaeological and philological evidence.

81

The Celts as a nation in the sixth century BC

Place-names, linguistically Celtic, are widespread in Spain and Portugal and correspond very generally with the distribution pattern of urnfields belonging to an intrusion whose antecedents can be traced back through Southern France, and the Rhône valley to within the south-western area of the North Alpine Urnfield province. This expansion, which had started in Late Bronze Age times and conditions, hardly reached Catalonia before the migrants were overtaken by metal and ornamental styles emanating from the new Hallstatt culture in the old homeland. The Catalonian urnfields would seem to date from not earlier than

26

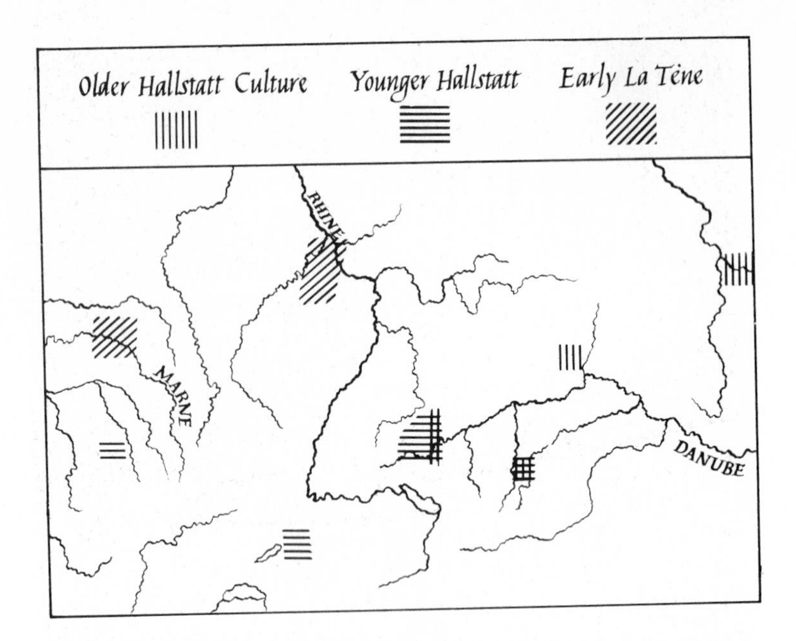

23 Principal areas of concentration of chieftains' graves with vehicles.

the beginning of the seventh century, but whatever their actual initial date, they represent the only satisfactory explanation for the introduction of Celtic place-names to the Peninsula. The Urnfield people eventually spread widely south and west from Catalonia, and other somewhat later, groups entered the Peninsula from the western end of the Pyrenees, establishing themselves along the whole Atlantic coast. These western people were still largely unabsorbed by the older established inhabitants when this region came within the Roman Empire in the second century BC. Here, then, is the archaeological and philological background to the Celts of Herodotus who lived around Pyrene, and beyond the Pillars of Hercules.

The question now arises as to whether these Urnfield migrants to Catalonia already called themselves Celts, albeit Celtic-speaking in modern terminology, or if it was a follow-up of Hallstatt warriors that brought about the adoption of this name. The latter view is favoured by the present writer because it would seem that only after the emergence of Hallstatt warrior society did a mechanism come into being that could bring together, under a national name, barbarian tribes from Spain, through Middle Europe, to the eastern end of the Alps. Hecataeus' reference to Nyrax, the later Noreia, in Styria, will not have been forgotten. 26 But even if Hecataeus be dismissed, the distribution of Hallstatt culture, fully established in the sixth century, conforms with the full extension of the Celtic peoples in relation to Celtic place-

24* View of the town of Hallstatt.

25* View of the site of the Hallstatt cemetery.

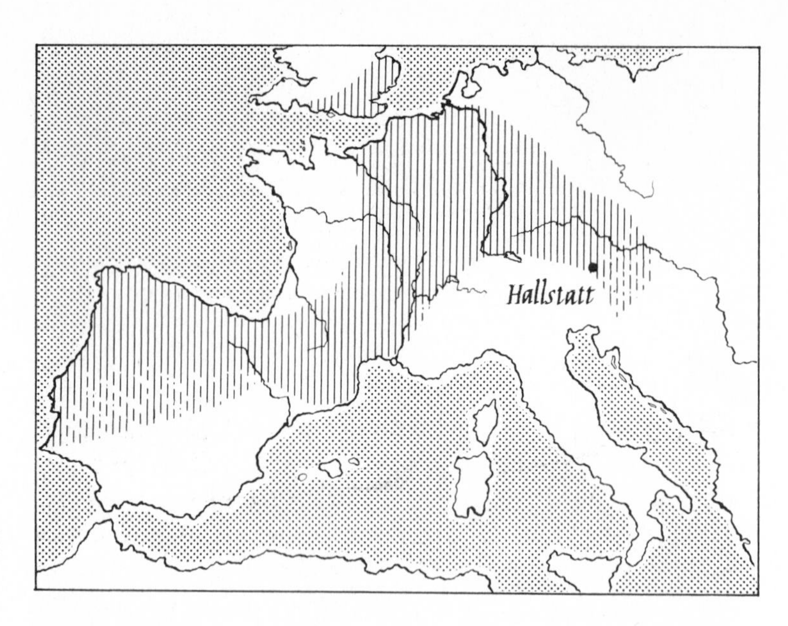

26 Extent of the Hallstatt Culture at the opening of the fifth century BC.

names, and the earliest Classical reference, more accurately than does the archaeological and historical evidence for the Celtic expansion period of the fifth and fourth centuries when the linguistic Celtic province south of the Pyrenees was not involved.

If history in trans-Alpine Europe had begun a thousand years before it actually did, the coming into being of the Celts would be followed not only through general economic and social trends but in terms of family or dynastic, and even individual, fortunes. The fact that history cannot reveal the more human aspects of events for the early Celts has necessitated the marshalling in this chapter of the results of more circuitous lines of inquiry. One advantage of this is that it demonstrates the many factors that were involved, and at the same time abolishes any need for an evocation of mystery in seeking national origins. It seems reasonable, too, that the formation of analogous confederations or nations more clearly within the light of history, may provide a fuller understanding of the uniting element.

Concerning the peoples living on the steppelands of Eastern Europe, Herodotus gives two useful descriptions of the composition of nations whose names he uses in the same descriptive way as he does that of the Celts. These are the Cimmerians, and the Scythians. In each case groups of tribes of different origins and occupations had been brought together through the overlordship of a warlike 'royal tribe'. When the royal tribe suffered reverses, then the nation fell apart, and new groupings and names incorporated the heterogeneous populaces. It may be said, in passing, that the bronze horse-gear of Caucasian connections, already mentioned as appearing at the end of the Urnfield Bronze Age, may well have had to do with Cimmerian riders. The Scythians were responsible for the collapse of Cimmerian suzerainty, and became the eastern neighbours of the Hallstatt culture province in the late sixth century. In their turn they were overthrown by yet another westward-moving nomadic people, the Sarmatians.

The situation amongst the Celts would not perhaps have been so simple, both on account of their mainly farming economy and the great diversity of their environment. It is in the regrouping of peoples on the decay of the Roman Empire, in the fourth and fifth centuries AD, that some possibly useful parallels can be drawn. In this period it was the name of the leading family, the 'royal tribe', that enveloped vaster populaces and territories. The Goths and the Franks are examples. On a smaller scale the name *English* illustrates the same point. There were few real Angles in the Anglo-Saxon invasion, but the immigrant populace soon considered themselves as English because it had been members of the Anglian royal house that had led the settlers from the Frisian coasts.

An hypothesis may therefore be most tentatively submitted. Namely, that the name *Keltoi*, known earliest in this Greek form, had become generally adopted by the people of the North Alpine cultural and linguistic province and its extensions, on the ascendancy of the Hallstatt, waggon-grave, 'royal tribe' whose tribal or family name it had originally been.

As to that other widespread name, *Galatae*, its origin may have been very similar, but it should be recalled that it only appears in Classical writers long after the centres of Hallstatt culture had decayed, and at a time when the Celts, now the creators of the La Tène culture, were again thrusting far afield. New circumstances and new allegiances would seem to have been involved.

Migrations to Britain

The final sections of this chapter must be devoted to questions of the Celtic settlement of Britain and Ireland, and to a brief consideration of the position of Old Irish literature and law as a mirror of ancient Celtic society at large.

It has already been said that the Belgae are the only people of Celtic, or part-Celtic, origin for whom there is direct documentary evidence of migration to Britain. This was an occurrence that history and archaeology agree in placing in the early part of the first century BC, but it will now be best to go back somewhat farther in time to note the archaeological events that should indicate the establishment of those Celtic-speaking population groups, foreshadowed in Pytheas, which are found, in the pages of Caesar, as the opponents of the Belgae, and, in Tacitus, as the opponents of the Romans in the areas beyond the erstwhile Belgic kingdoms.

The general archaeological position in Britain and Ireland at the end of the second millennium BC, when the North Alpine Urnfield province was coming into existence, was of a somewhat stagnant, but widespread, material culture with roots in the Beaker and Battle-Axe heritages on the one hand, and in Mesolithic and Western Neolithic sources on the other. A brilliant and diversified Early Bronze Age had flourished for some two or three hundred years centred on the fifteenth century BC. Thereafter followed this less remarkable period in which a mixed, and perhaps now largely undifferentiated, people, pursued a mainly pastoralist life. The bronzesmith's craft, however, kept abreast of northern Continental trends.

The first indication of impact from the North Alpine Urnfield province may be traced in the appearance, around the Thames Estuary, of bronze swords of Middle Rhenish types. It is arguable that these would have been objects of trade rather than that they should denote newly arrived adventurers. These swords may be placed in the tenth century BC. At about the same time a more likely trade object, the bronze socketed axe, came widely into use in both islands. This, the most efficient and utilitarian of bronze tools, together with the craft of sheet-metal working – both made possible throughout trans-Alpine Europe by the improved supply of metal from the beginning of Urnfield times – now created new opportunities for the indigenous metal trade. The home industry was thus able to meet the needs of a new era so that Continental weapons and tools were not brought in at any time in large quantities.

The first migrants to Southern Britain, as a result of the Urnfield expansion, were refugees from Northern France who are identifiable through their pottery made in French Middle Bronze Age styles. Evidence for such settlement has been found in Kent, but by the early part of the eighth century BC, more serious and large-scale immigrations had begun. The southern chalk-land of England was principally affected, and the bulk of the evidence comes from Sussex, Dorset and Wiltshire. It is not necessary in this book to distinguish the various archaeological cultures, but these invaders possessed certain common characteristics which are important to note. In the first place they brought with them a settled farming economy, and some of their farm sites and field systems have survived to the present day. This, as has been seen, is a distinctive element of the Urnfield culture foreign to the inhabitants of Western and Northern Europe in the second millennium. Secondly, cremation and urn burial was their funerary rite, but, to the older inhabitants of the island, this was no new thing because cremation had long been practised here; stemming apparently from a Late Neolithic ritual known widely in Britain and Ireland. Thirdly, the intrusive ceramic tradition was not mainly that of the North Alpine urnfields, but was again Middle Bronze Age from the opposing shores of the Channel. This conforms to what has already been said about the embracive nature of the Urnfield expansion northwards up the Rhine, and into France. It was only when colonists arrived who had come from within the heart of the North Alpine province, that real Urnfield pottery types make their appearance in England. This appearance was confined to the south coast, and was soon absorbed. These latest comers would appear to have included people from around the Swiss lakes, and they may have been essentially refugees from the disturbances caused by the iron-using Hallstatt warriors who entered that region during the seventh century.

The potential Celtic, or Celticized, immigrants so far reviewed do not appear to have spread greatly beyond their primary chalkland environment. The sterner tracts to the north and west were reserved for domination by warriors with swords and horse-gear of Hallstatt type. It is impossible to be sure on present evidence as to the precise nature of this new element. Did it represent the arrival of proper communities, including women, the bearers of domestic crafts, or only bands of adventurers? The latter seems most likely because widespread in Britain and Ireland are found what may be described as Hallstatt military trappings, but nowhere have they been related to remains of distinctive domestic crafts proper to their own Continental background. The issue may not of course be so simple. In outstripping the slower processes of migration, or even of trade, the Hallstatt warriors may have won to themselves mixed bands of followers from the peoples they overran. In this way the immigration to Britain and Ireland may have brought a more potent social organization than weapons and ornaments alone might be taken to imply.

It will be well to complete the survey of migrations to Britain before facing the rather different complexities in Ireland.

If an early or mid-sixth century date for the Massiliote Periplus be accepted, Albion, in its southern coastal areas, is the land of the various Late Bronze Age immigrants, now fully established, and perhaps subject to those Hallstatt warlords who had come armed with long bronze or iron swords and riding, or driving, horses bridled and adorned in the fashion of their Middle European homeland. By the time of Pytheas, Pretani had become a significant name in Albion. Is there a possible archaeological explanation? The reply must be that from the early part of the fifth century BC, Southern and Eastern Britain received colonists from the Low Countries and Northern France before whom, numerically and economically, earlier invaders pale to insignificance. The newcomers supported a provincial and outmoded material culture of Hallstatt type, but essentially they were the descendants of North Alpine Urnfield people who had expanded to the Lower Rhine, and, by other routes, to Champagne and the Seine valley.

It may help in clarification to refer to these latest arrivals by their archaeological label: the British Iron Age A Culture. Their importance as an element of the population in subsequent times can perhaps best be compared with that of the Anglo-Saxons in the Post-Roman period. They overran all previous settlers, submerging their differences. The total population of the island must have greatly increased; not least because of the opening-up of new farming land with the aid of iron tools.

The bearers of the Iron Age A Culture spread from their southern and eastern landfalls widely on areas of well drained soil, and later to heavier land along the Welsh Marches, in the Midlands, and to the Pennines. This expansion seems to have occupied some two centuries, but despite later Continental influxes, the Iron Age A people formed the bulk of the population down to the Roman Conquest. North of the Cheviots, the position is obscure for this period. The only intrusion on a retarded Middle Bronze Age population, who had adopted Late Bronze Age metal types, seems to have been that of Hallstatt wanderers. Iron Age A tribes seem to have invaded lowland Scotland only at the beginning of the Christian era as a result of the Belgic and Roman troubles farther south.

There can be no doubt that the Iron Age A people were Celts and the probability is strong that some if not all of them possessed the name Pretani, or its variant Preteni.

On the Continent, the reorganization of power and wealth at the end of Hallstatt times, in the fifth century BC, gave rise to

(*opposite*)
27 Chariot burial, with wheels dismantled and crouched skeleton, at Garton Slack, East Yorkshire. Early Iron Age, second century BC. The twelve-spoked wheels with iron tyres and gilded bronze nave-bands are 86 cm in diameter.

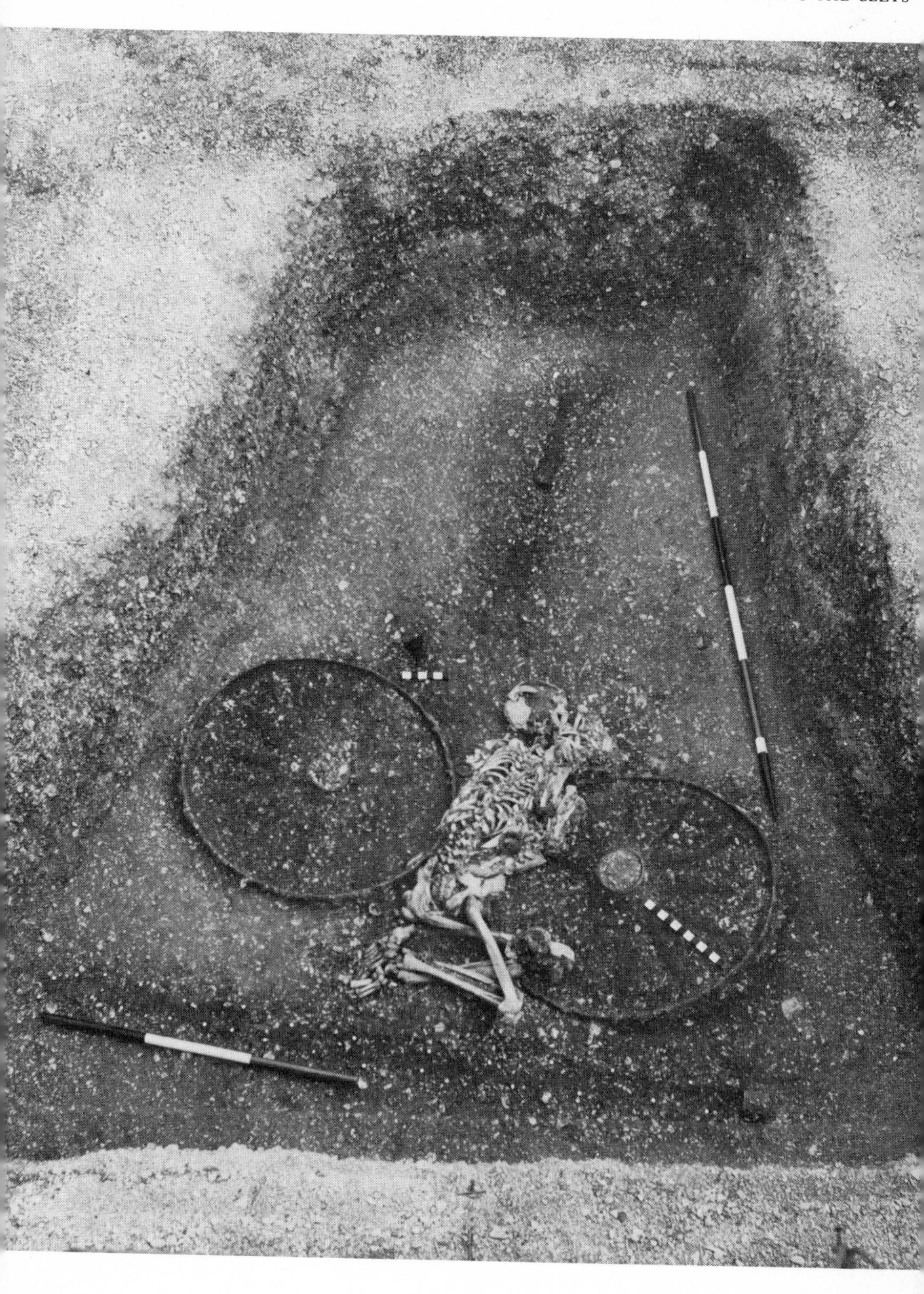

new fashions in material culture, and gave birth to a remarkable decorative art. The same populations were involved, and presumably the same ruling or aristocratic families. Archaeologically, the new trends are classified as of the La Tène culture, or of the La Tène art style. Principal amongst the patrons were the chieftains whose rich chariot graves have been found on the Middle Rhine, and, slightly later, in Champagne. These chieftains must be considered to have been in the forefront of the great expansion of Celtic tribes eastwards across Europe, and into Italy and the Balkans, as already related. They may in part have been responsible for the ejection of the Hallstatt-Iron Age A people to Britain, but this island was not itself threatened by La Tène invaders until the middle part of the third century BC. The intrusion was directed mainly to the south coast and to Sussex in particular. The invaders were probably small in number but it is clear that whole families, or social units, had moved, for domestic arts are represented in the material, not only weapons. The culture of these people, arrived in Britain, is known as Iron Age B. Sometimes they are known as 'Marnians', as their homeland appears to have been roughly the modern department of the Marne; but with this invasion, craftsmen in metal-work, if not chieftains, also seem to have come from the Middle Rhine. The Marnians seem to have formed an overlordship in the areas they occupied rather than to have driven out the older settlers, or formed independent enclaves. In the north, they established themselves on the Yorkshire Wolds, and extended perhaps into South-western Scotland. The Iron Age B, or Marnian, tribal aristocracy flourished in their new homeland, and became the patrons of a splendid insular school of La Tène art. This point is made here as their predominant position may be taken to have consolidated further the Celtic character of the island's population, south at least of the Cheviots. In the south-west, and Bristol Channel region – first as a result, perhaps, of the Cornish trade – settlers culturally La Tène, were establishing themselves from the third, or second, century to the time of Caesar, when the movement became a stream of refugees.

The final phase of colonization in Britain before the Roman Conquest comes with the Belgic settlements in the south-east. This event is very well documented in archaeology no less than in the pages of Caesar. The colonists were sprung from tribes within the Belgic confederation that occupied the territory between the Rhine, the Seine and the Marne. Some of the confederate tribes, those mainly along the sea coast, were of uncouth provincial Urnfield-Hallstatt origin and had come, or had been driven from across the Rhine. Other tribes in the confederation were largely descended from the La Tène people of Champagne, and the emigrants to Britain belonged to this latter division.

As settlers, the Belgae will be considered in the next chapter. Here it is sufficient to emphasize that in language and social organization they were Celts, and that they formed the backbone of native resistance to the Romans both in their own kingdoms, and later when dispossessed, in the west and north. It seems, indeed, that an actual tradition of Belgic royal genealogy survived in Wales throughout the Roman occupation, to be treasured by the resurgent Britons into Medieval times.

The Celts in Ireland

The rich store in Celtic language, and literary tradition, that has survived from ancient times in Ireland must contrast with the present very incomplete archaeological testimony from that island.

Since Early Bronze Age times, Ireland had played an important part in the bronze industry, and her metal-workers were not slow to adapt their craft to new techniques and improved forms. There is, however, no indication that any addition to the old native population took place before the sixth century BC, but it may be within this century that intruders first appear. There is a growing body of material, in bronzes and pottery, from areas as far apart as Antrim and Down in the north, Westmeath and Roscommon in the centre, and Clare and Limerick in the south-west, to indicate the arrival in Ireland of settlers bearing a version of Hallstatt material culture. Hallstatt adventurers may be suspected, as in Britain, but somewhat more distinctive pottery types may point to more close-knit immigrant groups. These people may in part represent an over-spill from the Iron Age A settlement of Britain, but, against this theory, there are certain archaeological factors that may be taken to suggest an earlier movement directly from the Lower Rhenish area, through, or around, Scotland. At least one site on the north-east Scottish coast would seem to bear testimony to this. There is also the problem of crannóg-type lake-dwellings, especially concentrated on the Upper Shannon, and the possibility must exist that these derive from some element whose antecedents lay in the West Alpine zone where similar structures were in use.

The next apparent signpost in the Irish archaeological record is provided by fine metal-work in the La Tène style. This material consists chiefly of engraved bronze scabbards for iron swords, ornamented bronze bridle-bits, and bronze trumpets. Stylistically, the oldest of these pieces are generally considered to date from the first century BC, and to be derived from British Iron Age B exemplars. The question must stand open for the present as to whether this La Tène metal-work represents the output of itinerant craftsmen, working for heretofore 'Hallstatt' chieftains, or indicates a new influx of aristocracy with their craftsmen in train. Certain philological evidence weighs in this direction, but is too complicated to warrant inclusion here. One thing is at least clear. If the metal-work in question is to be dated no earlier than the first century BC, its makers must have come from Britain, either from Yorkshire, or from South-western Scotland. Refugees, or other migrants from Gaul at this date could not have borne this elegant La Tène art heritage which had long waned on the Continent.

The probability that Ireland did in fact receive considerable bodies of Gaulish exiles, escaping from Roman subjugation, is one which has not yet been demonstrated archaeologically. Irish traditional literature, and some few tribal names recorded by the geographer Ptolemy in the second century AD, do make a case for such an inflow as well as for Britons, who presumably would have come over mainly in the first century AD when the full-scale conquest of Southern Britain was initiated under Claudius.

It seems really impossible to attempt at present an estimate of the contribution to life in Ireland of these settlers from Gaul and Britain. It may be asked if it was they who established the Celtic social system and culture that was found flourishing on the arrival of the Christian missionaries in the fifth century. Alternatively, did they form but a late augmentation to a Celtic Ireland that had been brought into being by 'Hallstatt' chieftains in the sixth century BC? This problem is not helped by linguistic considerations which, naturally, are dependent on much later documentary evidence. The following very brief summary of the philological position of the Irish language may, however, be ventured upon.

The Irish language of the ancient literature is the ancestor of the modern tongue generally called Gaelic. It belongs to that branch of the Celtic language family, designated Q-Celtic, which retained certain more archaic features than did the P-Celtic branch, to which Gaulish and British belonged, and of which Welsh is the principal modern representative. P-Celtic was predominant on the Continent, and in Britain, in the time of Caesar, and apparently for long before, but there are traces of Q-Celtic elements in place-names in Spain and Gaul, and in the latter country, in some very fragmentary epigraphy of Roman times. Philological opinion differs as to how ancient was the divergence between these two branches of Celtic, and as to whether the two were mutually intelligible prior to Latin influence on Gaulish and British.

Whatever view may be adopted on these problems, the fact remains that only in Ireland did there survive a language, and literature, that sprang directly from the ancient Celts, uncontaminated by Imperial Rome.

The continuity of native Irish traditional learning, and literature, from Medieval times backwards into prehistory is a matter of great significance, and one that has been little appreciated; and the final words of this chapter must therefore briefly state the circumstances of its survival.

Whereas in the early Teutonic kingdoms of Post-Roman Europe, the Church found but the most rudimentary machinery for rule and law, in Ireland the missionaries were confronted by a highly organized body of learned men with specialists in customary law, no less than in sacred arts, heroic literature, and genealogy. Paganism alone was supplanted, and the traditional oral schools continued to flourish, but now side by side with the monasteries. By the seventh century, if not earlier, there existed aristocratic Irish monks who had also been fully educated in the traditional native learning. This led to the first writing-down of the vernacular literature, which thus became the oldest in Europe next after Greek and Latin. The merit attached to accurate recitation of the oral learning continued to ensure a great measure of accuracy in committal to writing, and, later, in transcription from older manuscripts. In this way the language and form of a text first committed to writing in the seventh, or eighth centuries, can be found with only minor corruptions, in surviving manuscripts of the fifteenth or sixteenth centuries. The oldest surviving examples of written Irish are to be found in Church books of the eighth and ninth centuries where the Latin text is annotated with explanatory notes, and sometimes other comments, in the native tongue of contemporary monks. These dateable Church books provide the most important chronological yardstick for the language of tracts preserved only in late manuscripts.

It will be realized that the surviving literature can only represent a fragment of the body of oral composition as it stood in, say, the eighth century AD, and it is known that some of the early manuscripts contained important material now irretrievably lost. The systematic study of Old Irish language and literature is a thing of only the past hundred years, and, in some respects, only the preliminaries have been achieved. The content of the legal tracts, and of some of the epic and mythological stories, throws a flood of light on Irish life as it was from out of prehistory. It illuminates many Classical observations on the Continental Celts, and it provides important comparative data in the wider field of Indo-European institutions and mythology, no less than in philology. The Celts in Ireland preserved a western peripheral fastness of Indo-European tradition as, at the oriental end of the range, did the Aryans of Northern India. These long survived the disappearance of their geographically intermediate common parentage.

Notes to Chapter 1

FIRST REFERENCES: Herodotus, II, 33, and IV, 49. Hecataeus, F. Jacoby (1923).

CELTIC LANGUAGES: J. Vendryes (1937), R. Thurneysen (1946), K. H. Jackson (1953), for philology. H. M. Chadwick (1913), H. Rix (1954), are restricted place-name studies of value. A. Holder (1896–1907), for Celtic words recorded up to the Early Middle Ages.

CELTS IN HISTORY: A. Grenier (1945), is an invaluable study if somewhat outmoded in archaeology. It contains references to the principal earlier works not mentioned here. *Cambridge Ancient History* (1928), 101 ff., Celts in Greece; 554 ff., in Italy. For important chapter see bibliography under J. M. de Navarro (1928). K. J. Beloch (1926), for impact on Rome; G. E. F. Chilver (1941) on later Cis-Alpine Gaul; G. T. Griffith (1935) on Celtic mercenaries; F. Stahelin (1907), Celts in Asia Minor.

BELGAE: C. F. C. Hawkes and G. C. Dunning (1930); C. A. R. Radford (1955).

WESTERN SEAWAYS: *Cambridge Ancient History* VII, 53, and 770; P. Dixon (1940); C. F. C. Hawkes (1952).

PRETANI ETC.: K. H. Jackson (1954) and (1955).

PREHISTORY: V. G. Childe (1950) and (1957) for syntheses not necessarily followed here. *Grosser Historischer Weltatlas* I Teil, and Erläuterungen, München, 1954, for useful maps, and commentary. There is no general study of Iron Age Europe.

HORSES: M. Hilzheimer (1935); J. W. Amschler (1949); F. Hančar (1956).

INDO-EUROPEANS: H. Hencken (1955) provides an indispensable summary of current views and full bibliography.

NORTH ALPINE URNFIELD PROVINCE: V. G. Childe (1929) and (1948); W. Kimmig (1940b) and 1952–54); M. E. Mariën (1952) with map showing northern extensions. N. K. Sandars (1957) for France. M. A. Smith (1957) for important new survey.

MIDDLE DANUBE AND TRANSYLVANIA: V. G. Childe (1929); A. Mozsolics (1952); D. Popescu (1956).

MYCENAEAN SCRIPT: M. Ventris and J. Chadwick (1956).

HART AN-DER-ALZ: H. Müller-Karpe (1955).

HORSE-HARNESS IN BRONZE: G. Kossack (1953); A. Mozsolics (1956) for new dating evidence in Hungary.

HALLSTATT: E. von Sacken (1868) remains fundamental. F. Morton (1953) for description of the locality. R. Pittioni (1954) on the culture in Austria; G. Kossack (1954a) on Bavaria; K. Tackenberg (1954) for Rhine province, with full bibl., and maps.

WAGGON AND CHARIOT GRAVES: S. Schiek (1954) with map and bibl.

CATALONIAN URNFIELDS: W. Kimmig (1954), and references therein.

LATE BRONZE, AND EARLY IRON AGES IN BRITAIN: S. Piggott (1949) for general summary. C. F. C. Hawkes (1948) and (1956).

IRELAND: S. P. ÓRíordáin (1946) and (1953) for archaeological bibl. R. J. C. Atkinson and S. Piggott (1955) for dating Irish 'La Tène' art. J. F. Kenny (1929) for transmission of literature. The excellent series of small books on Irish Life and Culture, published by the Cultural Relations Committee of Ireland, Dublin, should be consulted. See particularly: M. Dillon, edit. (1954), and G. Murphy (1955a and b).

60

2
The Celts in Life

The Celts are now presented as a loosely knit barbaric nation that came into being in the region north of the Alps during the early centuries of the last millennium before Christ.

The common factors in material culture, and rural economy, no less than in social institutions and language, all of which derived from an amalgamation of at least partly intrusive Urnfield people together with more ancient local communities, seem to have gained cohesion on the rise of dynasties represented by the princely tombs of the Hallstatt and La Tène cultures. In the fifth and fourth centuries BC, the Celts achieved their greatest prosperity, and expansion over the face of Europe. In the recession that then ensued they were doomed to virtual continental oblivion, finally at the hands of Julius Caesar, but earlier through the natural processes of decline rather than from any other cause. It was only in Britain, and finally in Ireland, that population groups survived into Medieval times who preserved the Celtic heritage, but then under other, more local, names.

Physical characters of the Celts

This chapter will be mainly concerned with aspects of the life and mundane concerns of Celtic society as it seems to be quite uniformly reflected in insular native tradition no less than in archaeology and the Classical records. But it is first of all important to consider the physical appearance of the Celts, for this was a matter of frequent comment by Greek and Latin writers, and it leads to the need for a clarification of the term *race* in relation to these people.

It has already been suggested that the Greeks, in the time of Herodotus, were able to recognize Celts by various national traits just as the country dwellers of most of Europe could be distinguished one from another by regional differences in dress and physical features until quite recent times. It was in the period

(*opposite*)
28* Man's head, carved in soft stone, from Mšecké-Žebrovice, Bohemia. Height 24 cm.

after the great Celtic expansion, including the invasion of Northern Italy, that the dominant physical type amongst the Celts became a matter of note to Classical writers. Polybius, writing in the second century BC, and probably using earlier sources, remarked on the terrifying sight of well-built Gaulish warriors, but more explicit accounts come somewhat later in the writings, amongst others, of Strabo, Diodorus Siculus, and Pliny.

The Celts were remarkable to Mediterranean eyes for their height, their fair skin, muscularity, blue eyes and blond hair. It must be appreciated at once that these characteristics were relative to the physique and pigmentation of the Mediterranean observers, and that anyway they belonged to the most noticeable elements in Celtic society, the chieftains and freemen warriors, not necessarily to the whole population. The Classical descriptions accord well with the standards of beauty amongst the insular Celtic aristocracy extolled in early Irish literature, and thus many popular misconceptions of today as to what constitutes a typical Celt in, for instance, Wales or the Hebrides, must be abandoned. The question only remains as to the evaluation of the tall, fair, genetic type.

It may be said at once that the concept of pure races, exhibiting constant elements in structure and pigmentation, has long been refuted in science. The term *race* can have no accurate definition, but is useful only in such very general classifications as the black, white or yellow races. It does remain true, however, that within most definable population groups particular aggregations of physical characteristics may be expected. What impresses the non-specialist observer is the accumulation of, to him, novel features, but not more than a few of the total will probably be found in any one of the observed subjects.

29 Bronze mount from La Tène cremation grave, Mulheim, Koblenz. Height 4.6 cm.

So far as physical types representing the Celts are concerned, there are two other sources in addition to the literary descriptions. In the first place there are representations in plastic art both Classical and native, and secondly, there is skeletal material from Celtic graves. This latter body of evidence, which is still comparatively small, stands to increase in value with better standards of excavation and recovery of inhumation burials, but it is also dependent on conditions of soil chemistry from place to place no less than to the hazards of destruction, and even of discovery.

The anatomical evidence available from recognizable Celtic graves, containing Hallstatt or La Tène objects, indicates a mixture of both long- and round-headed subjects. The round-

heads would seem on the whole to represent the older established populations of the Bronze Age in the North Alpine zone, while the long-heads, which there is some reason to think formed the most aristocratic element, were evidently derived from a more Central European population that had expanded westwards. In general, the skeletal material so far studied would indicate a situation very similar to that in any modern ethnic group where considerable mixtures of genetic types are apparent, but where certain physical characteristics are prominent especially in relation to different grades or elements in the total population.

30* Bronze figure of Celtic warrior, from Italy. Height 13 cm.

31 Roman representation, from soon after AD 200, of a triumphal trophy flanked by captives, a Parthian (right) and a Briton (left). The Briton wears check *bracae* (or tartan trews). Inlaid bronze from a monumental statue at Volubilis, North Africa, probably commemorating the Emperor Caracalla's military achievements in Parthia, and in Britain during the Severan campaigns in the north.

The light thrown on this subject by representational art is quite considerable, and at the same time consistent. In the native, La Tène, art extreme stylization of human heads, and masks, prohibits any deductions on head form, but characteristics, attested elsewhere, such as flowing moustaches, and wild backward-swept hair give some direct evidence as to the ideal of facial appearance sought amongst the Celts.

The Classical sculpture of Celtic warriors, stemming principally from the Pergamene school, commemorating the defeat of the Galatians in Asia Minor, confirms the literary descriptions of tall, loose-limbed muscular bodies, with round or medium heads, and wavy or curly hair. Here, too, aspects of deliberate appearance are well illustrated, and it is to these, and styles of dress and ornamentation that attention must now turn.

Polybius' vivid description of the fateful battle of Telamon, fought between the Romans and the Gaulish invaders in 225 BC, provides the earliest account of Celtic dress and appearance. Presumably, he was able to make use of first-hand accounts of this battle, and his testimony may be regarded as sound. He describes how the Insubres and Boii, tribes already settled in Northern Italy, wore trousers (*bracae*, whence: breeches), and light cloaks. The *Gaesatae*, those fighting men brought in from beyond the Alps, paraded naked in the forefront of the battle line, adorned only with gold torcs around their necks, and gold armlets. Of the custom of going naked into battle more will be said later. It is Diodorus Siculus who gives perhaps the best general account of the appearance of the Celtic warrior, and here, too, an older and more direct report is probably repeated. First with regard to moustaches, he says that the nobles let these grow long, even covering the mouth, but that otherwise they were clean-shaven. This bears out the evidence, such as it is, in native metal-work, and also as seen in such sculpture as the well known 'Dying Gaul', and the 'Ludovisi' group of the defeated warrior committing suicide having already killed his wife. These two pieces had Pergamene originals and therefore depict those *Galatae* who invaded Asia Minor.

Diodorus states that short beards were worn by some men, presumably again warriors, but his most interesting piece of information is about the way the warriors wore their hair. He describes how they constantly smeared their hair with a thick wash of lime, and drew it back from the forehead to produce a weird effect like the mane of a horse. There seems to be only one extant piece of Greek sculpture which shows this peculiar hair style.

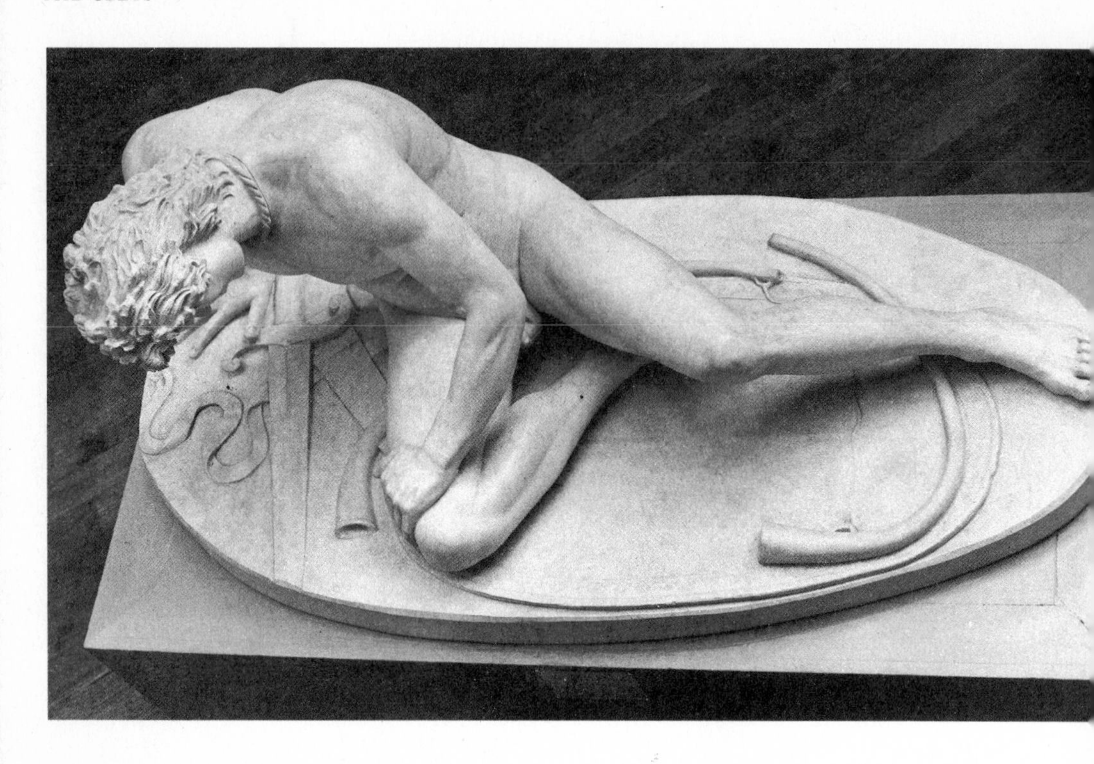

32* 'The Dying Gaul', the famous Roman marble copy of a Pergamene bronze. Third century BC. Slightly over life-size.

It is the mutilated head from Gizeh, now in the Cairo museum, and it seems to be in a style older than, and different from, the Pergamene school. Heads and masks in native metal-work have already been mentioned, but this hair style seems also to be depicted on some few Gaulish and British coins of the last phases of independence.

There is no actual description of lime-washing of hair in Irish texts, but it, or some similar practice, seems to have been observed. There are references to long stiff hair that would have been capable of impaling falling apples. This description, in one instance, is applied to Cú Chulainn, the paragon of tribal heroes, and elsewhere his hair is described as being in three colours, darkest near the scalp, and lightest at the extremities, with an intermediate colour between. This would certainly be the effect produced by lime-washing, and it can be paralleled in the colour sequence seen in hair let grow after dyeing.

Dress

The question of trousers, cloaks and costume generally must next be reviewed. Strabo explicitly states that the *bracae* were tight or close fitting, but it seems that looser forms were also in use, 31, 33, 134

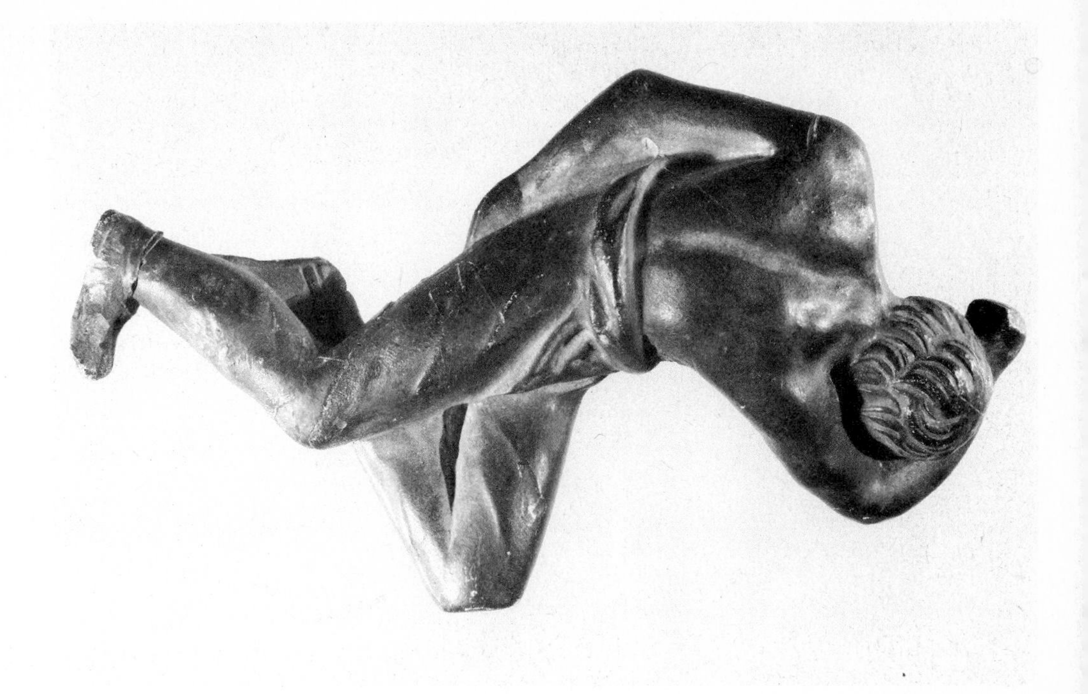

33* Bronze appliqué figure of recumbent Gaul, from Alesia, France. Length 10 cm.

at least in his own time in Gaul. Now, the use of trousers by the Celts raises some interesting questions as these are garments that do not seem to have originated in temperate Europe, and were quite foreign to Mediterranean dress. The evidence for European prehistoric dress is based on the evidence of Danish Bronze Age clothing so well preserved in tree-trunk coffins. If this evidence may be more widely applied, the normal male dress, in pre-Urnfield times, would have been a body garment passing over one shoulder and held round the waist by a belt. Over this was worn a cloak; everything being made of wool. It is on the Eurasiatic steppes that trousers were, and have remained, a principal male garment. Derived probably from dwellers in sub-Arctic regions farther to the north, trousers had obvious advantages for horsemen, and in this way they were widely propagated so that they became the normal wear of the Scythians, and amongst others, the Iranian horsemen who established the great Persian Empire. It is reasonable to assume that the various precursors of the Scythians on the fringes of Europe proper, the Thracians and Cimmerians, also knew the use of trousers, and it is from this source that they were most likely introduced amongst the Celts of Middle Europe. In the first chapter mention was made of the continuous influences, if not intrusions, from the Pontic grasslands that are evident in the archaeology of Urnfield and Hallstatt graves. This human garment would fit naturally into the horse-driving and horse-riding complex coming from the east.

So far as the Celts in Northern Italy are concerned, it is noteworthy that trousers were evidently appropriate to the warrior class amongst the Boii and Insubres even if wearing them was a departure from the more archaic custom of going naked into battle. This point emphasizes a problem in the Irish literary evidence which has been critically reviewed in recent years. The Irish aristocratic dress consisted of two garments, a tunic or shirt, in the earliest without sleeves, and a cloak. This costume was worn by both sexes. The tunic (*léine*) was made of linen, and was worn by men to the knee or below, by women to the ankles. 30 It was gathered round the waist by a belt or girdle (*criss*). Over this was worn the cloak (*brat*), made of wool, and four-cornered, so probably rectangular, but not oval as were those of the Danish Bronze Age. The Irish cloak had no sleeves or hood, being a plain piece of cloth held in position by a brooch. Its length probably depended on the wealth and status of its wearer. There are references to the cloaks of kings being five-folded, and in another text, a mythological personage stands in her chariot with her cloak trailing on the ground behind.

It is not known what word, if any, was used in Ireland for trousers prior to the introduction, through a Teutonic medium, of the word *bróc*. This, together with the fact that trousers are only mentioned in connection with the costume of servants – charioteers, however, included – would make it seem that either they never formed part of the original equipage of migrant Celtic warriors in the west, or they were early abandoned in conformity perhaps with some existing fashion that still carried prestige in the islands.

The Irish tunic and cloak find their counterparts, of course, in the Classical descriptions of continental Celtic dress. A light cloak is mentioned by Polybius, and it is seen worn by the warrior in the 'Ludovisi' group. Diodorus remarked on coloured cloaks fastened with a brooch, shirts that were dyed and embroidered and belts with gold or silver ornament. Strabo adds only to this in saying that the shirts (*tunicae*) were slit and had sleeves. Although the later Irish compositions give unduly elaborate descriptions of dress, the earlier texts consistently describe coloured cloaks chiefly of purple, crimson and green. Speckled and striped cloaks are also mentioned, and it would seem that ornamental

34 Gold torc, bracelets and rings from a woman's grave at Reinheim, Germany. Early fourth century BC. Diameter of torc 17 cm.

fringes or braids were worked separately and then sewn on. The colourful appearance of Celtic dress was noted by Diodorus, Pliny and others. Leather shoes and sandals were certainly worn in Ireland. Headgear does not seem to have been important anywhere, nor would this be expected in view of the nature of the hair style.

Finally, on the general subject of appearance, there is the matter of ornament to which the Celts were reputedly much attached.

Ornaments

The most characteristic Celtic ornament was a neck-ring of gold, or bronze, or more rarely of silver. This ornament is generally called a torc, and the word *torquis* was used by Latin writers to describe these objects although in fact the use of twisted metal was exceptional. The term remains, however, because of its antiquity and brevity. The torc first came into use amongst the Celts during that phase of enrichment comprehended archaeologically in the rapid development of the La Tène art style. This was an event of the mid-fifth century BC, and reflects the continued growth of contacts, mainly in trade and plunder, between the Celts at their optimum as a barbarian political and military force, and their neighbours to the south and east. The idea of the torc was a borrowing from the east, and certain Celtic specimens suggest ultimate Persian exemplars.

34–37

38

35* Gold torc and bracelets from a chariot grave at Waldalgesheim, Germany. Late fourth century BC. Diameter of torc 18 cm.

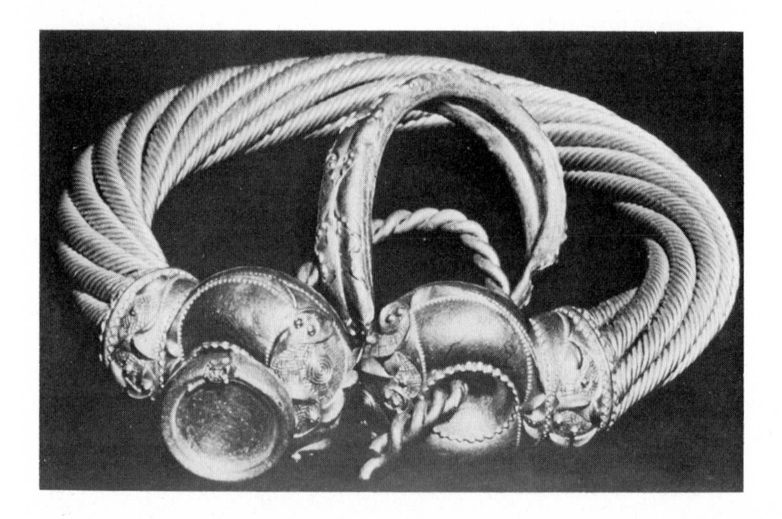

36* Hoard of gold objects from Snettisham, Norfolk, as found. Late first century BC.

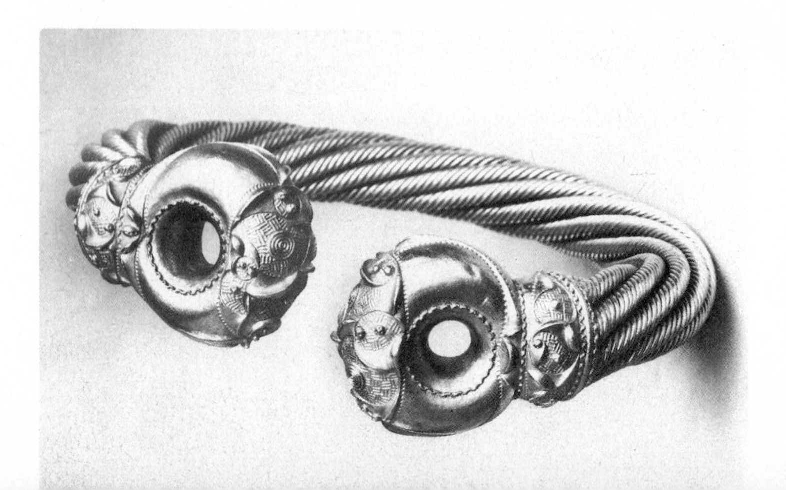

37* Gold torc from the Snettisham find. Diameter 20.5 cm.

The principle of the torc is that of a curved rod, or hollow tube, of metal with free terminals touching, or nearly so. Pliancy must be allowed so that the ring will open sufficiently to embrace the neck, but in some torcs a movable piece was arranged to that there were no free terminals and the ornament appeared as a continuous ring encircling the neck. The most characteristic torcs possessed various forms of enlarged terminals, and these were portrayed in Greek and Roman sculpture as well as in the native plastic art.

The most splendid gold torcs, and bracelets, belong to the first phase of La Tène art between approximately the mid-fifth and

v, vi

38* Massive silver torc from Trichtingen, South Germany. Diameter 25 cm.

39* Detail of the bulls' heads on the Trichtingen torc.

late fourth centuries BC. It is interesting that these mainly come from women's tombs, and there are examples from only very few warrior chariot graves. It is possible that the torc was not necessarily a neck ornament for women, and it must be asked if they could not have been head ornaments following the tradition of elaborate head-rings of bronze from women's graves of the Hallstatt period or of the gold diadem recently found in a princess's grave at Vix near Châtillon-sur-Seine. For the living, as opposed to the dead, it is clear that the torc was essentially a male ornament, proper not only to mortals but to the deities.

40

Torcs were not placed even in the wealthiest of women's graves after the early La Tène phase, and later specimens are known from other kinds of discoveries.

In view of the fact that sacred images are shown wearing the torc, it seems most probable that it possessed a socio-religious significance proper to all freemen whose status, as will be seen, was ritual as well as social. In this case a man's torc might well have been inheritable as an essential symbol of the headship of the family or tribe. This is only put forward as a possible explanation for the general absence of gold torcs from men's graves; but while gold was appropriate to the higher ranks, bronze torcs are known from warrior graves of a humbler kind, and these were doubtless ordinary fighting men of free status.

111, 112

Gold bracelets and finger-rings were also worn in the early La Tène phase, but with a change to less richly equipped graves, it is more difficult to estimate the range of gold ornaments that might have been worn by any one individual in later times.

34

Important, archaeologically, are bronze brooches of the safety-pin type. These first made their appearance in trans-Alpine Europe in Urnfield times, and they have, in essentials, remained popular to the present day. Their wide range in shape, and embellishment, reflecting changes in fashion, in external influences, and in regional predilections, make them of great value in establishing the chronology of graves, and sometimes of settlements. In graves, a pair of brooches, lying on the chest, indicates that they were used principally for securing the cloak, but the number of brooches is variable, and often only one is present. The most interesting brooches worn by the Celts are of the early La Tène phase, and display stylized human and bird masks on the cast bronze bow and foot. Other brooch forms were embellished with studs of coral indicating a southern trade in this exotic material, but, later, coral was abandoned for enamel which became an important native craft.

41, 43

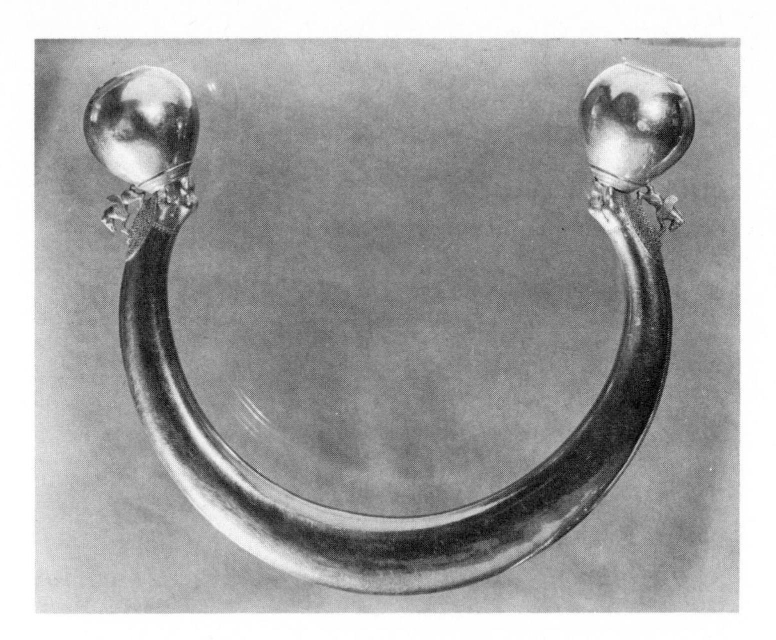

40 Gold diadem or torc found by the head of the 'Princess' in the Late Hallstatt princely grave at Vix, Châtillon-sur-Seine, France, with pegasus figures at the terminals. Diameter 20 cm; *below*, Detail of terminal.

41 Bronze brooch from Oberwittighausen, Germany, with complex human and animal heads. Late fifth or early fourth century BC. 10.5 cm long.

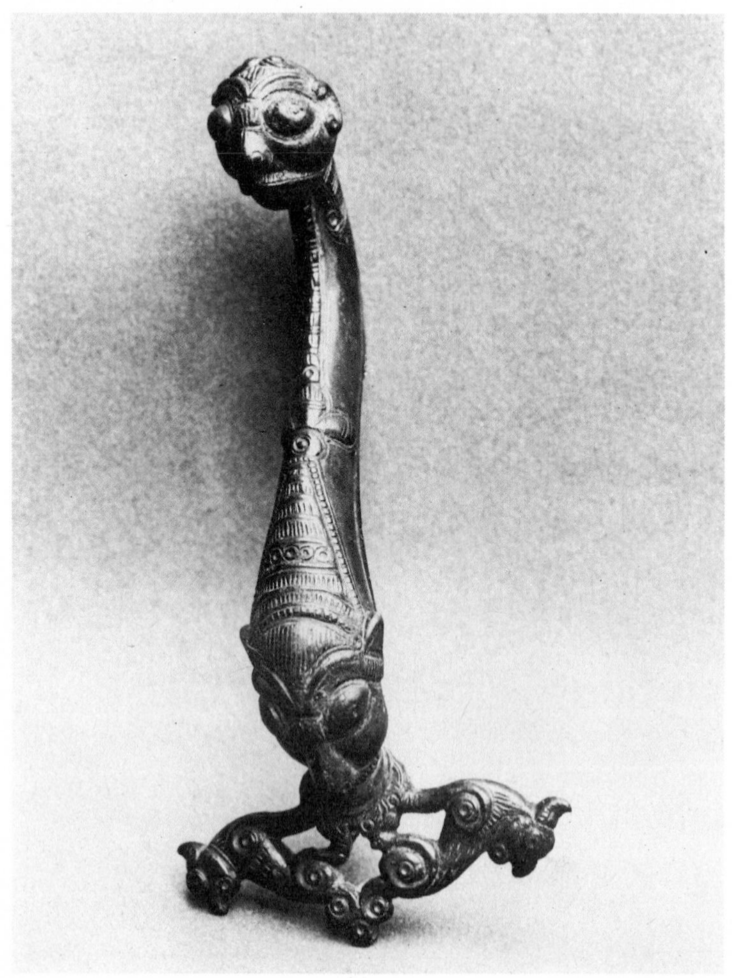

42 Bronze brooch from Parsberg, Germany, with human head and satyr's mask. *c.* 400 BC. 9 cm long.

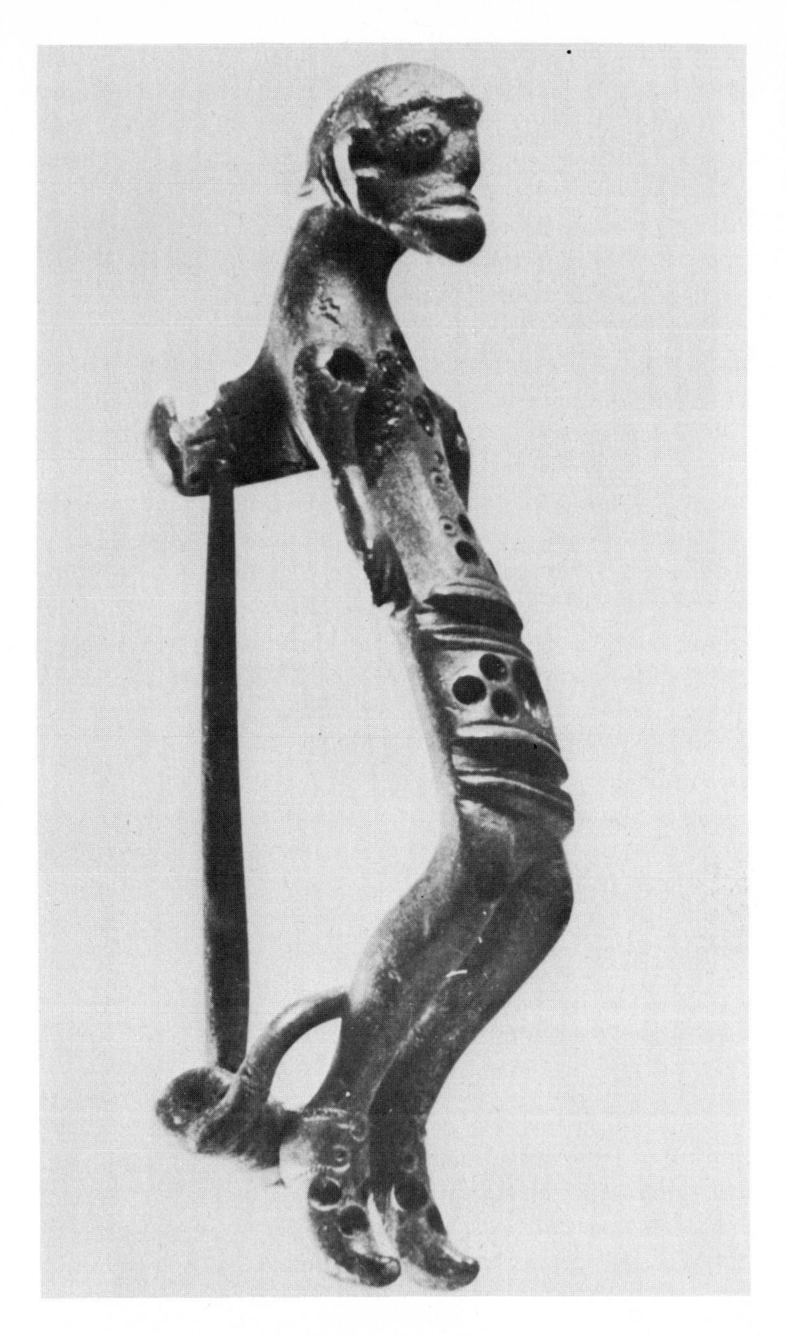

43 Bronze brooch in the form of a man, from Manětín Hrádek, Bohemia. The details of costume, including the pointed shoes recalling Etruscan fashions, are interesting: it was originally inlaid, probably with coral. *c.* 400 BC. 9 cm long.

The Celtic temperament

The Celtic ideal of personal good looks has now been identified, clothed to some extent and adorned. It may be asked next what can be learnt of the spirit of the Celts, and here fortunately Classical authors are again able to throw some considerable light.

'The whole nation ... is war-mad, and both high-spirited and quick for battle although otherwise simple and not uncouth.' These few words by Strabo perfectly express the impression gained of the Celts as a living people from all the written sources, and not least from the native Irish tradition. Strabo makes it clear that his description applied to the time of Celtic independence before Roman rule, and it is well to remember that he, as well as Diodorus Siculus, and other writers, made extensive use of earlier authors who had been able to make personal observations of Celtic life. Personal bravery, amounting to recklessness on the battlefield, and, at home, hospitality and a strict code of etiquette towards visitors, shows the Celtic householder as comparable to, if not a better person than, many of his more historical successors in the European countryside. Against the general impression of high spirits, if not excitability, and the impermanence of concerted action, there must be set the evidence for individual responsibility, and duties within a well-defined social system. The love of bright colours, adornment, praise and entertainment, feasting and quarrelling, all have remained European foibles when conditions have allowed, and none would be more natural than amongst a rustic people dwelling in the temperate regions of Europe.

Not much can be recounted specifically about Celtic women, but this section may end by noting the brief but not unappreciative comment of Diodorus Siculus who wrote that the Gaulish women were not only like their men in their great stature, but that they were also their equals in courage.

Social institutions

The social institutions of the Celts are of the greatest value in providing a mirror to life in Pre-Romanized trans-Alpine Europe, no less than for their wider connections remounting to that common social and linguistic heritage that was to survive in various forms amongst the leading Indo-European peoples. The archaeological setting has been outlined in the first chapter, but here, on the basis of comparative philology and jurisprudence, it may be said that the Celts possessed both a language and an institutional system showing them to have been but one member of a far-flung family. In Northern India, the Aryan heritage, preserved to modern times in a great body of oral learning, shows close relationships. The society of Homeric Greece offers parallels, and in Italy the Italic-speaking peoples possessed per-

44* Gallo-Roman bronze head of an idealized woman, from Finthen near Mainz, Germany. Height 31 cm.

haps the closest links with the Celts until the supervention of Etruscan, and, then, urban Roman institutions. The Celtic and Aryan traditions survived in largely uncontaminated form because they had come to rest in regions on the extreme periphery of the Ancient World, and so escaped succeeding periods of turmoil and replacement at the centre.

In view of these considerations it is unlikely that Irish customary law – in its oldest elements – can diverge very greatly from that observed by the continental Celts from whom it must have been derived, and here again some confirmation is forthcoming from Classical sources.

Social institutions in Ireland

In Ireland the community was embodied in the *túath*, a word that originally meant 'the people', but which had acquired a territorial connotation. The *túath* in population and in extent was quite small, and normally conformed to an area with natural topographical boundaries. The social structure within the *túath* was threefold: king, nobles and free commoners. The king was elected from within the kin of his predecessor, but he was not necessarily one of his sons. The king's family belonged to the noble grade, who were the warriors, but in pagan times the class of magician-sage, druid, seer or otherwise, was accorded the highest status, although these did not form an hereditary caste. The freemen commoners were mainly farmers, but the grade also included certain categories of craftsmen. It should be emphasized that in pagan times the ritual functions of the king were of as great importance as were his executive ones in the assembly or on the battlefield. It is also important that the threefold system formed a social and ritual entity within which all were of free status (*saor*), and of sacred, or ritual qualification (*nemed*). There was also an unfree population, without status or claims to possession, formed of such subjugated communities, slaves, and degraded families as existed.

Within the *túath*, the effective social unit was the kin (*fine*), but for purposes of inheritance, and most forms of obligation, a closer kinship was reckoned on the agnatic descendants of a common great-grandfather. In this more restricted sense (*derbfine*) kinship extended therefore to second cousins in the male line. The family within this kinship system was of the joint type: a householder with his wife, or wives, and children, including grown sons with their wives and offspring. It seems that marriages were contracted outside the kin, and perhaps in the case of the noble grade outside the *túath*.

The ownership of land was not held by an individual, even the head of a household, but by the kin from whom it could not be alienated. It should be said here that there is no evidence amongst the Celts for the king as a disposer of land in return for armed service, or on the other hand, for the existence of common or village land. Neither of these systems would have been appropriate to conditions in prehistoric Europe, although it has been recently claimed that these were early Indo-European forms of land tenure. This claim is based on Hittite and Mycenaean Greek documentary evidence, but in both cases the Indo-European overlords had adapted themselves to a form of urban civilization and polity quite divorced from their ancestral rural modes which were, however, to be conserved, amongst other peoples, by the Celts and Aryans.

These small kingdoms, formed of a single *túath*, can in no way be considered as States. There was no public administration or enforcement of law, and the procurement of redress, within the terms of the law, was the responsibility of the kin of the contending parties. Indeed, the kin was responsible for maintaining all its rights and procurements of settlements.

The individual freeman, of whatever grade, possessed an honour-price (*lóg n-enech*) which was an assessment of his dignity ('face', or present weight in the community), and this was directly related to his material wealth. In this way a prosperous man might ascend considerably in rank, but the honour-price fluctuated according to a man's fortunes, and this was an important matter as compensation for wrongs were directly related to it. In addition to the ties and duties of kinship, there was also the institution of clientship (*célsine*). In its simplest form this involved armed attendance, and other services, by the *céle*, normally a commoner, on his lord (*flaith*). In return the *céle* enjoyed pretection and material support without, however, losing anything of his independent status, or right to hold property in cattle, and interests in land. Clientship, however complicated it later became, should never be confused with feudalism.

Another important aspect of individual participation in the social order was suretyship, of which there were several kinds. In general, a man undertaking suretyship was guarantor, in his own person, by his property or by his power of supervision, for the fulfilment of another's engagements. The guarantor's honour-price entered into suretyship in that he might suffer its reduction, or even deprivation, if his principal defaulted. It is probable that at least one kind of suretyship was a development from the taking and giving of hostages, and these latter of course, also had their part in Irish law, more especially in relation to sureties given to a king.

In principle, an individual's rights and status existed only within his own *túath*, and beyond it he was at the mercy of circumstances. This would have certainly been the situation under primitive conditions.

It will be clear that the maintenance of customary law was not due to the power of any central authority, but it in fact rested on its own venerability, ritual potency, and popular acceptability.

The threat of sanctions, in the loss or reduction of status, was a paramount factor in upholding its effectiveness.

The knowledge of customary law was the concern of the learned order of society. Originally perhaps not distinguished from magico-religious and other offices, the law was in the hands of specialists for some time before it came to be written down in the eighth, possibly seventh, century AD. The *brithem*, jurist, was not a judge in the modern sense. He was an expounder of the law, and might so assist the king in delivering judgments, or he might act as arbitrator in disputes between kin, or even between kings. The jurist was trained in a law school where a great body of traditional knowledge was accurately committed to memory, and of this kind of learning something more will be said in the next chapter.

The law schools tended to differ from region to region in minor aspects of their teaching, but jurists, like others of their social and sacred grade, were free to move about the country at large, and in this way there was frequent interchange of professional knowledge, and a consequent over-all preservation of the learnedly archaic language in which the law was recited. The adjustment of customary law to changing conditions seems to have rested with the interpretative powers of the jurist, but some local alterations were also effected by the king in the assembly (*óenach*) of the whole *túath*. Assemblies were held at certain festivals in each year, and if need be at other times. In addition to their legal function, they fulfilled important ritual and economic needs, and were held, if not at the king's residence, at a sacred site often associated with the burial place of the dynasty.

The king's prerogative at an assembly included the enjoining of various kinds of public action, or undertaking, such as raising a host for warfare, or the conducting of a pact of friendship with another *túath*. The establishment of friendly relations between one *túath* and another may have concerned kings of equal strength, but more often it had to do with the extension of overlordship. In this way a powerful king could become overlord of others less potent, and these arrangements were essentially the same as in individual clientship; the lesser king pledging, with hostages and tribute, his *túath* for service in exchange for greater military security.

It can be seen how larger political combinations thus came about, forming, as they did in Ireland, considerable regional kingships, but this phenomenon is also well illustrated in Gaul, and it is to the continental evidence that inquiry must now turn.

I Gold openwork mountings on a bronze backing for a probably wooden bowl (here restored). A fine example of the 'First Style' of Early La Tène art, close to classical prototypes, and of the later fifth century BC. From a grave at Schwarzenbach, St Wendel, Germany. Height 8.5 cm.

II Gold plaque on iron base, with human masks framed in leaf motifs in the Early La Tène style of the early fourth century BC. From a grave at Weiskirchen, Merzig-Wadern, Germany. Width 8 cm.

I

II

III

IV

Social institutions in Gaul

The only considerable divergence between the Irish social system and that in part revealed by Classical authors for the continental Celts, lies in the matter of kingship. It is well known that in Caesar's time some of the principal Gaulish tribes were governed by the aristocracy with one or more appointed chief magistrates (*vergobret*). The reason for the suppression of kingship in these tribes was understood by Caesar as being due to the great increase, and abuse, of the system of clientship so that factions of the aristocracy were of such strength as to be able to abandon their higher allegiances.

It is interesting that these kingless tribes would all appear to have lain within Celtica, that largest division of Gaul as defined by Caesar. Again, it is perhaps significant that the principal of these tribes, the Arverni, Aedui, and Helvetii, all lay in the zone most open to influences from the *Provincia Narbonensis* which had been under Roman rule since the late second century. It was probably due to the emulation of Roman ways as well as to internal disruption, brought about in consequence of Roman advances from the south and barbarian incursions from the north, that these tribes had abandoned kings for magistrates. In the other two divisions of Gaul, in Aquitania, where the populace were largely akin to the Iberians, and in Belgica, where the tribes were of trans-Rhenine origins, kings held sway. Even within Celtica there were kings, as in the case of Cavarinus who ruled the Senones, but this tribe lay along part of the frontier with Belgica, and remote from the Roman province.

The whole body of evidence from ancient authors as well as from the philology of many Celtic personal names, shows that kingship was both ancient and normal amongst the continental Celts.

There was another factor operative in Gaul from the late second century BC which, in somewhat earlier times, may have done much to alter Celtic institutions in Northern Italy. This was the growth of defendable conglomerations of dwellings, hardly to be called towns or cities but making a real break with the essentially dispersed rural character of archaic Celtic society. In Italy there had been the example of Etruscan cities, but in trans-Alpine Gaul, although small tribal strongholds had long existed, the permanent bringing together of large numbers of people was a phenomenon of the late second century BC partly occasioned by the incursion of the Cimbri and Teutones, but chiefly as a reflection of the development of urban life along the

III Bronze flagon with human masks and animal figures of the late fifth or early fourth century BC, a very individual piece within the Early La Tène repertoire. From Grave XVI of the Dürrnberg cemetery, Salzburg, Austria. Height of whole flagon 46.5 cm.

IV Detail of bronze flagon with coral inlay, one of a pair probably from a grave at Basse-Yutz, Moselle, France. Like the Dürrnberg flagon, these date from the late fifth-early fourth century BC, and show another highly accomplished master at work. Height of whole flagon 39.5 cm.

Mediterranean littoral and within the Roman province generally. This development cannot but have had its consequences in tribal life, and certainly presupposes a diminution of the ritual importance of the old rural kingship.

By comparison with the Irish *túath*, the tribal areas in Gaul, as earlier in Northern Italy, appear to have been very large. In the case of the Gaulish tribes, whose boundaries largely survived through corresponding Roman administrative areas to the dioceses of medieval France, it is clear that the great names represent overlordships embracing numerous smaller population-groups.

This is the evident implication of Strabo's statement that there were the names of sixty tribes inscribed on an altar dedicated to Caesar Augustus at Lugudunum (Lyons), which place was used as their centre. To have been a common centre accessibility must have been possible, necessitating, even under Roman administration, not more than a day or two's travel. On the other hand, the political unit amongst the continental Celts may normally have been a good deal larger than in Ireland and Britain, where the smallness and diversity of natural regions, and the constraint of the ocean, imposed a higher degree of fixation than may ever have come about in the older homelands prior to the development of towns. It seems probable, too, that some oscillation between small and large tribal organizations was likely to have occurred under different circumstances. The agricultural communities, established in the Urnfield Culture expansion of Late Bronze Age times, would have been numerous and self-contained. This is apparent also in the case of the Iron Age A settlers in Britain. The rise of the mobile and warlike Hallstatt and La Tène dynasties may be taken to imply larger dominions, but fragmentation is likely to have ensued after the early conquests, mainly through the divisions of inheritance. Larger regroupings may be expected in times of crisis, and migration, as into Italy or the Balkans. Under these, last, conditions, heterogeneous bands would have been won to the tribal names of leading chieftains, but it is unlikely that whole tribal populations ever completely deserted their original territory. In witness of this may be mentioned the Boii who took part in the settlement of Northern Italy, but who also remained in Bohemia, later to seek refuge in Gaul in the time of Caesar. The Volcae were neighbours of the Boii in Middle Europe, and it may be safely presumed that the Volcae Tectosages in Southern Gaul, and in Asia Minor, were off-shoots from them. In other cases ancient geography does not help in pointing to the early centre of tribal dispersion, and the peripheral off-shoots only are known. Examples may be cited in the Senones in Northern Italy, and in North Central Gaul, the Suessiones whose name occurs in Central Spain no less than in Belgic Gaul, although from this latter area settlers are reported by Caesar to have been sent to Britain. The tribal name Bituriges is known in two very different connections. In Caesar's times this tribe was located south of the Loire, and in a small area west of the Gironde. A legend preserved by Livy tells of a powerful king of this tribe, Ambigatus, whose nephews led forces into Italy and the regions of the Upper Danube and the Rhine. This story probably embodies some memory of the migrations in the fifth century BC from an area north of the Central Alps. The western peripheral position of one branch of the tribe by the first century BC indicates that it had been driven westwards in all probability by the Belgic overrunning of Champagne, that important centre of early La Tène culture. More fully within the light of history are the Catuvellauni, Belgic settlers in Britain, probably in the first quarter of the first century BC. Their parent tribe had become a client to the Remi by the time of the Roman conquest of the Belgae, and the Catuvellauni are not mentioned by name before Ammianus Marcellinus in the fourth century AD.

To return to the questions of political and social structure amongst the continental Celts, an example of the obligations of overlordship and tribal clientage seems to exist in the sequence of events concerning the embroilment of the powerful Arverni with the Romans; an event which precipitated the annexation of *Gallia Transalpina.*

In the year 124 BC, a Roman army defeated the Salyes, a tribe of at least partly Celtic composition, who had begun hostilities with Massilia. Thirty years earlier the Greek city had obtained armed help from Rome in quelling Ligurian tribes who had interfered with her trade. When the Salyes were defeated, a Roman fort was established at Aquae Sextiae (Aix-en-Provence), but no assault was made by any other tribe. The Romans then required the surrender of Salyian fugitives who had sought sanctuary amongst the Allobroges, but this was refused. The Allobroges were then attacked and defeated, but on this occasion, unlike where the Salyes were concerned, the Arverni moved to retaliate. The motive, in view of the continuous success of Roman arms, must have been something stronger than a hope to remove a threat. The overlord's obligation to protect must have been involved, and on its fulfilment would have depended the continuance of allegiance from all the other tribes over whom the

Arverni claimed paramountcy. The inter-tribal politics revealed in Caesar's *Gallic War* are full of the ties of overlord and tributary peoples, and the securement of agreements with hostages, a basic element in tribal clientage.

Within the tribal unit, personal clientship amongst the continental Celts is first attested by Polybius who describes the advantages to a Gaulish noble of a numerous body of retainers and clients. Caesar also noted the mutual advantages of clientship to lord and follower. The system is clearly parallel to that already described for Ireland. So, too, is Caesar's recognition of the threefold division of Gaulish society into *druides*, *equites*, and *plebs*. He may have exaggerated the debased condition of the Gaulish *plebs*, but they would not of course have had any direct say in the kind of affairs with which he was concerned. It is true, however, that the trend of events in Gaul from the second century BC, involving the decline of rural society, may have done much to lower the status of the freeman commoner, but this must remain an hypothesis.

Another interesting parallel to Irish custom is found in Caesar's statement that persons who failed to comply with judicial decisions suffered exclusion from sacrifices, and were deprived of honour and normal society. Here may be seen the relevance of the Irish terms *nemed*, and *ṣaor* already mentioned. Caesar's note that in Gaul sons might not appear in public in the company of their fathers until they were of age to bear arms is perhaps best interpreted as meaning that, as in Ireland, sons were placed in fosterage. In Ireland they would normally have been taken at an early age into a household of higher rank, and would not have returned to the parental roof until, at the age of seventeen, they reached manhood. Girls also were sent to foster-parents, and returned home at the age of fourteen, 'the age of choice', when their betrothal would have been arranged. Their training in household crafts and arts, commensurate with their rank, was the responsibility of their foster-parents who, as also in the case of boys, received payment for their care and instruction.

Some doubt arises as to the accuracy of Caesar's description of dowry provisions, especially in regard to its disposal on the death of either partner. The Irish evidence indicates a basic situation of wife purchase, but with the development of a dowry system in which the woman brought a determined fraction of her husband's wealth. In Ireland, as in Gaul, a number of wives might be held, but the Irish evidence shows that there was a

45* Modern replica of a gilded bronze wine-flagon found in a corroded state in a richly furnished woman's grave at Reinheim, Germany. The gold torc, bracelets and rings in Ill. 34 came from the same grave, as did a bronze mirror. Height of flagon 51.5 cm.

single principal wife (*cétmuinter*), the others being of various subordinate classification.

As to the absolute power of the householder over his wives and children, the evidence from Gaul and Ireland speaks with the same voice, and illustrates this basic Indo-European principle of patriarchal authority. A further word may perhaps be ventured here on the status of women and their capacity to own property. It is generally assumed that the right of a wife to hold independent property, or of a daughter to inherit, is a late development appearing in parallel form in different Indo-European legal systems. On the other hand, a more liberal, but still common, practice seems to have been operative at very varying dates as illu-

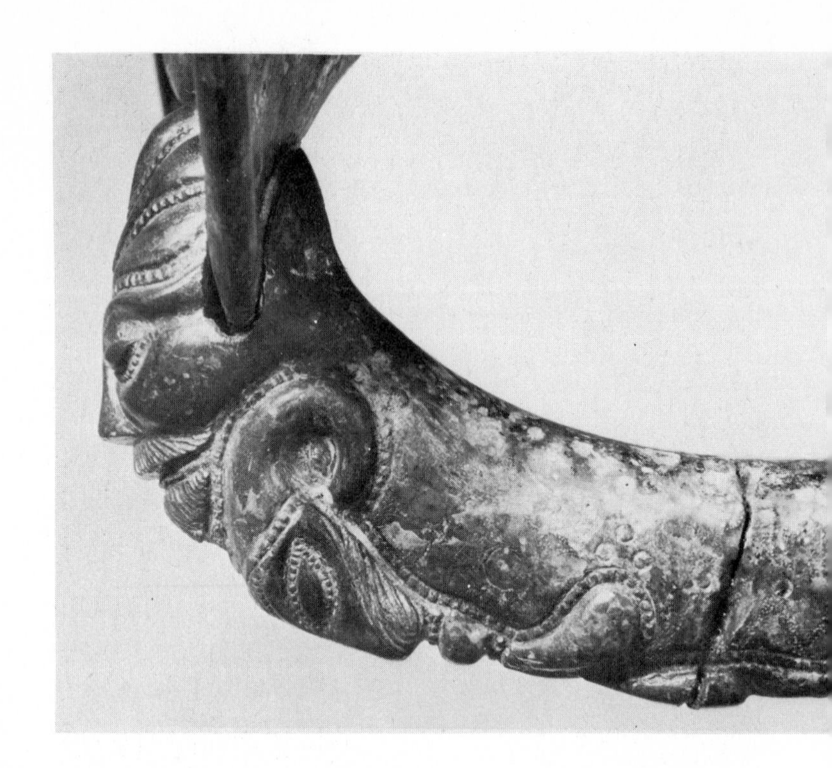

46* Human and animal masks on the bronze flagon-handle from the Reinheim grave. Early fourth century BC.

47* Detail of the human figure on the gold armlet from the Reinheim grave. Early fourth century BC.

strated in Aryan, Roman and Celtic legal custom. There is also the question of the very rich Celtic women's graves, as at Vix, and Reinheim, to take but two recently discovered examples. Here women, buried singly, had been accorded the most splendid funerary chambers, and the most sumptuous adornment and accessories. Personal prestige and the right to possess property may account for such instances, while all the considerations taken together seem to suggest that incapacity of women was a reflection of primitive conditions, predominant in times of migration or hardship, though the legal system was always sufficiently elastic in periods of prosperity, from place to place, to permit greater female freedom in public and family interests.

Rural economy

When the diversity of territory occupied by the Celts is considered, it follows that the balance of rural economy, on which their livelihood essentially depended, must have varied a good deal from region to region. Apart from special opportunities in crafts, and trade, or indeed in pillage, the average Celtic *túath*, or tribe, was mainly engaged in its own food production by agri-

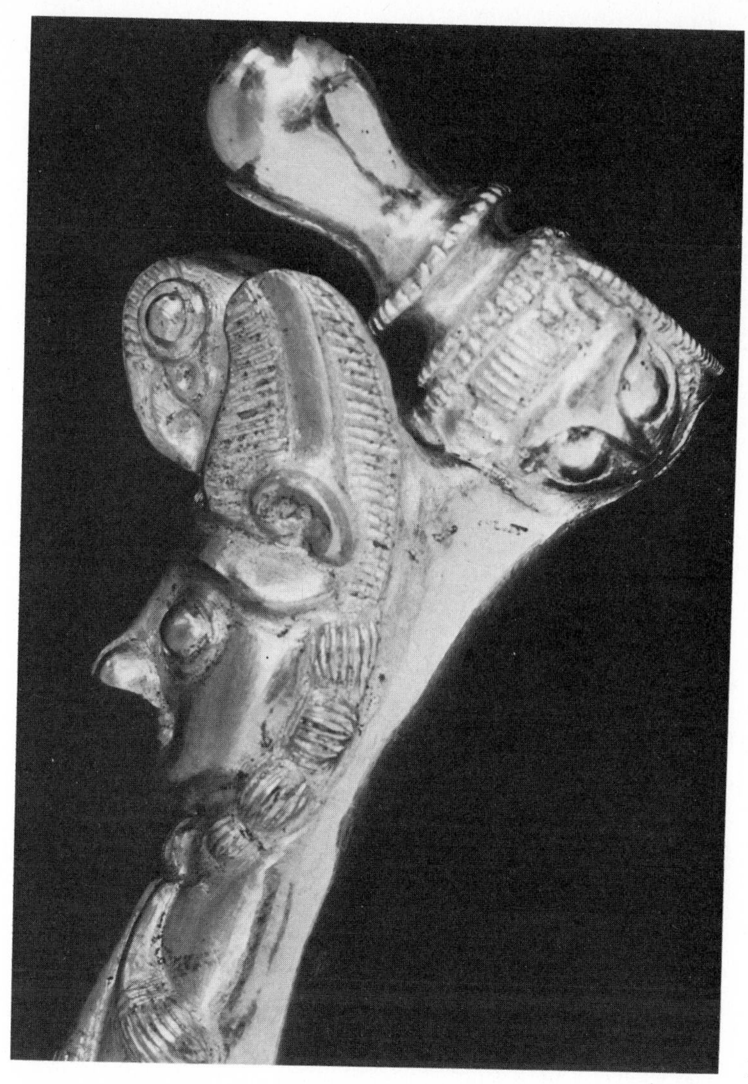

48* Detail of human mask on the gold torc from the Reinheim grave. Early fourth century BC.

culture, cattle raising, or both combined as mixed farming. In this the Celts stand in contrast to the contemporary barbarian nations lying to their east, such as the Scythians, and Thracians, whose uninterrupted grasslands imposed a high degree of uniformity.

From such material as is available from competent excavations, it would appear that in addition to cereal crops, mainly wheat and barley, the normal Celtic farm stocked cattle, swine and sheep. The evidence is derived principally from the debris of the farmstead, in arrangements for the drying and storage of grain, and in the types and relative quantities of domestic animal bones

49 Air photograph of prehistoric field systems of 'Celtic' type on a limestone spur near Corfe Castle, Dorset.

found in rubbish pits. Only under exceptional circumstances can the actual lay-out of these farms be apprehended. For the most part the land has been in use throughout subsequent centuries, and all traces of ancient field systems have disappeared. But in Southern Britain, on the higher slopes of the chalk downs, field systems from the Late Bronze Age and the Iron Age have been preserved together with the house and cattle enclosures, drove-ways, and boundary ditches. This has come about because the land was subsequently abandoned for richer soils at lower levels. Similar field systems have survived in Western Denmark, an area not properly within the Celtic zone; but in the older Celtic home-lands it is only the recognition through excavations of the farm-house, with its appurtenances, that can throw light on farming practice; extensive evidence for ploughing and fields has disappeared.

Contrasts in settlement

It will be remembered that in the formation period of the Celts, the Urnfield settlers of the Upper Danubian region were mainly distinguished as farmers on the plains, while the older native tradition was that of pastoralism on the uplands and hills. Although there was undoubtedly a great intermixture of peoples and cultures during the ensuing centuries, it is possible to observe some continuation of this duality in rural economy although it may often have been a necessary adaptation to local conditions rather than the result of conservatism. It is worth instancing two cases, different in nature, but both significant for their wider aspects. In the first place there is the Celtic settlement of Languedoc, an area in which Greek traders in the Western Mediterranean may first have heard of the Celts, and in the second place there is Ireland where native literary tradition stems directly from a prehistoric past.

Languedoc

It was mentioned in the first chapter how people of North Alpine derivation spread across Southern France, and beyond the Pyrenees. Confining attention for the present purpose only to Languedoc, it may be said that the coastal plain was settled by immigrants who established themselves in permanent communities, cultivating the soil in the immediate neighbourhood of their settlements which were placed on hill-tops, or projecting plateaux, overlooking the low ground. These places were later fortified, and became the *oppida* held against the Romans. Notwithstanding the presence of indigenous inhabitants, and the enormous influence of Greek trade, the continuing cultural characteristics of the *oppida* dwellers showed their North Alpine origins, and it is very difficult not to see these people as predominantly Celts.

Largely contemporary, if not appearing quite so early, there is evidence for pastoralist communities living on the limestone *garrigues* that form the southern fringe of the Cevennes, and which provide the hinterland of the coastal plain. Similar herdsmen roamed the foothills of the Pyrenees, and all were accustomed to raise small tumuli over cremation graves that were equipped with pottery and metal types showing a culture parallel and interrelated to that of the plainsmen, being also of North Alpine and Hallstatt inspiration.

50* Air photograph of hill-fort, Old Oswestry, Shropshire.

51* Air photograph of hill-fort, Cissbury, Sussex.

These pastoralists were thus also intruders, and are generally regarded as having been Celts, but it would be rash to claim, on present evidence, that their way of life resulted from an ancient pastoral heritage in Middle Europe rather than from the exigencies of migration. It should not be supposed that these upland pastoralists were mere nomads, and although no dwellings have been excavated, it is considered that small stone forts may well be of their building. Probably a recurrent aspect of pastoralism was the construction of burial mounds, forming as they did lasting monuments, and landmarks, whereas flat urnfields could be provided with perishable demarcations, wooden posts or fences, in areas of continuous habitation, as on the plains, where the *oppida* presuppose a denser population.

Britain

The achievement of compact settlements within *oppida*, as in Languedoc, infers some density of population requiring permanence to cultivate the soil, but also with the economic, as well as the social, ability to establish effective strongholds. This capacity has already emerged amongst the Urnfielders in the North Alpine zone, as fortifications of those people attest, but in Southern Britain, as well, the distribution of hill-forts is mainly that of the settlement areas of the Iron Age A people who were agriculturalists, and mixed farmers. Here, the hill-forts do

52* Air photograph of Iron Age hill-fort, Uffington Castle, Oxfordshire, above the chalk-cut White Horse, probably also an Iron Age monument.

not appear to have been much used by permanent residents; they existed mainly as refuges and tribal centres, and the Celtic freeman occupied his own farmstead elsewhere.

In the areas where the Iron Age A settlement was lightest, and where the Iron Age B immigrants had territory largely to themselves, as in Lincolnshire and Yorkshire, hill-forts are rare and not certainly the work of the newcomers. It would appear that these people, with their Rhenish La Tène, or Marnian, antecedents did not require large strongholds, and this should cause little surprise, for in the old Celtic homelands it was migration and warfare, set against the cumulative results of the Sub-Atlantic climatic deterioration, that had necessitated an economic swing to mobility: wealth in livestock rather than in crops. That this was not necessarily an enduring condition is manifest in the avidity with which the Celtic settlers took to cereal cultivation in Cis-Alpine Gaul, a matter of surprised note to Classical writers. In Britain, also, in areas where the 'B' and 'A' folk intermingled, the agricultural tradition continued, and was of course greatly strengthened as a result of the Belgic settlement in imme-

53 Hill-fort at Crickley Hill, Gloucestershire: Reconstruction of stone-walled entrance defences, from before the fifth century BC, and of entrance and long houses, from sixth or seventh century BC.

54* Iron Age hill-fort of Otzenhausen near Trier, Germany.

diately Pre-Roman times. The Belgae were themselves within the same Urnfield-Hallstatt cultural tradition as the Iron Age A people, although their rural economy, and methods of fortification, had meanwhile undergone considerable development.

Ireland

The recognition of a mainly pastoral zone in Eastern and North-eastern Britain, during the Iron Age, is relevant to the Irish scene. In that island, large prehistoric fortifications are rare, and of such as can be regarded as hill-forts, or *oppida*, some were never completed. They appear to have been the work of refugee communities who were not the bearers to Ireland of La Tène fine metal-work, chariotry, and the other manifestations of heroic society. These things are revealed in the early epic literature of Ireland as the concomitants of a warrior society whose wealth was counted in cattle, and whose heroic exploits centred on

55* Ruined stone wall of the Otzenhausen hill-fort.

cattle-raiding. As will be seen, too, the pagan festivals in Ireland belonged to a pastoral rather than to an agricultural cycle.

These factors, taken with the wetter climate of Ireland, show how cattle-raising continued to be the livelihood of the more significant body of Celtic overlords. It explains, too, the essentially dispersed nature of the population, and how there came into being the innumerable small circular earthworks (*ráth*, *lios*, etc.) that formed the defences of individual permanent households from which could be operated the short-range transhumance, and general animal husbandry, determined by Irish geography. These considerations have specially to do with those northern and western parts of Ireland, where the archaeological evidence is strongest, for derivations going back through the Iron Age B culture of Eastern Britain to Continental La Tène origins, and the heroic concepts of the cattle-raiding epics might well have been equally apt for the splendidly turned out chariot warriors of the Middle Rhine, or of Champagne, in earlier centuries.

If this dominant strain amongst the Irish Celts was but little concerned with agriculture, there were other elements in the population who supplied the need. One may suspect, amongst others, the crannóg-dwellers, but the archaeology of the subject has yet to be evolved. The literary evidence, in some mythological and kingship stories, perhaps of somewhat different geographical distribution within Ireland from the cattle-raiding epics, show the importance of the success of corn harvests. The laws also contain many provisions about ploughing and corn lands, but these may chiefly be a reflection of the great advances in Irish agriculture resulting from the establishment of the monasteries in the fifth and sixth centuries AD. From that period, and throughout Medieval times, corn-growing was a prominent aspect of Irish farming, but the settlement pattern remained that of the independent farm-steading within its own entrenchment or wall.

Fields and ploughs

49 The prehistoric 'Celtic' or 'square' field, as best exemplified in Southern Britain, is rarely bigger than some one hundred and twenty by eighty metres, and is frequently much smaller. The fields are more often rectangular than truly square, but their width is great in proportion to their length, and this was evidently intended to assist in ploughing both along and across the area within the boundaries. This cross-ploughing was necessary under dry climatic conditions in order to break the soil as finely as possible to conserve moisture. It was only with the change to a consistently damp climate in North-western Europe that ploughing in one line, up and down a field, became expedient, and this led to the appearance of long, strip ploughlands, and the emergence of a heavy plough capable of cutting and turning the heavy, moisture-laden sod. These innovations seem to have been first achieved by the Celtic, or mixed Celtic-Teutonic, tribes living in North-western Germany. The Belgae brought these practices to South-eastern Britain, although their full development is only seen as a result of that final, and Post-Roman, 'Iron Age' invasion of Britain: the Anglo-Saxon settlement.

V Pair of gold torcs from a hoard of four torcs and three armlets from Erstfeld, north of the St Gotthard Pass in the Swiss Alps, about 400 BC. Here again the extraordinary individuality and virtuosity of the Early La Tène artist is apparent. Diameter 14.5 cm.

VI Gold arm and neck rings from the chariot grave at Waldalgesheim, Kreuznach, Germany, of the later fourth century BC and representative of the stylistic phase of Early La Tène art named from this find. Diameter of torc 18 cm.

The older type of field, determined by the need to cross-plough, was broken by a light plough with neither coulter nor mould board, but with a simple share, of wood or stone, then of iron, which did little more than scratch the surface. Both field and plough of this archaic mode have remained in use in the drier and poorer parts of Europe, especially in Mediterranean lands,

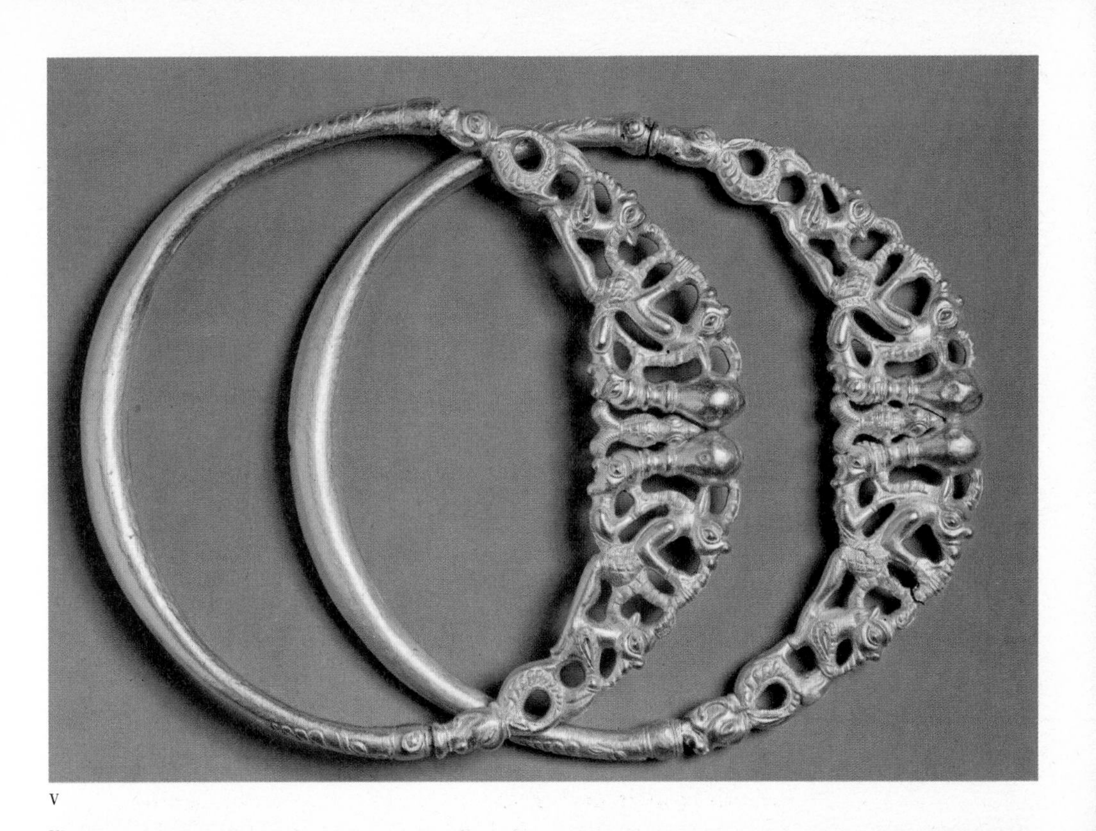

V

VI

VII

but they also continued, despite the damper climate, in the western and northern parts of Britain, and in Ireland where the hand cultivation of corn plots has also to be taken into account.

Houses

The study of house sites in relationship to field systems, cattle drove-ways, and boundary ditches, is still in its initial stage, but so far as the evidence from Britain and Ireland is concerned, it would seem that the arrangements can best be interpreted in terms of the Celtic social structure already outlined. One may envisage greater and lesser land-owning families of the joint type, each under their patriarchal head, dwelling in their own farmsteads, or strongholds, together with their unfree retainers, and themselves in various conditions of patronage or clientship according to their rank.

In a social system such as this, where material assets greatly determined the size of the family dwelling-place, the variety of house types, and in dwelling-place units, revealed by archaeology, is not surprising. Of actual house plans, rectangular forms are predominant in Urnfield-Hallstatt and La Tène cultural associations everywhere on the Continent where they have been excavated, but in the hill-forts of Spain and Portugal round houses were also common, and in Britain and Ireland, round houses again appear to be the commonest form. Without an exhaustive discussion, it would be unwise to draw any deductions from individual house plans; it must suffice to say that generally speaking the rectangular house has a very great antiquity in Middle Europe, while along the Atlantic coasts, the round house also goes back to Neolithic and Early Bronze Age times. There is unfortunately little clarification to be found in Greek and Latin writers on this subject, but Strabo does mention dome-shaped houses in Gaul, and these should surely have been of round-house type. The possibility may have also to be considered that in the case of some mixed farming tribes, their house forms may reflect an earlier, more mobile and pastoralist, condition when lightly constructed circular wooden frameworks for skin-covered huts had been the rule. These would have been the most likely forms of human shelter for tribes on migration with wheeled vehicles, and Strabo's description of the Suevi and related peoples, wandering with their goods on waggons, may well have been appropriate to Celtic as well as Teutonic tribes in Middle Europe.

56, 57–59

VII Helmet of bronze with iron and gold mountings, from Amfreville, Eure, France. It lacks its knobbed finial and its cheekguards and attachments, but is a splendid piece in the Waldalgesheim style of the fourth century BC. Height 17.5 cm.

56* Stone-built houses in the Citaña de Sanfins, Portugal.

57* Air photograph of the hill-fort of Citaña de Sanfins.

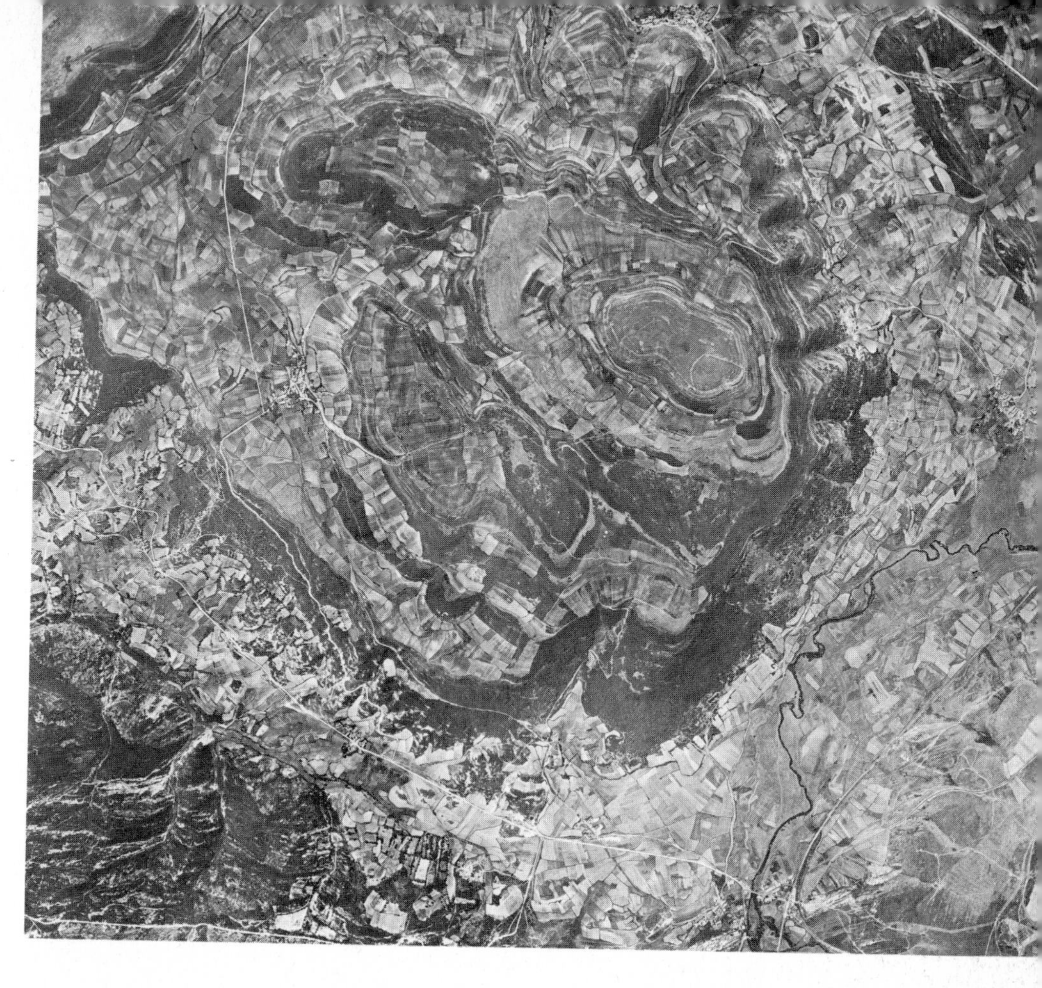

58* Air photograph of the Castro de Monte Bernorio, Palencia, Spain.

59* Air photograph of the Citañia de Briteiros, Portugal.

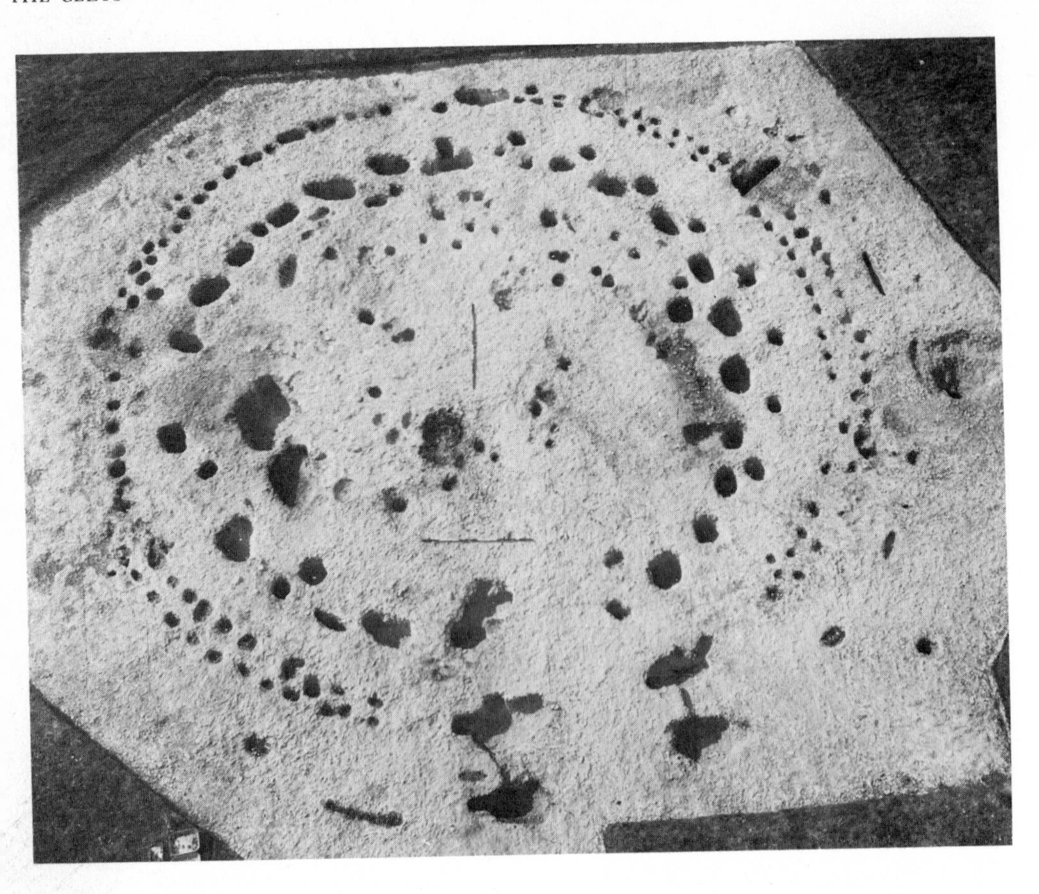

60 Excavated post-holes of circular timber-framed house of the Early Iron Age at Pimperne, Dorset. Fifth–fourth century BC.

It is so far only in Britain that round houses of post-built wooden construction for permanent residence have been excavated. The principal site is that of Little Woodbury, in Wiltshire, where a single large house stood in its own stockade. At West Harling, in Norfolk, two round houses and a rectangular building formed one farm-steading, and both these sites belong to the Iron Age A culture. In Ireland, excavated houses so far have proved to be of Early Christian times, but they show considerable intermixture of round and rectangular dwellings contemporary with each other on the same site. It is clear that the sample of properly studied house sites is as yet too small, and geographically too scattered, to permit even the possibility that the full range has yet been discovered.

Strongholds and 'towns'

In some few excavated sites where a number of house foundations bespeak a large social and economic unit, sometimes possibly a chieftain's household, the range in size of house plan may be expected to reflect differences in status amongst the one-time residents. More particularly, the special siting and greater size of one or two buildings may indicate the overlord's residence, and this is well exemplified in the Urnfield culture defended site at Altjoch on the Kochel See, in Bavaria, where a single large rectangular house occupied the inner fortification, below which stood the smaller houses and farm structures. Similarly at the Hallstatt culture site on the Goldberg, in Württemberg, a rectangular post-built house, and another large building, stood within a timber stockade, outside which were more than two dozen structures of various kinds, both houses and other farm buildings, the whole having been included within an outer fortification.

The sites so far mentioned, were essentially rural, but when it comes to a consideration of large permanent settlements, such as the Languedocian *oppida*, it must be supposed that the normal Celtic social system had undergone some modification, and this must certainly have been true of the great 'townships' of Central Gaul such as Gerovia Bibracte and Avaricum, which played so prominent a part in Caesar's conquest.

Grain storage

A remarkable feature of some Celtic agricultural settlements that cannot be passed over in silence, was the use of deep storage pits,

61 Plan of the excavated settlement of Hallstatt date on the Goldberg, South Germany, showing post-holes of buildings and palisades.

or silos, sunk into the underlying ground within the house or farm-stead enclosure. It would appear that these pits were used mainly for corn storage, and in Britain, at least, they were lined with basketry, and used for a few seasons only owing to the effects of humidity. They were then filled up with rubbish and earth, and new pits excavated. They are, therefore, valuable sources for archaeological material, but they are peculiar to the Iron Age A culture in this island. In the Languedocian *oppida* of Cayla de Mailhac, and Ensérune, which have been excavated, very deep silos had been sunk into the limestone, and they, too, had been filled with rubbish as had their smaller counterparts in Britain. The practice of using silos was later given up in Languedoc when large earthenware jars, *dolia*, came into use as a result of Greek influence.

The distribution of storage pits in prehistoric Europe has not yet been worked out, but their use was an ancient practice in the Eastern Mediterranean world, and is also testified at some of the Middle Bronze Age village sites in Hungary. It would appear that the use of storage pits, with its inference for greater harvests resulting from improved agriculture, was one of the eastern intrusive elements that took root in the Urnfield culture of the North Alpine zone.

62

Crafts and trade

It was perhaps the very diversity of their environment and material resources, together with their lively disposition, and the elasticity of their social structure within the free grades, that brought to the Celts a standard of achievement in arts and crafts unparalleled amongst the ancient inhabitants of trans-Alpine Europe, rivalled only by their Eurasiatic neighbours, the Scythians. It would be impossible to describe and discuss in a short book the immense range of objects in durable substances, in gold, silver, bronze and iron, in pottery, and even in fragments of wood and textiles that bear witness to the excellence of Celtic manual skills and artistic perception. That would be more properly the function of a specifically archaeological study, and here only some general considerations can be taken into account.

I, II

The essential aspect of the economy of any Celtic community was its capacity to feed and clothe itself, and at the same time to produce enough in purchasing power of some sort to acquire the tools and weapons, and less utilitarian accessories of life, that only intercommunication with craftsmen or traders could bring.

(*opposite*)
62 Storage pits and other features within the hill-fort of Danebury, Hampshire. Mainly fifth-third century BC.

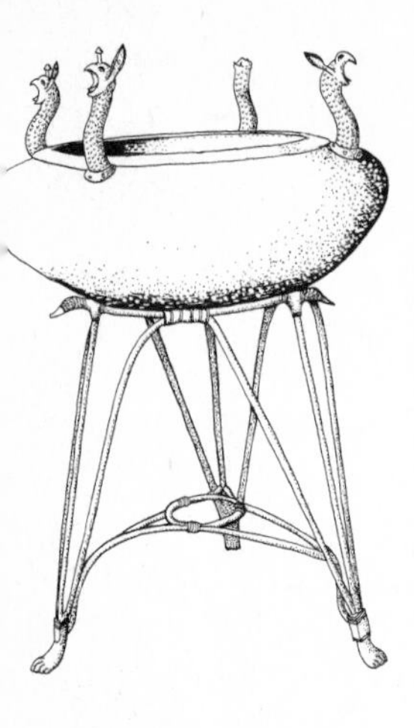

63 Greek 'griffon cauldron' of bronze with iron tripod. Ste-Colombe-sur-Seine, Côte d'Or. Height of tripod 56 cm.

Except, therefore, amongst the most unfavourably situated communities, one may look for some degree of specialization which enabled any unit, from a family to a tribe, to augment its wealth. With many, it must have been wool, hides, and other farm produce, but the widespread occurrence of iron ore throughout the Celtic domain provided an important negotiable substance which was more easily worked, and in greater demand, than bronze had ever been with its technical limitations, and the natural scarcity of its components.

The richness of many Celtic communities, expressed archaeologically in their graves, can be interpreted in relation to metal resources, and this is especially so in areas where production in quantity could be made to serve the insatiable markets of the urban world beyond the Alps; first in trade with the Greeks and Etruscans, and later with the Romans. As examples, the graves at Hallstatt itself, situated in the Salzkammergut, bespeak the trading relations of the local salt merchants with distant North-eastern Italy. The late Hallstatt culture chieftains' graves in Burgandy bear witness, in their Etruscan and Western Greek imports, to the result of extensive local iron working, and export by way of the Rhône. The tin trade from Cornwall and Brittany to the Mediterranean shores of Southern Gaul may also be cited, but with less spectacular remains, as an important economic and cultural factor amongst the Celts along the Atlantic seaboard.

Cultural significance of the wine trade

The most important development in long-distance trade was that affecting the Celts in Burgundy, already mentioned, together with tribes on the Middle Rhine and the Upper Danube. From the Celtic point of view the real objective of this commerce seems to have been wine, and one may envisage gold and slaves, as well as iron, as important export items in the exchange. The final significance of all this lay not so much in economics as in the flowering of 'La Tène' art, a native creation in just that wine-drinking zone, centred on the Middle Rhine, where the most novel and luxurious Greek and Etruscan drinking services, brought in with the wine, had their full impact in forms, and decorative plant motifs, on the minds of Celtic craftsmen and patrons alike.

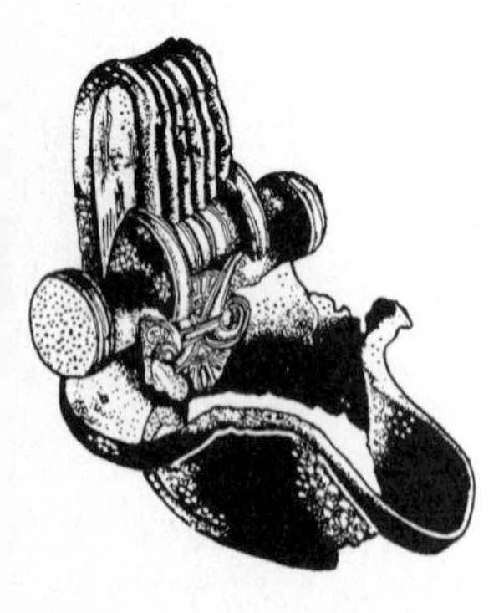

64 Upper fragment of Rhodian bronze flagon, Vilsingen, Württemberg. About a quarter actual size.

In archaeological terms, the story began in the middle of the sixth century BC, and is testified in late Hallstatt cultural associations by the presence of Rhodian bronze wine jugs in the princely waggon graves at Kappel-am-Rhein in Baden, and at Vilsingen

65* Fifth-century Greek cup with Celtic gold appliqué ornament, from the grave of Klein Aspergle, South Germany. Diameter 15.5 cm.

in Württemberg. These jugs may have preceded the actual transport of Greek Black Figure drinking cups, but the latter form an especially important chronological horizon in their occurrence at such important strongholds as the Heuneburg, near Riedlingen, which overlooks the Danube in its course through Württemberg, at the Camp de Château in the French Jura, and at the great hill-top *oppidum* on Mount Lassois near Châtillon-sur-Seine in the Côte d'Or. The prelude to the creation of La Tène art

72

71

66* Gold terminals of drinking horns, Klein Aspergle grave. Fifth century BC. Larger head about 2 cm long.

is set in just this kind of stronghold, the centre of political authority and far-flung trade relations, and to these places there is now some reason to think that there came southern craftsmen as well as material imports. These men were able to modify Greek styles in weapons and decorative forms to native requirements, but also introduced new ideas in building as in the case of the brick wall and bastions found during the recent important excavations at the Heuneburg. 72, 73

It was the advent of Etruscan influence, embodied again in fine metal vessels, but also in more utilitarian crafts, as probably

67* Flagon and stamnos from the Klein Aspergle grave. Height of flagon 35 cm.

(*opposite*)
68* Bronze spouted-flagon from the chariot grave of Waldalgesheim, Germany. Height 32.5 cm.

in an improved model of a fast two-wheeled war chariot, that would seem to have touched off the spark of native Celtic creativeness; for the first flowering of La Tène art comes in objects from the war-chariot graves of the Middle Rhine, and the art is throughout a part of the aristocratic culture sprung from this source. What factors in politics and wealth brought this about must remain obscure, but it is certain that La Tène art was not the creation of the Celts at large, but of the overlords of this central group. It is interesting to consider that the Celts in Lan-

74

I, IV

69* Detail of handle of the flagon from the Waldalgesheim grave.

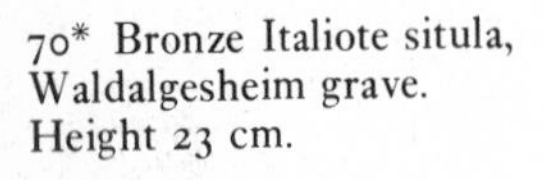

70* Bronze Italiote situla, Waldalgesheim grave. Height 23 cm.

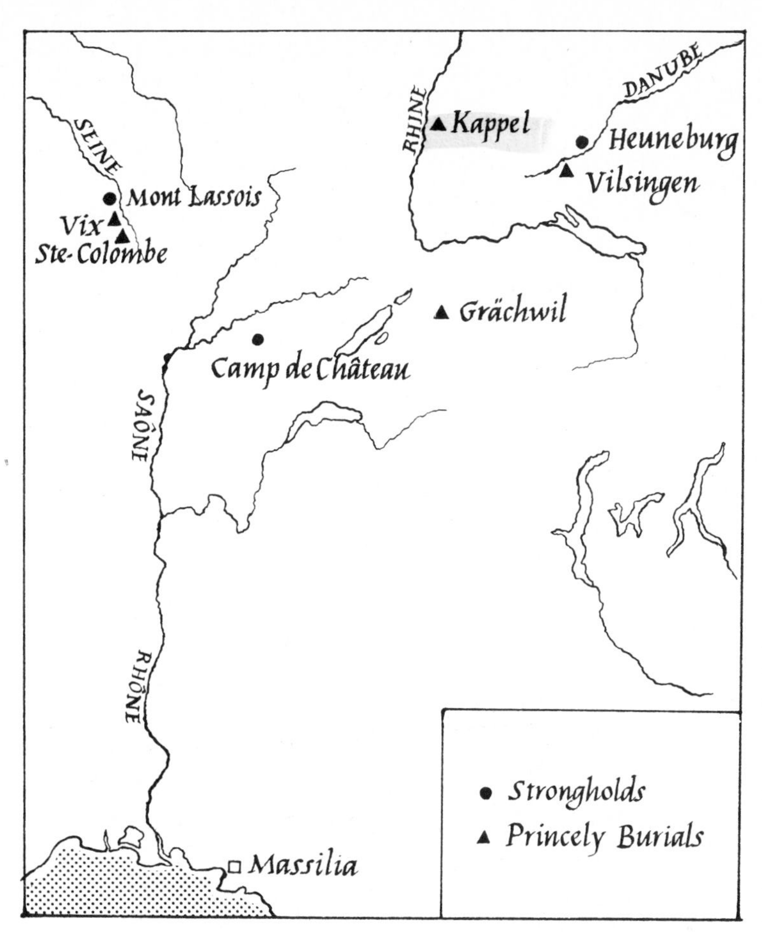

71 Greek wine trade with the Celts, showing strongholds and princely burials in the 'Burgundian' region of the late Hallstatt culture containing fine Greek metal and ceramic imports. *c.* 550–470 BC.

72* The Heuneburg hill-fort, South Germany.

73* The Heuneburg: foundations of defensive bastion.

guedoc, open as they were to Greek and Etruscan influence, played no part in the creation of the new art style, and the explanation must largely lie in the fact that their rulers did not share in that tradition of heroic glorification, on the battlefield and in the feasting hall, which was at home amongst the waggon- and chariot-burying dynasties, and which found its ultimate literary memorial in Ireland.

However much the originating patrons and craftsmen were indebted to southern stimuli in appreciation and in technical training, it was the native Celtic craftsmen who developed and spread the new art, and the fashions in weapons, brooches, and pottery, that went with it. This is the moment to remember the special status enjoyed by men of skill (*aes dána*) in early Ireland. They formed almost a special grade between the warriors and the farmers, but they were closer to the warriors both in the nature of their privileges, and in consequence of their mutual interests.

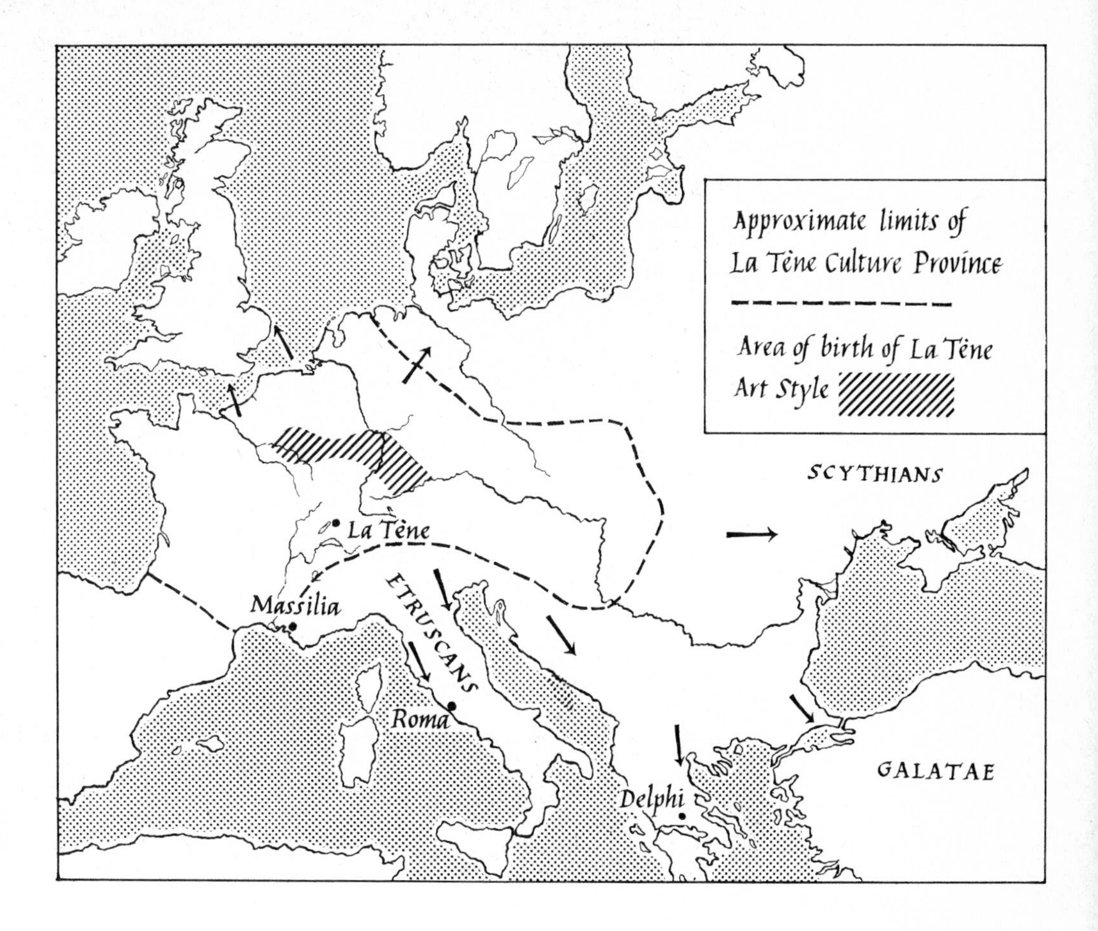

74 The expansion of the Celts between the late fifth and mid third century BC.

'La Tène' art

It would be impossible to expound adequately the full nature of Celtic (La Tène) art in the present general study. The Bibliography (p. 219) gives references to the authorities, and the Supplementary Notes on pages 210–217 are designed to point out the characteristics of the specimens illustrated. It would be wrong, however, if the subject was left, even here, without a note on the sources, additional to Graeco-Etruscan, from which Celtic art drew its inspiration. In the first place, there was of course the old native tradition in trans-Alpine Europe of abstract geometric decoration, and this had been strengthened during the period of the Urnfield and Hallstatt cultures by East Mediterranean motifs such as the meander, sun symbols and stylized birds, especially waterfowl.

I–VII

In the second place there was Scythian, and other oriental, influence from which the Celts drew ideas especially about animal

75 Black graphite polished pottery dish with meander pattern, Eschenfelden, Bavaria. Diameter 43 cm.

representation: stylized beasts from the Scythians, more naturalistic ones from as far afield as Iran. To this latter source seem also due the concept of the elaborate neck ornament, the torc, as well as the motif of opposed pairs of creatures, or of heads alone, as in the remarkable silver torc from Trichtingen in Württemberg. The Celts were careful not to copy this eastern art any more than they did the Graeco-Etruscan; they merely made use of suggestions from both, and it is not always easy to decide from which they were borrowing, for Etruscan art also incorporated an oriental tradition of weird animal and human shapes.

V, VI

38

Although pottery and, doubtless, other material played their part, the great vehicle of Celtic art was a fine metal-work in gold and bronze, less often in silver, and its expression was characterized by a rhythmical linear, and plastic, treatment of surfaces involving infinite variations on a comparatively small number of basic curvilinear designs. These were applied with great skill and sensitivity, with an especial joy in asymmetry, and in allusions to naturalistic forms, within the discipline of an essentially geometric and abstract method of composition.

Celtic coinage and barter

There was another medium in which the Celts, in the final two centuries of their independence, showed their peculiar artistic flair. This was at a time when La Tène art had declined everywhere except in Britain, and it involved tribes who had played

76* Roman and Celtic coins: (a) Denarius, *c.* 48 BC; (b) Denarius, *c.* 54–44 BC; (c) Coin of the Carnutes: (d) Coin of the Baiocasses; (e) Coin of the Arverni.

a

b

c

d

e

77* Coins illustrating the Celtic world: (a) Tetradrachm of Aetolia, *c*. 279 BC; (b) Coin of the Remi; (c) Denarius, 118 BC; (d) Denarius, AD 69–70.

no great share in that art. The new art was a coinage, from the time of the first issues in the late third century BC to its cessation in Gaul with Julius Caesar, and in Britain with the Claudian conquest. There were two main streams in Celtic coinage; in the first, in gold, inspired by the staters of Alexander III, or less probably of Philip II, of Macedon, and carried west by way of the Danube to Central Gaul, and, through the Belgae, to South-eastern Britain; the second, in silver, from Southern Gaul where the beautiful coins in this metal of the western Colonial Greeks, and of Massilia itself, formed the exemplars. The native numismatic art was one of extreme stylization of heads, animals and chariots, with an apparent profusion of mythological symbolism. The stylization led to accentuation of particular elements – as of hair at the expense of the face – and to distintegretation – as in the dismemberment of body and legs in portraying the horse. Inscriptions are late in the series, and are usually confined to abbreviations of recognizable Celtic proper names, and of titles. The selective distribution of coin types has made possible their identification with particular tribes in the great majority of cases, and their value in reflecting political conditions, and changes, is of the greatest importance.

Units of value

Coinage leads to the question of units of value amongst the Celts, and Caesar's note that in Britain iron ingots of fixed weight, as well as gold and bronze coins, were used as money has been substantiated by the discovery of iron 'currency bars'. These long strips of iron, with one end pinched up, are suggestive of sword blades, and may in fact be the metal equivalent of an unworked blade. These currency bars have a selective distribution in Britain, and it is clear that outside the çoin and currency bar areas, and in earlier times – for neither is earlier than the late second century BC – the unit of value was of another kind. Here philology, and the Irish texts, supply useful information, and it was cattle, as universally amongst the Indo-Europeans, that formed the oldest standard of value. In Ireland, units of value in terms of six heifers, or three milch cows, came into use, and to these

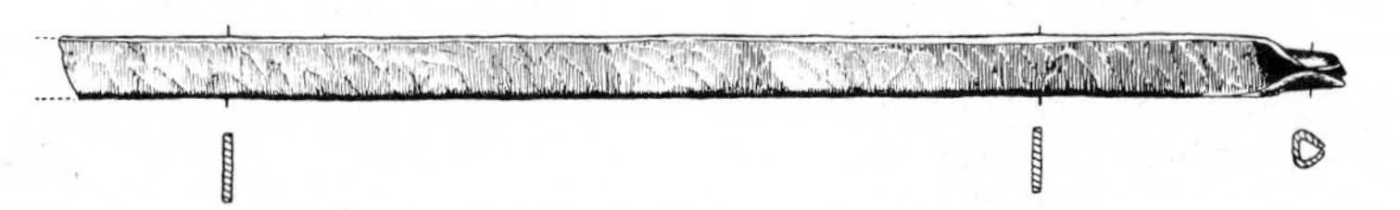

78 Iron 'currency bar'. Llyn Cerrig Bach, Anglesey. Existing length 50 cm.

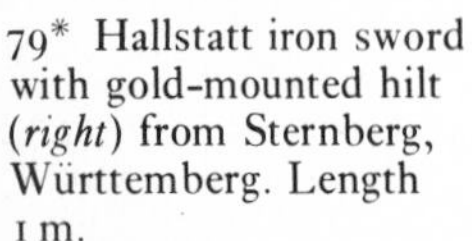

79* Hallstatt iron sword with gold-mounted hilt (*right*) from Sternberg, Württemberg. Length 1 m.

a female slave (*cumal*) came to be regarded as roughly equivalent. The term *cumal* then came into very general use, as in estimating the worth of a chariot, or of land holdings. The choice of the bondswoman in this connection suggests that at some stage she had become a direct negotiable asset on her own account, and the Roman slave market may well be suspected as having brought this about.

In Ireland, as in Scotland and some other parts of Britain, no native coins were ever produced, but even where coinage had been adopted, on the Continent or in Britain, the more ancient forms of estimating worth, and effecting exchange, would have continued for the bulk of rural transactions. Coins had been at first only necessary in dealing with foreign merchants who would not always accept the animate or more bulky forms of exchange.

Warfare

The final pages of this chapter must be devoted to Celtic warfare. The profound impression made upon the minds of Romans and Greeks by the appearance and behaviour of Celtic warriors is evident from the numerous literary descriptions and allusions, as well as from the sculpture at Pergamon, and representations in minor art in Italy. In the oral literature of the Celts, it may be reasonably assumed that in epic, and eulogy, martial deeds took pride of place, as they are so so found in the Irish tradition which depicts an heroic society differing in no way, except in chronological position, from the ancestral continental mode of life.

For the completely prehistoric period, during the centuries which saw the formation of the Celts, the archaeology of graves is the main source for information on the warrior's equipment. Throughout the Late Bronze Age, the principal weapon was the cut and thrust sword, but spears were also in use, and there is some evidence for round wooden shields with bronze studs, and for leather shields. Bronze arrow-heads are known, especially from the Upper Danubian region, but the bow seems to have been going out of fashion. Helmets, shields, and even cuirasses, of sheet bronze are known, but must be regarded as having always been great rarities. VII

The feat of arms

The introduction of iron to the general economy of the North Alpine peoples, in, or a little before, the seventh century BC, had a great effect on the quantity and toughness of weapons. Associated particularly with the waggon-grave chieftains of the first phase of the Hallstatt culture are long iron swords of proportions specially serviceable for cut and thrust fighting. Because horse-gear also becomes conspicuous in these tombs, it has often been asserted that cavalry had now come into use, and that these long iron swords had been evolved for this new type of combat. This view is unsound because to be mounted on a horse is not to presuppose concerted action by a body of armed riders. That is the 16, 18

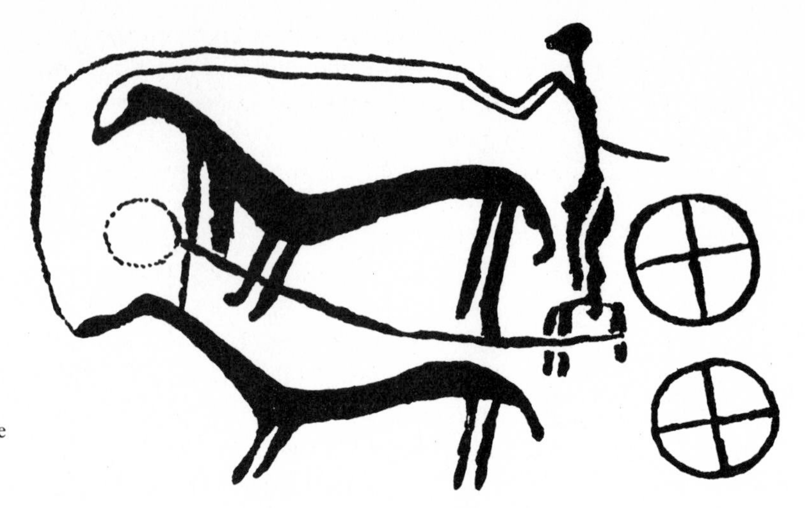

80 Depiction of spoke-wheeled chariot on stone wall of tomb at Kivik, Scania, Sweden.

proper meaning of cavalry, and, moreover, this type of sword would have been very difficult to use on horseback, especially without stirrups, then unknown. For swordsmen, as opposed to bowmen, the horse anciently provided a useful means of arrival at, and departure from, battle, but the whole essence of European fighting, as earliest shown by Homer, was the individual feat of arms by champions standing in front of their battle lines.

Although the majority of vehicles found in Hallstatt-culture chieftains' tombs were four-wheeled waggons for ceremonial or ordinary transport purposes, there are some indications that the two-wheeled chariot had come into use in trans-Alpine Europe by this time. The depiction of a vehicle of this kind on the stone walls of a Bronze Age tomb at Kivik, in Sweden, dating from about the tenth century BC, is significant in this connection, and in some Hallstatt culture graves, a pair of wheels only have been found, although this does not rule out the possibility that the vehicle had originally possessed four. In addition to the cut and thrust sword, both of iron and bronze, spears of various sizes, mainly for casting rather than thrusting, were in use. This was during the first phase of the Hallstatt culture, a time, as has been suggested, that saw the political cohesion of the Celts under a warlike dynasty. During the ensuing period of the sixth, and early fifth centuries BC, when Greek, and then Etruscan, trade was able to penetrate to the Upper Danube, and to the head waters of the Seine, implying a period of comparative peace and unitary control throughout the Celtic dominions, the long sword gave way to a broad-bladed dagger, and this, with a pair of casting spears, became the standard equipment. It has been suggested that this modification in personal armament is another indication of more settled conditions, at least in the central Celtic areas, and that it was a combination of weapons equally suitable for the chase.

It is in the archaeological material contemporary with the great expansion of the Celts, beginning at the end of the fifth century BC, that the full characteristics of Celtic warfare, so vividly to be illustrated in Classical and native literature in later centuries, comes first to light. The transition from Hallstatt style to that of La Tène had been achieved shortly before this irruption began, and now, equipped with a light thrusting iron sword, as well as a dagger, for close fighting, and with casting-spears, the Celtic warrior lord was conveyed by his charioteer in a fast two-wheeled war chariot drawn by a pair of small horses. The weapons of the early La Tène period show a mingling of Hallstatt and outmoded Greek ideas, and in the fine workmanship of the chariot design, Etruscan influence is strong. From tombs of the late fifth, and of the fourth centuries BC, from the Middle Rhine, and from Champagne, can be drawn a fairly clear idea of the turn-out of

27

81* Reconstruction of the Early La Tène chariot burial at La Gorge Meillet, Marne, France.

82* Bronze helmet from the chariot burial at La Gorge Meillet. Height 37 cm.

83* Pottery vessel from the La Gorge Meillet chariot grave. Height 32 cm.

84* Bronze beaked flagon from the La Gorge Meillet chariot grave. Height 27 cm.

the greater warriors. The iron sword was carried in a bronze scabbard with ornamental foot or chape, and with a design in the La Tène style chased on the outer face. A dagger, similarly sheathed, might also be carried as well as a complement of spears. A few particularly wealthy chieftains possessed helmets of cap, or high conical, shape, made of bronze and sometimes covered with gold worked in La Tène motifs, and embellished with coral studs. The horses were handsomely fitted out with snaffle-bits and harness mounts, and the chariot also had bronze fittings, with iron tyres and other components. The normal metal snaffle-bit in prehistoric Europe was of the two-link type, but in Champagne, and later in Britain and Ireland, a three-link type is found which would have been less severe on the horse's mouth. This suggests the emergence of a finer breed, more sensitive to skilled control.

87

Fighting methods

With Polybius, and subsequent authors, the procedure on the battlefield can be brought into view. Taking all the evidence into consideration, it may be deduced that the initial purpose of the

85* Helmet of bronze, iron and gold from Amfreville, Eure, France. Late fourth century BC. Height 16 cm.

86 Helmet of iron and bronze with coral mounts, from a grave at Canosa, Apulia, Italy. A Celtic piece of the later fourth century BC, perhaps a mercenary's trophy. Height 25 cm.

chariot warrior was to drive furiously towards and along the front of the enemy ranks to instil terror by sight, and by the delivery of missiles, no less than by the tremendous noise that was kept up by shouting, horn blowing, and beating on the sides of the waggons drawn up to the flanks or in the rear. The warriors then descended from their chariots, which the charioteer held in readiness for a quick retreat if need be, while the warrior, with casting spear, or drawn sword, stood out to deliver a challenge to an opposing champion. The challenge was evidently in a set formula of boasts of prowess, and perhaps of lineage, incorporated in a war song. Indeed, a kind of frenzy was probably worked up. In inter-tribal fighting, it would appear that the main body of troops became involved only after this phase of individual contest, and perhaps only if one side had become certain of success in a general mêlée. The course of events against Roman armies must have involved the whole body of fighting men more directly, and it led to considerable modifications in battle order.

The archaic mode of individual challenge, and encounter by champions, recalls the scenes in the *Iliad*, and the Celts were indeed the inheritors of the tradition which had long become outmoded south of the Balkans and of the Alps.

The battle of Telamon, fought in 225 BC, in which the Romans turned the tide of Gaulish supremacy in Italy, is the earliest Celtic battle of which a proper description exists. Polybius' vivid account, based on contemporary sources, should be read without fail. One point made by him is that the Gaulish swords could only be used for cutting, and not for thrusting. Archaeology shows that by this date Celtic swords had become heavier and broader. The importance of the short dagger remained, but not all warriors would seem to have been in possession of both. The majority of graves of ordinary foot warriors, presumably the client freemen, throughout the third and second centuries BC, indicate that the heavy sword, with one or two spears, comprised the most typical armament. It is at this time, too, from the mid-third century BC on, that the long Celtic shield comes into evidence. The earliest portrayals of it are on Greek coins and in the Pergamon sculptures, and it figures towards the end of its life on Roman monuments in Gaul. The shield was normally straight-sided with rounded ends, or oval; it was made of wood, perhaps occasionally of basketry, and the wooden shields came to be fitted with iron umbos, and more rarely with iron edges. Actual wooden shields of Celtic type are known from a great peat deposit at Hjortspring in Denmark, where they would appear to

IX

32, 77, 88, 90, 91

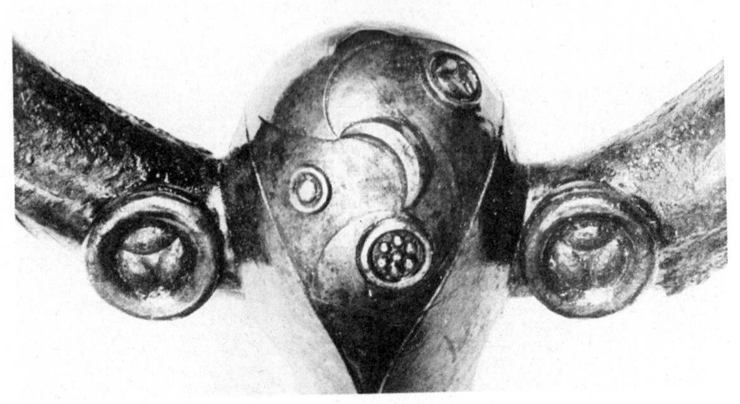

87* Pair of bronze horse-bits from Ringstead, Norfolk. First century BC. Length 26 cm. Below, detail of ornament.

have been carried as votive offerings, and from a single specimen preserved in the sands of the Egyptian Fayûm. This latter must have belonged to a Celtic mercenary, for whom there is evidence in Egypt as early as 274 BC.

The naked Gaesatae

Polybius' account of the body of Gaulish troops he calls *Gaesatae*, at Telamon, is of particular interest. He thought the name meant 'mercenaries', but it is a Celtic term meaning 'spear-men'. The *Gaesatae* had been brought in from beyond the Alps to assist the tribes already settled in Northern Italy. It is, first, of great interest that a large force of men, separated from tribal commitments should have been available, but this organization invites comparison with the bodies of warriors known later in Ireland as *fiana*,

Opposite
88* Celtic trophies in a carving from Pergamon in Asia Minor, including shields, chain-mail shirts, and an animal-headed trumpet. Second century BC.

89* Further Celtic trophies from the Pergamon reliefs, with shields, yoke, helmets, etc.

who led a roving warrior life divorced from tribal society. The second particular point about the *Gaesatae* was their appearance in battle naked, carrying only their weapons. This again was an archaic custom amongst the Celts which died out as successive tribes came under more sophisticated influence, but it is witnessed in the Pegamene sculptures, on Roman and native coins, and is alluded to in old Irish texts. The custom was not mere bravado as the Romans thought; it was an invocation for magical protection, and it was a practice that had also been widespread in Greece and Italy in earlier times.

Decapitation

A more horrifying Celtic custom was that of the decapitation of foes, and the suspension of the heads on horses' bridles, eventually to be exhibited at home, or in sanctuaries, as at Roquepertuse. It would be hazardous to dismiss this custom amongst the Celts as being merely a desire to collect trophies for the accumulation of martial prestige. It is more likely that it originated in cult practices to do with fertility, and with bringing the ghost into servitude.

90* Celtic trophies on triumphal arch at Orange, Vaucluse, France. Late first century BC.

91* Battle scenes of Gauls and Romans on the Orange arch.

Horsemen

Although the idea of Celtic cavalry, in the sense that one might speak of Assyrian or Roman cavalry, is decried in these pages, it is clear that the number of mounted horsemen present in battles with the Romans increased as time went on. The *equites* in Gaul, described by Caesar, had replaced the chariot warriors of earlier generations, but they were persons of rank, acting independently, and brought together only for the contingencies of the immediate action. An interesting Celtic term was preserved by Pausanias

92 Wooden shields of La Tène type from a votive find in a bog at Hjortspring, Als, Denmark, which included shirts of mail as on the Pergamon relief. Third century BC. Length of larger shield 88 cm.

from earlier Greek authors, and presumably goes back to the descent of the Celts into Greece in the third century BC. Pausanias speaks of *trimarcisia*, three riders, comprising a noble with two attendants who could supply him with a fresh horse, and act in his defence. There is nothing to suggest that these three formed any kind of attacking unit. That was the function of the principal only, but whether the subsidiary horsemen were kinsmen or clients, rather than servants, it is not possible to tell. It may be wondered if the 'three riders' who occur in some Irish stories have anything in common with the *trimarcisia*.

Insular warfare

When it comes to the insular Celts, two things are outstanding. In the first place, the archaeology of the developed Iron Age B culture of Britain shows to what heights, in the second and first centuries BC, the art of fine metal-work rose for the aggrandisement of the warrior, his horses, and his chariot. Remarkable are the chased sword-scabbards, the bronze shields, the pairs of ornamented snaffle-bits, and other harness pieces with enamel settings, as well as the bronze fittings for the chariot. The majority of the material comes from chance finds rather than burials, but sufficient pieces of actual chariots and wheels have come to light to demonstrate the high standard of the wheelwright's and 'coach-builder's' craft in these islands.

87, 93

VIII One of the rare surviving pieces of finely painted pottery in a style related to that of Waldalgesheim and of the late fourth or early third century BC. From a grave at Prunay, Cher, France. Height 31 cm.

VIII

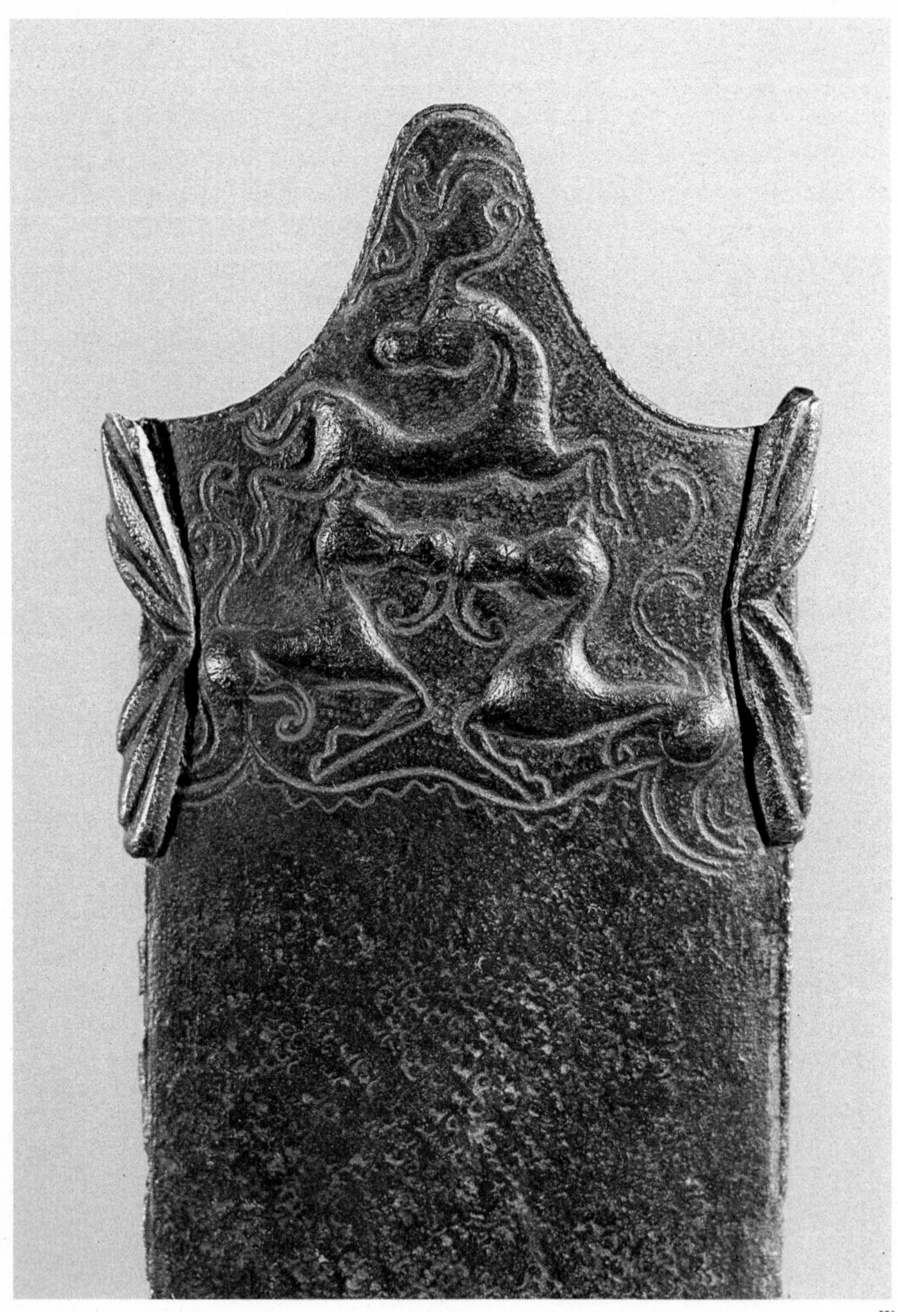

IX

It must be mentioned here that there is so far no archaeological evidence for scythed chariots. Nor are they mentioned by the more reputable Classical authors. They are referred to in Irish literature, and at least one passage suggests that the scythes were carried in the chariot until need arose to fix them. The use of scythes would suggest a closer employment of the chariot against the enemy, and something of this sort is also suggested in Caesar's description of chariot warriors in Britain running up the draught pole to stand on the yoke, although it is not certain that this was anything more than a display of agility.

The second outstanding point to do with insular Celtic warfare is the interpenetration of archaeology and traditional literature in Ireland, and the close parallels in description between the latter and Classical authors, only some of which can be mentioned here. In particular, the body of epic centred on the hero Cú Chulainn, and the hostilities between the kingdoms of Ulster and Connacht, display all the characteristics of chariot fighting, the champion's challenge, sword-fighting on foot, decorated long shields, the taking of heads and the tumult kept up by the hosts. This was the most spectacular and aristocratic of the warrior traditions in Ireland, but there were other Celtic communities whose warfare figures in the literature, but on whom only two comments can be made here. These have to do with the sling, and perhaps the thrusting spear, and both are associated with peoples who would appear to have come from Western Gaul.

Archaeologically, the use of the sling is attested in Brittany and in South-western Britain in the first century BC. This was a weapon not typical of the central Celts, but was evidently derived from Western Mediterranean sources by way of the tin trade routes. The spear in question (*laigen*) seems to have been something different from the accepted throwing weapon – the heavier *gae*, or the lighter *sleg*. Traditionally, it was described as having had a broad blade, and that it was introduced by certain newcomers. The particular fighting qualities of its bearers, and the fact that it was worthy of notice, rather suggests its use as a hand-held lance, perhaps comparable to the *lanciae* mentioned, but not very closely described, by Diodorus.

IX Detail of the mouth of a wrought iron sword-scabbard with embossed incised and chased ornament. This unique piece gives us a glimpse of a fine tradition of working in iron in the Celtic world of the third or early second century BC. From La Tène, Lake Neuchâtel, Switzerland. Width 5 cm.

The Celtic feast

The reward of warriors in all heroic societies was feasting and gifts provided by the king, and the Celts were no exception to this custom. Again, the Irish and Classical descriptions are com-

93* Engraved bronze terminals, perhaps of drinking horns, from Torrs, Kirkudbright, Scotland. Second half of third century BC. The bird-head is 4 cm long. *Below*, Reconstructed horn.

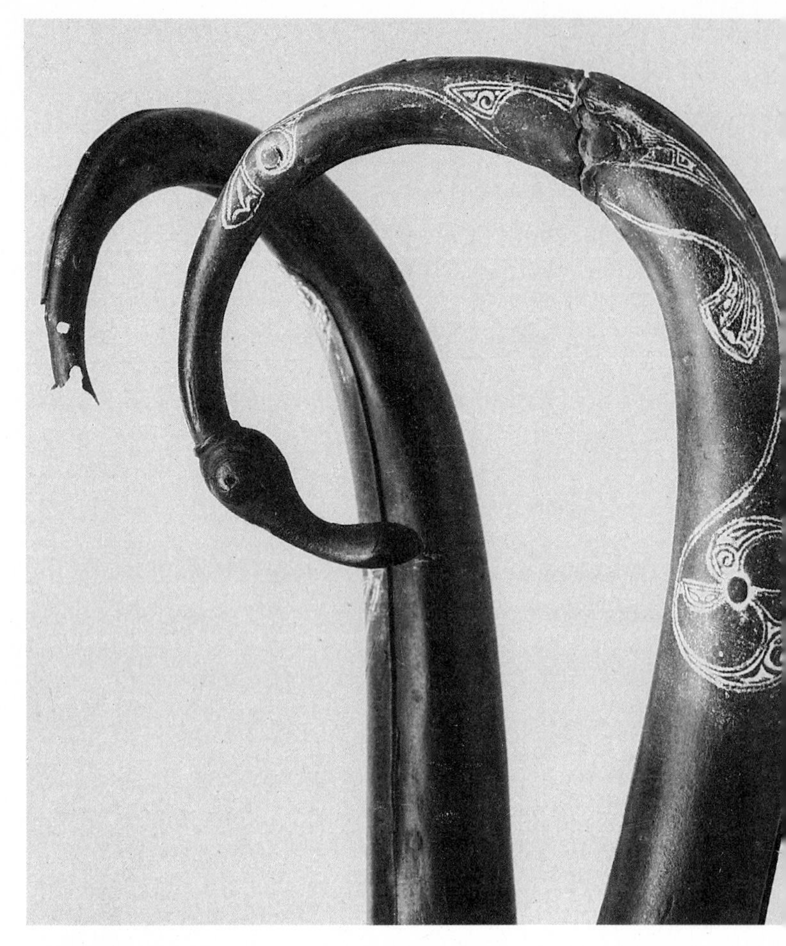

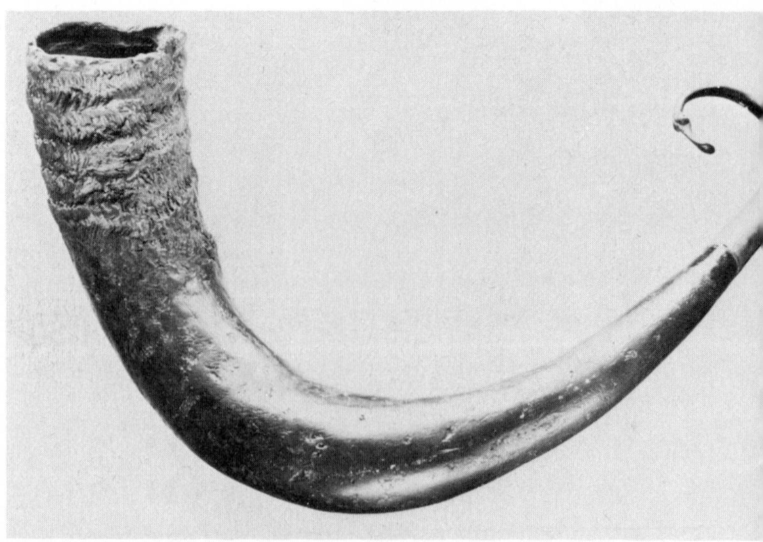

plementary, and one may first note Polybius' remark on the Celtic warrior's inordinate love of drinking and surfeiting. The long-distance portage of wine, beginning in the sixth century BC, is one indication, and, in the last phase of independence in Britain, Belgic princes went to the grave with a generous supply of wine stored in Roman amphorae. Beer was everywhere the drink of home production. Pork, either roast, or boiled in a great cauldron, was the favourite dish. In Ireland, a whole porker was reputedly the champion's portion *par excellence*, and the skeleton of an entire boar was found in a chariot burial in Champagne. The champion's portion was often in dispute, and led to fighting on the spot, as Diodorus, and Athenaeus, report, and as is so well illustrated in the Irish stories of Bricriu's Feast (*Fled Bricrend*), and the Story of MacDatho's Pig (*Scéla Mucce Meic Dathó*). Everywhere the etiquette of precedence and hospitality was observed. Seating at the feast was according to rank and prowess, strangers were fed before their business was inquired, and every-one had his appropriate joint of meat. In Ireland it was a leg of pork for a king, a haunch for a queen, and the boar's head for

93

94* Mouth roundel of bronze trumpet, Lough na Shade, Co. Armagh, Ireland. Probably first century AD. Diameter 20 cm.

95 Iron bull-headed firedog and frame, perhaps for holding wine amphorae, from a grave of *c.* 50–10 BC at Welwyn, Hertfordshire. Fire-dog about 1 m high.

a charioteer. Animal bones in continental Celtic graves point to a similar system, and Athenaeus, quoting Poseidonius, says that the thigh went to the best man present.

The continental Celts sat on hay or skins strewn on the ground, if eating out-of-doors, otherwise on the floor of the house. They sat in a circle with low tables before them, and in addition to meat and drink, bread was also served. Beef and mutton, salted pork, and baked salted fish were other dishes known to the Celts. Athenaeus noted with approval their cleanly, if voracious, way of eating, but the refinements of the banquet lay in the music and oral compositions of the bards, and on their praise or satire hung the reputation of a prince. So, too, in Ireland where the ancient tradition of courtly eulogistic verse continued far into historical times. Indeed, as long as there were Irish chieftains to receive and reward it.

96 Iron cauldron and suspension from La Tène, Switzerland. Length of suspension 1.5 m.

Notes to Chapter 2

ANCIENT DESCRIPTIONS: Polybius, II 28–29; Strabo, IV, *passim;* Diodorus Siculus, V, 28–31; Pliny, *Nat. Hist.* VIII, 196. These are the principal refs. only. E. Hull (1907) for Irish comparisons.

CELTIC IMAGERY: P. Jacobsthal (1941).

PHYSICAL ANTHROPOLOGY: J. Huxley and A. C. Haddon (1935); C. S. Coon (1939).

CELTS IN GREEK SCULPTURE: P. Bieńkowski (1908) and (1928); W. B. Dinsmoor (1950) for bibl. on Pergamon. Convenient illustrations of Gizeh head, and 'Ludovisi' group in A. Grenier (1945), and G. Lippold (1950).

IRISH DRESS: H. F. McClintock (1950), and (1948) on Cú Chulainn's hair.

TROUSERS: Possibly introduced by such people as the Sigynnae of Herodotus, see J. L. Myres (1907). On philological difficulties see M. Dillon (1943), and F. Shaw in H. F. McClintock (1950). O. Klindt-Jensen (1950), Pls. 83 and 87 for trousers depicted on Gundestrup bowl. J. Brøndsted (1940, fig. 230, for Thorsbjerg peat find.

SOCIAL INSTITUTIONS: A. Grenier (1945) for Gaul; D. A. Binchy (1943) with bibl., and M. Dillon, edit. (1954) for Ireland. D. A. Binchy (1941) for important glossary of Irish legal terms.

FOSTERAGE AND STATUS OF WOMEN: D. A. Binchy, edit. (1936).

VIX: R. Joffroy (1954).

REINHEIM: J. Keller (1955).

RURAL ECONOMY: J. G. D. Clark (1952); M. Louis, and O. and J. Taffanel (1955) for Languedoc. G. Bersu (1940); H. Helbaek (1952). S. Applebaum (1954); E. C. Curwen (1954) for Britain. M. Duignan (1944); G. F. Mitchell (1946) for Ireland. G. Hatt (1944) for Continental field systems. C. ÓDanachair (1955) augments previous information on threshing methods.

HOUSES: J. G. D. Clark (1952), generally, and, with bibl.; J. Maluquer de Motes (1954) for village at Cortes de Navarra. Domed houses referred to by Strabo, IV, 4, 3.

CORNISH TIN TRADE: H. O'N. Hencken (1932).

WINE TRADE: Recent important studies are: W. Kimmig and W. Rest (1955); J. J. Hatt (1955); F. Benoit (1956).

HEUNEBURG: K. Bittel and A. Rieth (1951); W. Dehn (1957) for important developments, and full bibl. to date. Summaries by W. Dehn in *Antiquity* XXVII (1953), 164, and in W. Krämer, edit. (1958), 127–145.

MONT LASSOIS: R. Joffroy (1954).

LA TÈNE ART: P. Jacobsthal (1944) is the standard work, but now out of print. S. Piggott and G. E. Daniel (1951); J. M. de Navarro (1952); R. J. C. Atkinson and S. Piggott (1955) for the British material.

CONTRIBUTORY ARTS: G. Kossack (1954b) for Hallstatt symbolism. T. Talbot Rice (1956) for Scythians. M. Rostovtzeff (1922) for Iran. A. Riegl (1893) is still valuable for the basic Greek patterns.

COINAGE: A. Blanchet (1905); L. Lengyel (1954) for Gaul. K. Pink (1939); G. Behrens (1950); R. Pittioni (1954); J. Filip (1956) for Central and Eastern Celts. D. Allen (1944); R. P. Mack (1953) for Britain. J. G. Milne (1940) is important for gold currency and prototypes.

CURRENCY BARS: C. Fox (1946), and refs. therein.

KIVIK: C. A. Althin (1945); V. G. Childe (1950), fig. 154.

CHARIOTS: J. Déchelette (1914); P. Coussin (1926); P. Jacobsthal (1944); C. Fox (1946); S. Piggott (1946) and (1952). Strabo, IV, 5, 2, seems to imply that chariots were still in use in parts of Gaul. The encounter reported by Livy, X, 28, was not a chariot charge, as alleged by Coussin.

BATTLE DESCRIPTIONS: E. Hull (1907) for Classical and Irish parallels, but see especially: Polybius, II, 28–29; Diodorus Siculus, V, 29, and 32; Strabo, VII, 2, 3, on the Cimbri in battle. The Champion's Challenge is splendidly illustrated by that Indo-European Philistine, Goliath, see: I Samuel, xvii. 8–10. M. L. Sjoestedt (1940 and 1949) for ritual and social aspects of Irish hero warrior.

TRUMPETS: F. Behn (1954).

HJORTSPRING: G. Rosenbërg (1927); Brøndsted (1940).

FAYÛM SHIELD: W. Kimmig (1940b).

FIANA: M. L. Sjoestedt (1940 and 1949); T. G. E. Powell (1950).

NAKEDNESS: A. Grenier (1945).

IRISH TEXTS ON HEROIC LIFE: T. P. Cross and C. H. Slover (1936) for English translations of the principal exploits and feastings. See further: M. Dillon's augmented bibl. in M. L. Sjoestedt (1949).

FEASTING: E. Hull (1907) for comparisons, but see especially Polybius, II, 19; Diodorus Siculus, V, 26, 28; Strabo, IV, 3, 2, on Gaulish salt pork. Athenaeus, *Deipnosophists* IV, *passim*, for much information on Celtic food and table manners M. E. Dobbs (1913) on joints according to rank.

BARDS: Diodorus Siculus, V, 31, and comments by D. Greene in M. Dillon, edit. (1954), 22. Also I. Williams (1944). It would seem that in Ireland, at least, the bard had been the skilled performer in recitation or song, while the *fili* (poet) was the learned composer of the verse.

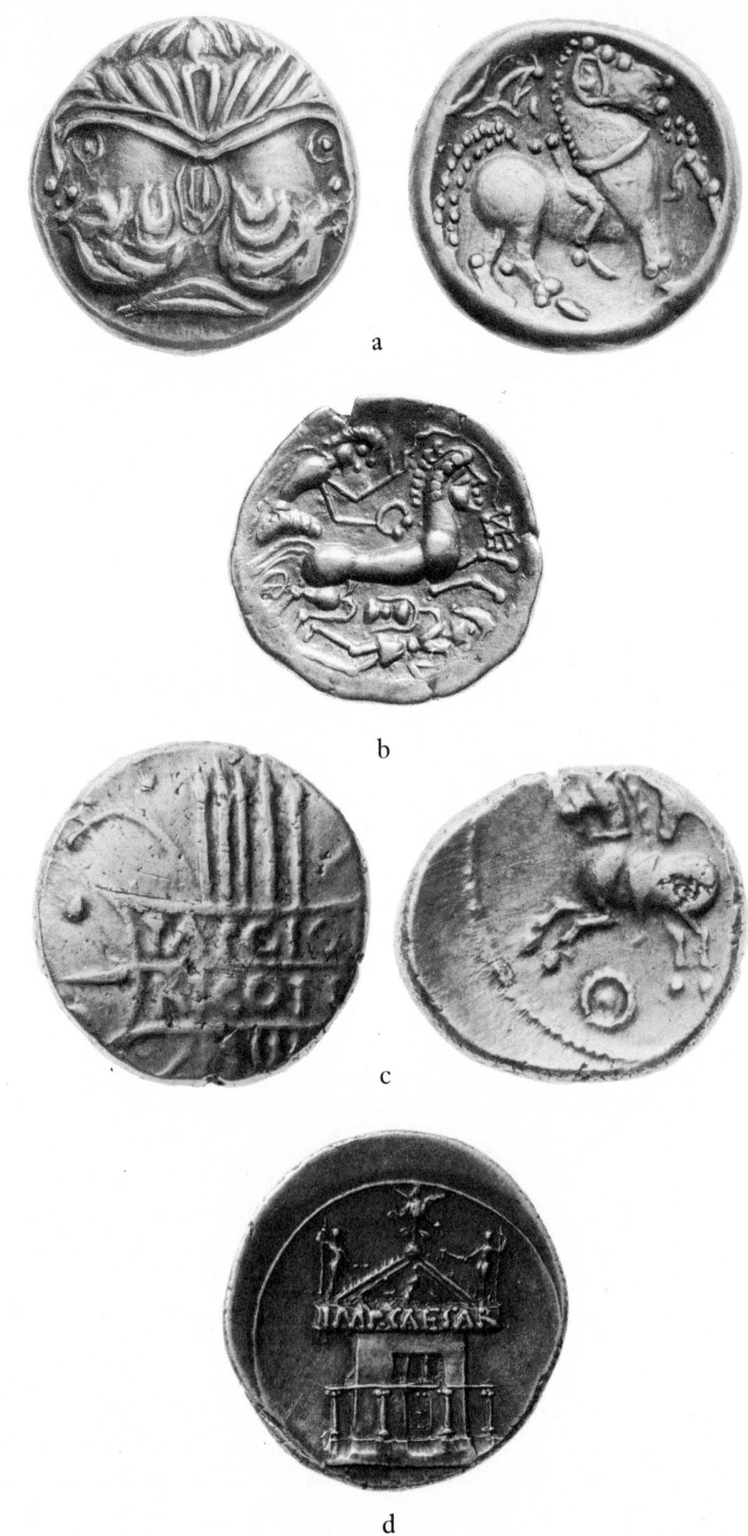

97* Celtic and Roman coins: (a) Gold coin from Pannonia; (b) Gold coin of the Aulerci Cenomani; (c) Gold coin of Tasciovanus; (d) Denarius of Augustus.

3
The Celtic Supernatural

Celtic primitive religion

The Celts were obsessed probably no more, but certainly no less, with magic, and the observance of ritual, than any other unsophisticated people of the Old World. It is well to stress the word magic, for of religion, except in the modern anthropological sense of primitive religion, it cannot be said that the Celts were at all conscious.

As with most simple country-dwellers, the Celts believed magical agencies to pervade every aspect of their lives and surroundings. They were concerned primarily, therefore, to constrain the powers of magic to beneficent ends. This was to be achieved through ritual and sacrifice, and by the recitation of myths: those sacred tales which were thought to move the deities, by precedent and remembrance, to acquiesce to mortal needs. To seek for a clear-cut body of belief, in the sense of the great historical religions, to expect consistency or conformity of views about life after death, or of the relation of man to the supernatural, whether gods or beings less defined, would be to mistake the whole nature of trans-Alpine barbarism in Pre-Roman times. In the same way, an organized pantheon, as popularly accredited to the Greeks and Romans, finds no place in the Celtic world, but there are many vestiges in myth, cult and sacred terminology, springing from a common Indo-European tradition which the Celts shared in particular with the Aryan ancestors of the Hindus, and with the Italic forerunners of the Romans.

The sources on which the Celtic inquiry can be based are remarkably abundant although largely misinterpreted until very recent times.

In the first place, there is a considerable volume of material, despite Church expurgation, in the ancient literature of Ireland. This comprises many mythological tracts surviving in the guise of history, the names of numerous deities, the principal pagan festivals, the activities of druids, and many related matters. Not to be forgotten are such fragments as remain of paganism in Welsh literature, and both Irish and Welsh evidence find many analogues in the continental sources.

The greatest body of continental evidence comes from inscriptions and monuments set up under Roman rule, and encouragement, in the Celtic areas brought within the Empire. The inscriptions are in Latin, rarely in Greek, and are generally to some well-known Roman god coupled with the name of a local Celtic one, or paired with a Celtic goddess. The monuments, normally altars of purely Roman type, do provide, however, an iconography where none existed, or hardly so, in earlier days. To this information must be added the remarks of various Classical writers, most explicit of whom is Caesar. On the druids, and on various tenets reported of the Celts, such Greek and Roman sources are more useful than they are on the gods. Information is also forthcoming from the comparative philological study of Celtic deity names, and words to do with cult, and there is finally the prehistoric archaeological, material in burial rites, votive offerings and, all too slightly, on sacred sites and temples. With these should be mentioned the iconography of some Gaulish and British coins of the period immediately before the loss of independence.

76, 77, 97

It seems most profitable to attempt to approach the Celtic supernatural by considering it firstly in its context of the ordinary life of its devotees, and here the Irish evidence is most helpful, for a beginning can be made by noting the festivals which marked the divisions of the farming year.

The ritual year

The Celtic year, certainly in Ireland and Gaul, was divided into two principal seasons: warm and cold. In Ireland, at least, these were further subdivided so that four festivals marked the turning-points. The greatest festival in Ireland was known as *Samain*. In terms of the modern calendar it was celebrated on the first of November, but the preceding night was perhaps the most significant period of the festival. *Samain* marked the end of one year and the beginning of the next. It was considered to stand independently between the two, and its position in relation to the natural seasons shows it clearly to have been the turning-point in a pastoralist rather than an agrarian cycle. It corresponds to the end of the grazing season when under primitive conditions the herds and flocks were brought together, and only those ani-

98

98* Part of bronze calendar of the Celtic year from Coligny, Ain, France. Late first century BC.

mals required for breeding were spared from slaughter. This was, of course, an age-old practice going back in temperate Europe to the Neolithic farmers, and imbued with immemorial custom no less than in providing the opportunity for unlimited feasting. The word *Samain* seems indeed best interpreted as meaning a reassembly or gathering together, and in Ireland the *túath* may be envisaged as reuniting at an *óenach* at this time. In the literature, the importance of this festival was so great that practically every event of note ascribed to the Pre-Christian period took place at it, but its real magical significance was that of ensuring the renewal of earthly prosperity and tribal success; the germination, as it were, of good fortune for the ensuing spring and summer.

At *Samain*, sacrifices were certainly offered although no material descriptions have survived. Types of sacrifice amongst the Celts will be described later, but here the nature of the *Samain* myths is of greater interest. These were concerned with the renewal of the fecundity of the earth and its inhabitants, and had to do with the union of the tribal god with the nature goddess who nourished the tribal territory, and who was sometimes personified in a river or other natural feature. Exemplifying this aspect are the stories of the union of a god, the Dagda, with a goddess, the Morrígan, or in another instance, with Boann, the deity of the river Boyne. It is worth considering what can be gleaned of the way in which these deities were conceived. The name Dagda, used normally with the definite article, means the Good God, but not good in the ethical sense, but good-at-everything, or all-competent. He is the father of the tribe, its protector and benefactor, and it may be said at once that this is the basic type of all the Celtic male deities whether in Ireland or beyond. There were no such gods exclusively as of war, wisdom or of the sun; these were but particular manifestations of the embracive nature of the tribal god. This fact helps greatly to explain why so many god names are known throughout the whole Celtic zone, while very restricted distributions are enjoyed by all but a few. It supports, too, the view that to the Celtic mortal it was only the tribal and local deities, male and female respectively, with whom he was concerned; the supernatural world, in existence alongside his own, was avoiding, and to be avoided, except in relation to specific ritual times and needs, and the tutelary powers of the individual community.

The Dagda's mate at *Samain* was, as has been indicated, a nature goddess. In the name Morrígan, Queen of Demons, she occurs frequently in Irish texts, but this name is interchangeable with other horrific ones such as *Nemain*, Panic, and *Badb Catha*, Raven of battle, while other conjunctions include goddess names, such as Macha and Medb (Maeve), that introduce a whole range of horse – more strictly, mare – attributes and symbolism. The Celtic goddesses in fact also conform to a general type, but not tribal, or social, for they are of the land or territory to be placated, taken over, or even enslaved, with the occupation of the ground. They display both fertility and destructress aspects, and may be symbolized in the sun and moon no less than in zoomorphism, and topography.

These, then, were the supernatural powers to be entreated at *Samain*, but the night of its eve was the great occasion in the year when the temporal world was thought to be overrun by the forces of magic. Magical troops issued from caves and mounds, individual men might even be received into these realms; whilst against the royal strongholds, assaults by flame and poison were attempted by monsters.

The second most important festival in Ireland was that of the first of May, the beginning of the warm season. Called *Beltine*, or *Cétshamain*, this also was a predominantly pastoralist festival corresponding to the season when the cattle could be driven to open grazing. The lighting of great fires was a characteristic of this festival, continued long into Christian times, and the practice of driving cattle between two large fires to protect them from disease has been recorded as a pagan rite supervised by the

99* Gaulish inscription from Alesia (Alise-Ste-Reine), France.

100* Bronze plaque dedicated to the Celtic goddess Epona, from Alesia, France. Height 14 cm.

101* Air photograph of the site of the Gaulish oppidum of Alesia, France.

druids. The word *Beltine*, incorporating the Celtic word for fire, is probably to be connected with a god name, Belenus, known widely in Northern Italy, South-eastern Gaul, and in Noricum. 121 Belenus appears to be one of the oldest Celtic gods descernible, associated particularly with the pastoralist element.

The other two Irish seasonal festivals were *Imbolc*, on the first of February, and *Lugnasad* on the first of August. Of all the festivals least is known of *Imbolc*. It was anciently explained as marking the beginning of the lactation of ewes, and it corresponds with the Feast of St Brigit in the Christian calendar. The Saint's pagan predecessor, Brigit 'a wise woman, daughter of the Dagda', was a potent fertility goddess with perhaps specially emphasized attributes of learning and healing. The goddess Brigit, whose name is cognate with the Sanskrit *Bṛhati*, The Exalted One, can also be traced on the Continent in place-names and inscriptions. That *Imbolc* may have been especially connected with the tending of sheep seems reasonable, for although this animal possessed no ritual status as did the ox, the boar and the dog, who figure as components in divine and mortal names, the working of wool was an important element in Celtic domestic economy.

The possibility should always be borne in mind that *Imbolc* may have been originally peculiar to some one cultural or occupational population group. That *Lugnasad* was a festival introduced, at least in name if not purpose, by a late-coming group of settlers to Ireland seems well indicated in the stories connected with the god Lug. This festival seems to be the most agrarian in character of those known from Ireland. Its date, the first of August, does not accord well with a pastoralist economy when summer transhumance would have been in full swing. It seems rather to have had to do with ensuring the ripening of the crops, and here one may note again the nature of the Celtic interchange with the supernatural, for the observances were undertaken to ensure the harvest, and not to thank for it. The concept of thankfulness did not enter into the magical scheme, for humanity initiated the ritual which, if correctly carried out, must necessarily culminate in the desired result.

The god Lug is portrayed in the mythological tracts as a latecomer to the society of Irish divine beings. He, also, was a tribal god, but of less archaic character than the others; his weapons are different, and his epithet (*samildánach*) denotes him as lord of every skill in particular rather than of knowledge in general. His name is, of course, well known in Lugudunum, the modern Lyons, and a number of other Continental town names. In Ireland, the centre of devotion at *Lugnasad* was not, apparently, the god himself, but the nature goddess, whether as Tailltu, in whose honour he was reputed to have founded the festival, or as Macha, who was entreated in Ulster at this time. The indications only await explicit archaeological testimony to show that Lug was brought into Ireland by Gaulish settlers, perhaps in the first century BC.

There was another name for the August festival, *Bron Trograin*, which has been interpreted as the 'Rage of Trograin'. To this otherwise unknown name, sacrifices were made for increase and plenty, and one may deduce an obscure tribal god who came to be overshadowed by Lug.

The calendar from which the festivals were computed is known both from Irish and Classical sources to have been based on lunar observations, and to have counted nights rather than days. It may be supposed that the actual choice of day lay in the hands of the druids, who would have decided what days were auspicious or otherwise.

So much for the ritual framework of the year based as it was on essential considerations of livelihood; but the welfare of the *túath*, or tribe, was also considered to be dependent on the ritual success of its king. This matter is well exemplified in the Irish texts, and it can be seen that the failure of crops, cattle disease, or other misfortunes, might be attributed to the supernatural unacceptability of the king resultant, in all probability, from some physical or ritual blemish, especially in regard to the numerous sanctions and observances that beset his every action.

The subject of kingship ritual is too elaborate to be discussed at length here, but some principal aspects may be mentioned. In the first place the Irish king was thought of as being the mortal mate of the territorial nature goddess. At Tara it was Étaín, or Medb, who accepted the kings as husbands. The goddess handed them the goblet, the symbolical act of marriage in Celtic society, and in other mythological stories, the young king meets her at a well or spring where she awaits him in the guise of a beautiful maiden. The king must needs also possess a mortal wife, although her ritual function is not so clear as is that of the queen in Aryan India. The Tara kingship stories are much concerned with instancing 'perfect reigns' in which there were plentiful harvests and other ideal conditions, but the king must grow old, and with his ageing came the risk of the decline in prosperity of the people and the land. At this stage the goddess takes on the aspect of a repulsive hag, withering with the king's declining powers, and emphasizing the need for a new mate who will ensure the continuation of prosperity. There can be little doubt that the Celtic king, in fully pagan times at least, met a violent but ritual end, and there are a number of somewhat veiled allusions to deaths by weapon wounds, drowning and burning, in the midst of high magic, in the presence of the hag and the tribal god.

X Bronze mirror with engraved back. This is representative of one of the distinctly insular schools of Early Celtic art developing in Britain in the last couple of centuries BC. The design is very precisely executed to a compass-drawn scheme. Early first century AD. From Desborough, Northants. Diameter 36 cm.

XI Engraved bronze mounts on an iron spear-head, examples of the balanced asymmetry achieved in insular Celtic art, contemporary with the 'mirror style' in the early first century AD. From the River Thames at London. Right-hand mount 9 cm long.

Tribal and nature deities

It may be more in sympathy with archaic Celtic thought to begin a discussion of the principal named deities by a short description of their behaviour and appearance in Irish mythology than by an abstract classification from other sources such as the refined iconography of Roman sculpture.

In the stories connected with *Samain*, the Dagda is represented as a grotesque figure of immense strength and appetitites, he is clad in the short garment of a servant, his weapon is a great club, sometimes dragged on wheels, and he possesses a magical cauldron with properties of inexhaustibility, rejuvenation and inspiration. The great chalk-cut figure of a naked man wielding a club, at Cerne Abbas in Dorset, must surely represent such a god, and in Gaul the type is best exemplified, though in a more civilized fashion, by Sucellos, the Good Striker, with his hammer, and cup or dish which may be the counterpart of the cauldron.

X

XI

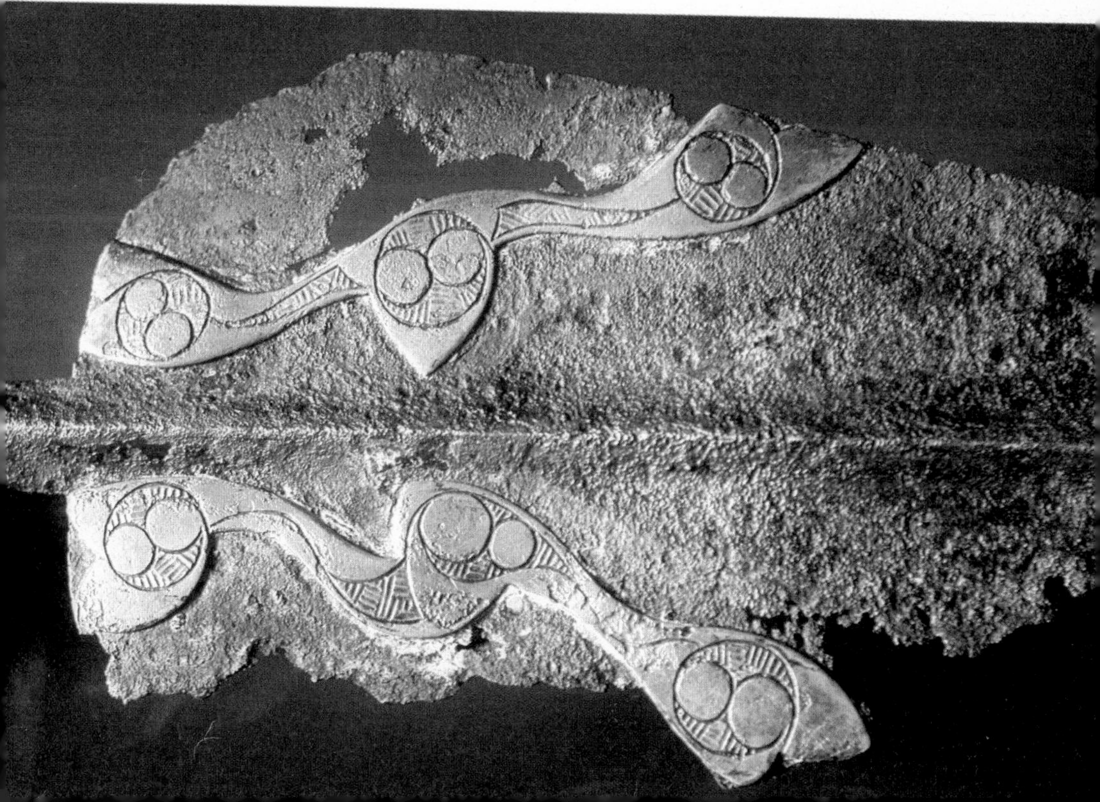

CVNO

102* Stone carving of horse goddess, from Beihingen, Württemberg. Height 60 cm.

The symbol of abundance in Ireland was this magical cauldron. Of the Dagda's it was said 'that no one goes away without being satisfied', but these vessels were possessed by other Irish gods such as Cú Roí, a Munster deity, and Gobniu who used his for the brewing of immortal beer. The tribal god's cauldron played its part also in the sacred building into which certain kings were brought for their deaths. To return to appearances, the grotesque male figure is found present in a number of other Irish mythological stories, and in Welsh literature, in the *mabinogi* of Branwen, Daughter of Llyr, he emerges from a lake with his cauldron and his wife. It is clear, however, that this story has to do with a tradition of the settlement in West Wales of pagan Irish in late Roman times.

By contrast, Lug is always portrayed as a young man representative of a much less primitive concept, and exhibiting none of the grosser characteristics of the Dagda. Although there is no such vivid description of his appearance as that given for the Dagda, it is at this point that mention should be made of another of his epithets: *Lámfhada*, 'Of the Long Arm', in the sense of far-reaching, and this is self-explanatory for his weapons were the great throwing-spear and the sling; new and impressive additions to Irish armament.

The transfiguration of the goddesses, from beautiful maiden to hag, have already been described, but there is one other manifestation which is important. This is their appearance as destructresses whether in predicting some calamity, or in their presence on the field of battle. The famous Ulster hero, Cú Chulainn,

XII Art on Celtic coinage: Silver coin with stylized head, and horse and rider, from Romania, second century BC; Gold stater of the Bellovaci with wreathed head and horse, found at Fenny Stratford, Buckinghamshire, late second century BC; Silver coin of the Coriosolites with characteristic treatment of head and horse motifs, from Jersey, mid first century BC; Gold stater of Cunobelinus (died *c.* AD 40) with wreath transformed into an ear of barley and classicizing horse. Struck at Camulodunum (Colchester).

103* Altar with dedication to the Celtic deity Taranucnus, from Böckingen, Württemberg. Height 1 m.

was confronted by the Badb attired in a red cloak, and with red eyebrows, mounted in a chariot drawn by a grotesque horse, and accompanied by a crude male figure driving a cow. Much might be made of the symbolism of this scene, but its intent was to inspire horror, as did the names which this weird pair recited of themselves. The Badb subsequently changes into her bird form, the raven or crow, and it is in this guise that she was said to gloat over the bloodshed, inducing panic and weakness among the contending warriors.

Badb Catha, the Raven of Battle, introduces the zoomorphic aspect of many Celtic deities of both sexes. This would seem to have been an expression of the powers of shape-shifting rather than a purely archaic concept of the supernatural in animal form. The comparative evidence would suggest that deities in human form had been too long known to the Indo-European peoples for any branch of them to retain only a zoomorphic concept. The male deities seem less markedly zoomorphic than the female, but the name Lug may mean a lynx, and from Gaul are known such names as *Cernunnos*, the Horned One, the *Tarvos Trigaranos*, the Three-Horned Bull. A name brought into Asia Minor, by the Galatae, was *Deiotaros*, the Divine Bull; bearers of this name being prominent in the first century BC.

The horse does not play a prominent part in male deity names, although from Ireland there are mythological names such as Eochaid, and Ro-Ech, the latter meaning 'Great Horse'. Horse symbolism is most closely attached to the goddesses, and the most widespread name is Epona, the goddess-mare depicted on numerous Gallo-Roman altars. She is the equivalent of Étaín Echraide, and Medb of Tara, and of Macha of Ulster. So, too, Rhiannon, 'Great Queen', is remembered in the *mabinogi* of Pwyll, Prince of Dyfed. This mare presentation of the typical Celtic goddess would appear to be of some significance in the common traditions of the Celts, both as a horse-using people, and in their early Eurasiatic connections. In India, the deified earth, 'Manu's Mare', played an important part in the ritual of kingship.

Triads

Another particular aspect of the Celtic deities, male and female, is that of triplism. This matter has been explored a good deal. It is not a tendency to trinitarian concepts, or of the union of three distinct supernatural beings. It is, in fact, an expression

of the extreme potency of any one deity. It may be likened 'to the power of three', and this number was sacred, and auspicious, far beyond the Celtic world as Indian parallels could again show.

104 Chalk-cut figure of club-bearing giant, probably Romano-Celtic, at Cerne Abbas, Dorset. Height 55 m.

It is worth while considering some examples of Celtic triplism, for there appear to be certain differences in its application according to the sex of the deity. It is perhaps also a more pronounced attribute amongst the goddesses, and here it takes the form of groups of three different names, as in Morrígan, Badb, Nemain, who are equivalent to Morrígna, in the plural. So, too, there are three Brigits, and three Macha; the triad Éire, Banba, and Fodla may be less ancient although the individual names can claim genuine antiquity. Of others, both Carmen, and Tlachtga, gave birth to triplet sons.

The goddess triad in Ireland is mirrored in the numerous Gallo-Roman dedications to the Mothers. These *Matres*, or *Matronae*, are usually depicted as three figures bearing symbols of fecundity. Amongst epithets, they sometimes possess locality

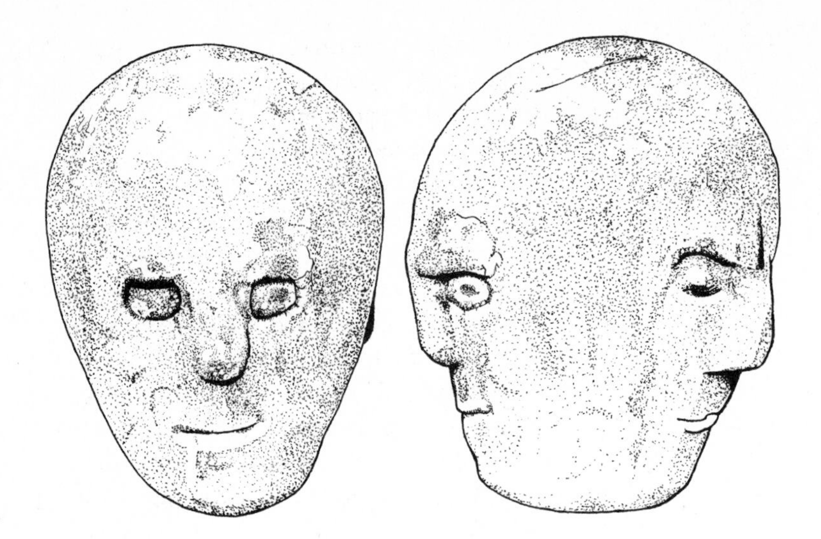

105 Three-faced stone head, Corleck, Cavan, Ireland. Height 32 cm.

names, demonstrating again their identity with the territorial nature goddess.

The triad amongst the male deities in Ireland takes several forms. Principal characters such as the Dagda, and Lug, are not strongly triple, although the Dagda had ascribed to him two other names, and Lug had two brothers, and arrived at Tara with two companions. The inscriptions to the *Lugoves* known in Switzerland, and in Spain, would seem best explained as a retention of the triple form of Lug who, as will be remembered, was also widely celebrated, in the singular, in the place-name *Lugudunum*. From Roman Gaul are known three-headed, or three-faced, sculptures of a native god, and from Ireland one three-faced stone head is known. A direct reference to such an horrific member of the supernatural world is found in Éllen Trechend who issued from the cave of Cruachain, and devastated Ireland, but this type of representation might well have been applied to any tribal god, although in Gaul it can be seen that while attributes were interchangeable, there were regional or tribal preferences in iconography.

It has to be continually borne in mind that the information on Celtic deities thus gleaned from various sources must rest on traditions of varying age and differences as amongst archaic or more advanced population-groups. It would be wrong to attempt to reconcile all the indications as if they emanated from a single century or a common centre. This warning thought brings to present attention certain other Irish triads. The Three Gods of Skill (*Na tri dee dána*), usually personified in Gobniu, Credne and Luchta, do not appear to have any direct mortal connections at least in this form. They play a part in mythological scenes wholly within the supernatural world. On the other hand, the triad cited as Mac Cuill (son of hazel?, or, of one-eye?), Mac Cecht (son of plough?), and Mac Gréne (son of sun) may well be a presentation of the typical tribal god. Somewhere between these two concepts may perhaps be placed the Three Sons of the King of Iruath who are connected in story not with a normal tribal organization but with the *fiana*, that age-occupation group devoted to hunting and warfare, that was characteristic of some, but perhaps not all, Irish peoples. Here the relationship of the triad to mortals seems to be impermanent, and the magical services rendered to the *fiana* had to be requited not by any attention or gifts, but by avoidance. It may suggest some particular ritual status for the *fiana* divorced, at least temporarily, from ordinary tribal custom.

A supernatural community

So much for the divine triads, but the Three Gods of Skill bring forward the difficult question as to whether there was in fact some kind of Celtic pantheon notwithstanding the embracive functions of the tribal and nature deities. In Ireland, this question must primarily revolve around the nature of the *Túatha Dé Danann*, a title that may be interpreted as the Peoples of the Goddess Danu. Many of the gods already mentioned are included in this association. The Dagda, Lug, Gobniu, are there, and a king is found in the personage of Nuadu Argatlám (of the silver arm). Nuadu, whose weapon was the sword, gives place to Lug as king on account of his blemish, through the loss of an arm in battle. The most significant pointer to the reality, within Celtic mythology, of this association of deities lies in the myth known as *Fled Gobniu*, the feast of Gobniu, which is concerned with the brewing of a magical beer for the sustenance of the deities in their battle against the powers of ill-intent and misfortune (*fomoire*). This appears to be a very ancient mythological concept, but it may not have had any bearing on tribal cult, being rather the concern of the magico-religious men of learning who supported a tradition more ancient than the cults of fragmented, tribal, populations.

It must remain a question beyond the present inquiry as to whether there can in fact have been an original Indo-European divine society, but the specialization of gods according to function or attribute, as in the case of Mars and Mercury, or Jupiter, is something Mediterranean and urban, unknown to the Celts before, or beyond, the Roman conquests. This is not, however, to deny that the Celts, in some way, envisaged their deities as maintaining their own families and retinues, largely reflecting the mortal social order, but also because these conveniently termed gods and goddesses, being more strictly supernatural magicians, themselves required magic for their own continuance.

Another and more complicative factor contributing to the development of the *Túatha Dé Danann* would have been the political federation of several tribes or the emergence of a paramount tribe whose god would presumably have been thought to take into clientage the gods of the tutelary peoples. This development seems to be indicated in the iconography of some Gaulish monuments, and a good case might be made out for its operation amongst the *Túatha Dé Danann* on account of the inclusion of unquestionable tribal gods as well as purely other-world personages.

Gallo-Roman monuments

It is now time to turn to the monuments of Roman Gaul and the Rhineland to learn something of the iconography in which native deities were portrayed, and how they were sometimes matched with Roman gods, both ends bearing out the policy of *interpretatio Romana*.

Caesar, who was not concerned in perpetuating accurate information on Gaulish cults, merely claimed that Mercury was accounted the greatest of the gods, and that Apollo, Mars, Jupiter and Minerva, were also worshipped. The Latin inscriptions on subsequent Gallo-Roman monuments show how misleading it would be to take Caesar's statement at face value. With the very large number of local Celtic deity names recorded in inscriptions, Mars is predominant in native associations, followed by Mercury, Apollo, Jupiter and others. But these assimilations can be seen to mean nothing more than the approximation of a particular Roman god to the corresponding facets of any tribal god, and in some cases a Celtic name occurs allied both to Mars and Mercury – ascription does not define the whole nature of the Celtic deity.

In the same way, misunderstanding or indifference, led Lucan, writing in the first century AD, to give inordinate prominence to three Celtic god names of which he had heard: Taranis, Teutates and Esus. The corpus of Gallo-Roman inscriptions which

103

is very representative, shows these names to be quite obscure, but at best they might be epithets applicable to any tribal god. The scholiasts on Lucan's poem *Pharsalia* variously equated Taranis with Dispater and Jupiter, while Teutates and Esus are both allied to Mercury and Mars. The general applicability of the Celtic names is evident, for Taranis is cognate with words for 'thunder', Teutates for 'people', and Esus probably for 'master'.

Many of the dedications incorporating Celtic deity names are found on altars or votive tablets without iconography, but in other cases characteristic representations are in direct relation to inscriptions. Monuments to *Cernunnos*, the horned god, to Epona, the great queen and mare-goddess, and to Sucellos with Nantosuelta, may be instanced, but it does not follow that where no inscription elucidates the sculpture the attributes may determine the name; certainly not outside the region in which the name can be confirmed. There are also a number of deity representations and symbols to which no native name can anywhere be attached. Principal amongst these are figures of a three-headed or three-faced god, a squatting god, one with a snake, a wheel, or mounted on a horse supported by a kneeling giant. These monuments are found to conform to distribution patterns generally showing a particular concentration as well as a wide scatter. The three-headed god is best represented in the territory of the Belgae, between the Oise, Marne and Moselle, but is also found in Burgundy and farther south. By contrast, the god with the wheel is found in the Massif Central, and the lower Rhône valley, but also sporadically north-eastwards to Champagne, and the Rhine. The horseman and kneeling giant are concentrated in a wide area on either side of the Middle Rhine, but also sporadically throughout Eastern and Central Gaul. These examples could be multiplied, but the inference to be drawn seems again to be that of regional, but not exclusive, preferences on a common stock of illustration. With the deep geographical interpenetration of these types must go the large number of tribal areas involved, and one is almost tempted to see those whose duty it was to Romanize native cults promoting a selection of illustrations any of which might be adopted.

106

There is no doubt, however, that by the time these monuments were being set up there was also great intermingling of deity names. This may not have been so marked at an earlier period, but, to take one example, there were celebrated, in the territory of the Treveri, goddesses under the names of Matronae, Epona, Sirona, and Rosmerta. Others might be added.

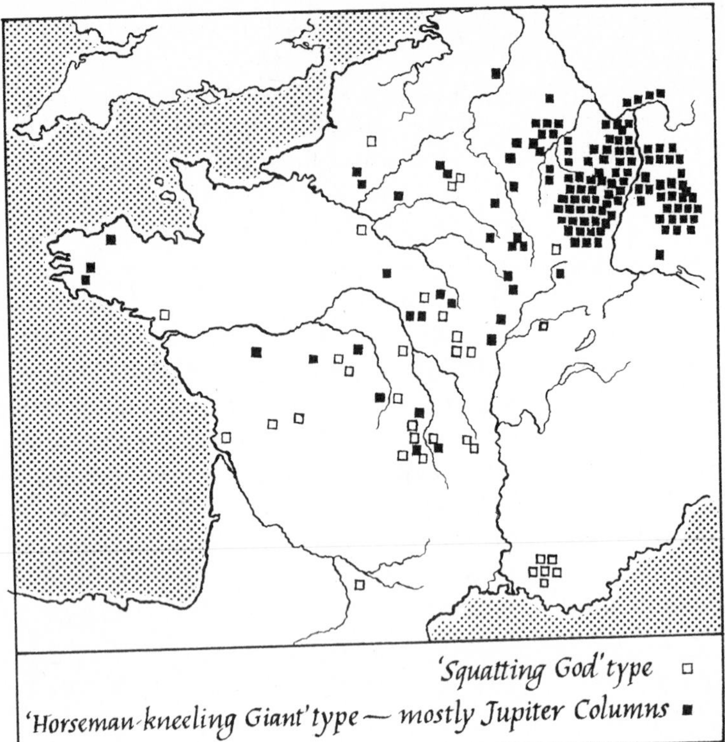

106 Map contrasting the distribution of two leading iconographical types among the Gaulish deities.

107 Carved wooden figures from a Gallo-Roman sanctuary at the source of the River Seine, France. Mid first century AD.

Roman Britain

In Roman Britain a somewhat parallel situation came into being, and the epigraphy has been a valuable if somewhat slight source for insular deity names. There is, however, nothing comparable to the great range of the Gaulish material, and the inscriptions seem to be restricted to a few areas of military and commercial importance.

It is unfortunate that, with perhaps one exception, the mythological figures of the Welsh Mabinogion, such as Manawyddan son of Llyr, Gofannyon and Lleu Llaw Gyffes, are not recorded in epigraphy. The exception is Mabon, generally equated with Maponus who is known from inscriptions and place-names in an area on either side of the western end of Hadrian's Wall. The dedication at Lydney in Gloucestershire to Nodens, who may be identical with the Irish Nuadu, and the Welsh Nudd, is now considered to result from an Irish settlement of the fourth century AD. It may be to this period of Irish expansion, to which Wales was fully subjected, that the bulk of mythological material in the Mabinogion belongs.

In making use of the monuments and inscriptions of Roman times in Gaul and Britain, it must be remembered that the later they fall in date the less trustworthy they are for regional investigations. The movement of auxiliary troops, and individuals, in both directions across the Channel was such that deity transplantations were not infrequent.

Native iconography

Although it has been suggested on a previous page that in the Romanization of native cults a selection of seemingly standardized representations were largely employed, this is not to deny that the essential symbols – horned or squatting figures, horses, wheels and so forth – were already in use in the days of independence. These things cannot be dismissed as borrowings from any Mediterranean iconography, however much their presentation was influenced from that quarter. The great majority of Pre-Roman images must have been made of wood, and have not survived, but that some were recognizably anthropomorphic seems a reasonable deduction for those *plurima simulacra* assigned by Caesar to Mercury.

In Northern Europe, and in Britain and Ireland, where peat has preserved many wooden objects, there exist a number of rough human images of which the earliest remount to the Late Bronze Age. These, and a sprinkling of certainly Celtic stone figures, to be described later, go some way to redress a commonly held view that human representation was repugnant to trans-Alpine barbaric cult. One has only to think, too, of the ever-increasing number of La Tène style masks and heads, and of the heads and figures on Celtic coins. It must have been largely a matter of available craftsmanship, and it was only in rare cases that images in stone or bronze could be achieved. The hazards of the intervening centuries have of course further reduced the possibility of appreciating the number or significance of such creations.

Of the representational types already mentioned from Gaul, the squatting figure can be shown to go back at least to the second century BC, for it is found in the monumental sculpture at the great sanctuaries of Entremont and Roquepertuse near Aix-en-Provence. Entremont was a sanctuary of the Salyes and was destroyed by the Romans in 124 BC. These places cannot be regarded as typical of Celtic practice. They lie in just that area most open to Mediterranean civilization, whether in the form of

108 Stone figure from Roquepertuse, Bouches-du-Rhône. Height about 1.5 m.

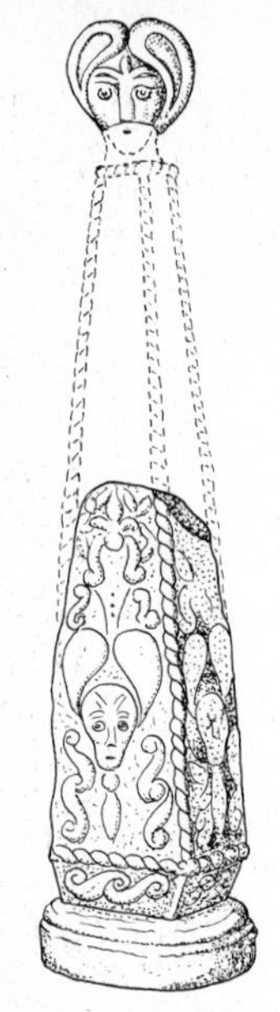

109 Reconstruction of the Pfalzfeld pillar (see Ill. 110).

110* Carved stone pillar from Pfalzfeld, St Goar, Germany. Fourth/fifth century BC. Surviving height about 1.5 m.

Colonial Greek at Massilia, or in that from the Graeco-Etruscan sphere of Northern Italy. At most, the Celtic element around the Lower Rhône was composed of warrior overlords, and their material culture was predominantly that of their Ligurian subjects, and their more civilized neighbours. However unusual Entremont, Roquepertuse and the other sanctuaries in the same region may have been, they gave expression to certain purely Celtic elements in symbolism and ritual. The outline friezes of horses, the carved birds, and the niches for the display of human heads, agree well with the kind of symbolism already deduced for more primitive regions. The large human stone sculptures at Roquepertuse sit cross-legged with the legs drawn close to the hips, and the soles of the feet turned upwards. This has appeared as something very oriental to many writers, but in all probability it was the normal ground-sitting posture amongst the Celts as it remains amongst many Asiatic peoples. It provides a more comfortable arrangement of the legs for people accustomed to it, learnt in the agility of childhood. Here was something of the Eurasiatic way of life abandoned in the west on the general adoption of chairs and stools. This pose would none the less have been also appropriate in ritual for gods and devotees whether in receiving or offering gifts, or, in the recitation of sacred texts, but to which category the Roquepertuse figures belong it is not at all clear. A fuller discussion of these sanctuaries must be foregone in the present survey, but one other point should be noted. The dress of the Roquepertuse figures, with the exception of the ceremonial square-cut cape, consists of the short tunic gathered at the waist with a belt, and so illustrates this type of Celtic apparel by more than a century in advance of Diodorus Siculus.

In the absence of intermediate examples of cult art in Gaul, between the Roquepertuse statuary and the very various Gallo-Roman pieces, it is impossible to say what influence, if any, the southern sanctuaries may have had in areas northwards. It is not anyway likely that the squatting pose was propagated from that quarter.

An earlier, and perhaps more potent, exotic influence in Celtic cult art was that of the Etruscans, and this is manifest in a few surviving sculptures mainly from the Middle Rhenish zone. Here, individual motifs of Etruscan origin are found in sculpture that is wholly Celtic in general composition, but this evidence is important in showing the extent to which ideas about sacred monuments may have developed at a time when, in artistic sensibility generally, the Celts were most receptive.

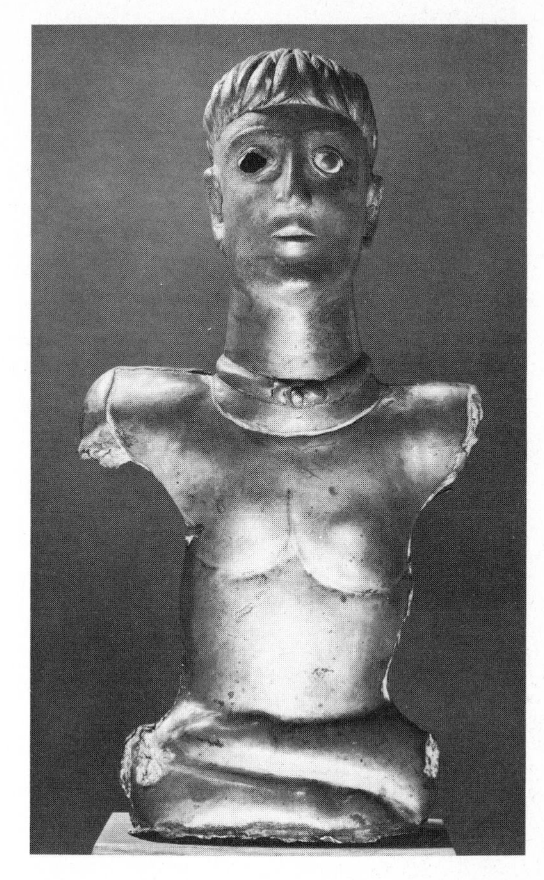

The relief-carved, four-sided pillar from Pfalzfeld, in the Hunsrück, is the most outstanding of the existing monuments. It is described in detail on page 216, and here its cult significance only will be discussed. Its essential character is that of a tapering monolith decorated on all sides with floriate motifs in the early La Tène style, and in the midst of each panel peers forth a human face surmounted by great paired lobes, the so-called 'leaf-crown' considered to be a mark of deity in early La Tène art. The monument was originally surmounted by a similarly carved head, but this has disappeared within recent centuries. There is unfortunately no other known comparable pillar, but a stone head from Heidelberg may well have surmounted such another. On stylistic grounds, and bearing in mind the historical setting for the period of direct Etruscan influences north of the Alps, the Pfalzfeld stone should date to within the fourth century BC, if not slightly earlier. Its explanation in terms of cult is perhaps hazardous, but whether or not it stood originally on a grave mound, there is something to be said for believing it to represent the idea of a sacred tree, the home, if not the embodiment, of a tribal deity.

111* Stone figure from Euffigneix, Haute Marne, France. First century BC. Height 26 cm.

112* Bronze figure from Bouray, Seine-et-Oise, France. Third century BC? Height 42 cm.

113 Fragmentary stone head from Heidelberg. Height 30 cm.

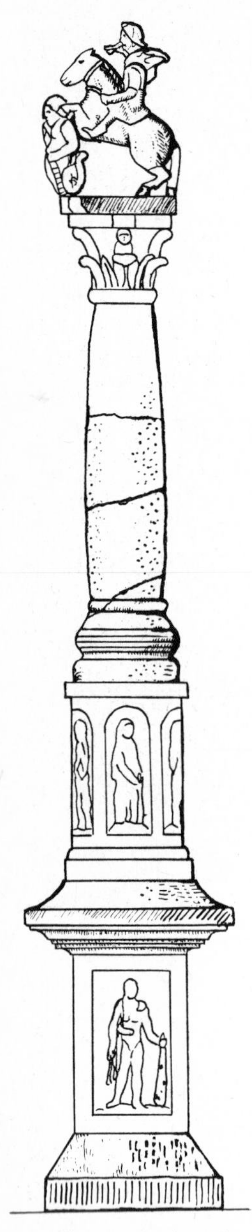

114 Reconstruction of Jupiter Column from Cannstatt, Stuttgart. Estimated height 4.5 m.

Sacred columns and trees

Of a much later date, but in line with this possibility, is the evidence of a type of Gallo-Roman monument not hitherto mentioned. This is the 'Jupiter column', so called from the epigraphical testimony of dedication to Jupiter. These monuments have their main distribution in the Middle Rhenish zone, both east and west, and extend into the Vosges with a wide dispersal in North-eastern and Central Gaul. The over-all appearance of the monument is Roman, and it essentially consists of a square base surmounted by a swelling and slightly tapered column, with capital, and surmounting sculptured device. The base, and even the column, are often decorated with figures of Roman gods, but the topmost element portrays a composition more at home in native cult. This, usually, is a sculpture of the horseman and emergent giant who supports the horse's front feet. The bearded rider is garbed in Roman military attire, but may carry a wheel as well as weapons. In a few cases a seated male figure, or a male and female couple, take the place of the equestrian group, but all these subjects can be reconciled with the general theme of the all-purpose Celtic god as already expounded.

It is not, however, the iconography so much as the column itself that is of prime interest. Its unusual form, as a subject within the *interpretatio Romana*, and its concentration within the Middle Rhenish zone, strongly suggest that it had native forerunners in wood, and again, that its ultimate prototype was the growing sacred tree.

It remains to say that both Gallo-Roman epigraphy, and Irish texts throw light on the significance of sacred trees amongst the Celts. Gods of oak and beech are known from dedications. The tribal name *Eburones* incorporates the word for yew, and Gaulish proper names include *Guidgen*, son of wood, and *Guerngen*, son of alder. In Ireland there are a number of allusions to a sacred tree (*bile*), and this word is to be compared with the French place name Billom, originally Gaulish *Biliomagus*, the plain or clearing of the sacred tree. Again, Irish mythological names such as *Mac Cuilinn*, son of holly, and *Mac Ibar*, son of yew, tell the same story.

The Middle Rhenish Celts may be credited with adopting for their own purposes the Etruscan practice of raising sculptured stone monuments, but it is probably from that quarter also that they received the idea of portraying two-headed, or two-faced, Janus-like, images. The finest surviving example is the tall stone from Holzgerlingen in Württemberg which shows on two opposing sides identical shallow-cut human faces with below, the right forearm extended horizontally across the body. This figure also appears to have had a 'leaf-crown' standing free, and shared by the two faces. The Holzgerlingen stone has no ornamental carving, and the emphasis is on the severe, inscrutable, face, whichever is confronted, for there is no real side view or profile. It seems very probable that this, and related stones, were set up in shrines and sanctuaries of types to be mentioned later, but one of the most arresting pieces from Roquepertuse was a Janus composition of two heads, and this may give strength to the case for the Rhône having been the route by which these new ideas in cult art found their way to the central Celtic area.

The ritual interest of these heads, together with the faces on the Pfalzfeld pillar looking in all four directions, lies in the expression they give to the superhuman abilities of the deity, and the purely Celtic embodiment of this, involving the sacred number of three, would have been a subsequent sculptural development.

Finally, an interesting stone of even earlier date deserves mention. It was found at Stockach, near Tübingen, in association with a cremation burial under a tumulus. The grave offerings

115* Janus statue (restored) from Holzgerlingen, Württemberg. Probably sixth–fifth century BC. Height 2.3 m.

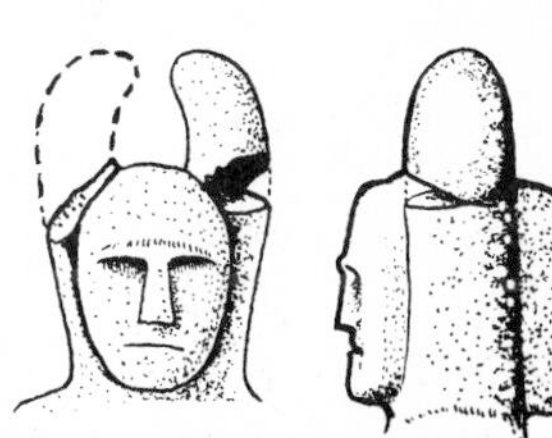

116 Reconstruction of the Holzgerlingen head, showing the two faces in profile and outline of the missing horn.

117* Two views of carved stone figure from Waldenbuch, Württemberg. Existing height 1.3 m.

118* Three views of stone Janus head from Leichlingen, Rhein-Wupper. Height 12 cm.

belong to the first phase of the Hallstatt iron-using culture. The stone, which was broken, shows the lower part of a roughly modelled head with a single face. Shoulders are marked but no neck, and the only other feature is a single zig-zag line running round all sides beneath the shoulders. It seems unnecessary to seek southern inspiration for this piece, but its witness for more widespread practice at this period is uncertain.

The sacred enclosure

119 Stone figure found in cremation burial at Stockach, Württemberg. Height 75 cm.

The precincts of sacred trees, images, and other objects of veneration, must now be considered. Except for sanctuaries such as Roquepertuse and Entremont, lying in an area particularly open to more sophisticated attainments, the sacred places of the Celts, prior to, or beyond, the Roman Empire, seem to have been of the simplest kind.

A widespread form appears to have been a sacred wood, or tract of ground on which stood groves of trees. This seems to have been the general implication of the word *nemeton* which is widely distributed in place-names throughout the Celtic lands. Some examples are *Drunemeton*, the sanctuary and meeting place of the Galatians in Asia Minor, Nemetobriga in Spanish Galicia, Nemetacum, in the territory of the Atrebates in North-eastern Gaul, and Nemetodurum from which is derived the modern name of Nanterre. In Britain there was a place Vernemeton in Nottinghamshire, and in Southern Scotland a Medionemeton.

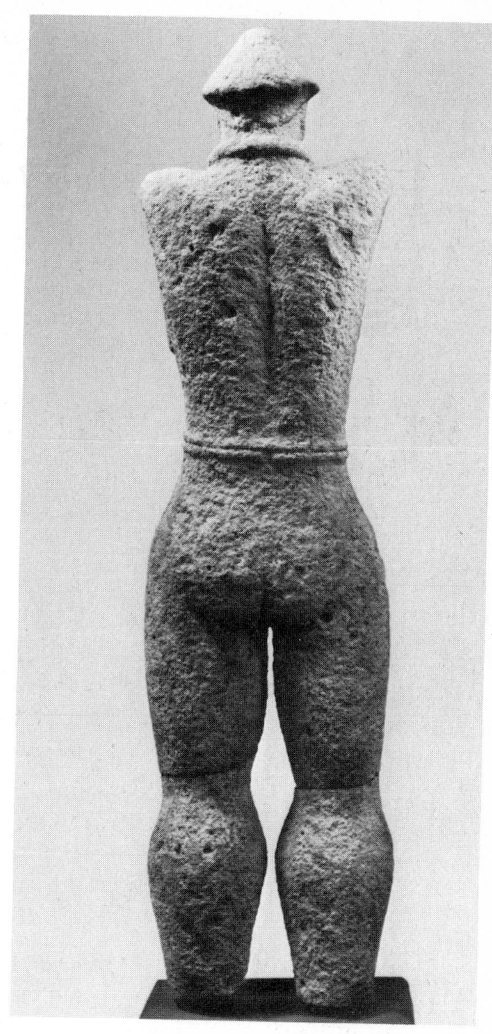

120 Stone statue of helmeted warrior, Hirschlanden, Württemberg. Originally standing on the top of a Hallstatt tumulus, this figure of local stone is in an idiom looking towards the south-east Alpine and North Italian regions. Late sixth–early fifth century BC. Height 1.5 m.

In Ireland, *fidnemed* meant a sacred wood, but a Latin gloss for *nemed* gives *sacellum* which suggests a small shrine or enclosure. An eighth-century glossary gives a plural word '*nimidas*', evidently derived from *nemeton*, and explains it in terms of the holy places of the woods, and the eleventh-century cartulary of the Abbey of Quimperlé refers to a wood called *Nemet*, thus showing the continuity of Celtic tradition in Brittany. There are, as well, the references by Classical writers to the woods in which the druids performed their rites and sacrifices, but the Celtic word in question is not mentioned in these passages.

Archaeology can do nothing to recapture the sanctity, even horror, of a natural wood, and from antiquity there is only Lucan's perhaps imaginary description of the sacred wood near

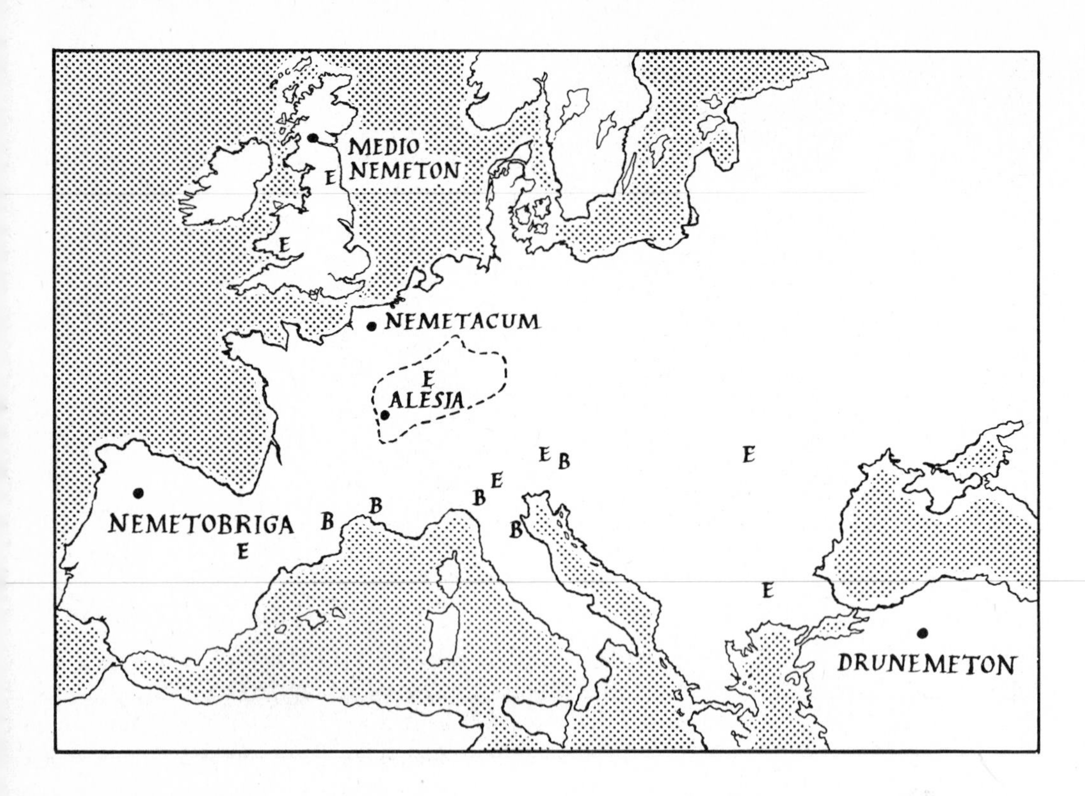

121 Map illustrating the geographical range of (i) Dedications to Belenus (B), (ii) Dedications to Epona (E). These are concentrated within the area enclosed by the broken line, together with the site of Alesia which was a principal centre of the cult. The outlying dedications result from devotees in Roman military service. (iii) Four selected *nemeton* place-names indicative of sacred woods or other kinds of sanctuary. (Note: This is not a detailed distribution map.)

Massilia which was destroyed by Caesar to provide timber for siege works. Lucan's word-picture of rotting wooden idols and branches smeared with human blood is graphic enough, but whether it is true – that is, of a genuinely Celtic cult – or based on an account from elsewhere, it is impossible to tell.

It seems, indeed, that *nemeton* may have come to have had a very wide application, and there are two categories of sites, in addition to woods, that may have been so called. Firstly, there were the places at which the seasonal gatherings of the *túath*, or tribe, took place. The Galatian centre, Drunemeton, and the various royal sites in Ireland, Emain Macha, Tara, Cruachain and others, are possible examples. These popular foregatherings could not have been conveniently held within a wood, as races, games and public meetings of various kinds were all essential elements of these festivals. In Ireland one finds that the traditional sites are in fact more remarkable for their funerary monuments than for signs of habitation or defence, and in the literature, it is the grave mounds that are remembered, and shown to have been the reason for the celebration at that place.

Secondly, however, *nemeton* seems to have been appropriate to lesser sanctuaries, or local shrines, if one may judge from the

122* Air photograph of Emain Macha (Navan Fort), Armagh, Ireland.

123 Excavations of the mound within Navan Fort, revealing complex timber-framed houses superseded by ritual post-circles. Sixth to third century BC.

124* Air photograph of the central group of earthworks on the Hill of Tara, Co. Meath Ireland.

equation of the term with *sacellum*, and with an inscription of Roman times from Vaison, Vaucluse, which commemorates the setting-up of a *nemeton* in honour of Belesama. This must surely refer to some kind of structure.

Before discussing some of the few archaeological sites which throw any light on these two categories of sacred place, it should be said that we are not justified in concluding that all Celtic sanctuaries were fundamentally places of burial, as has sometimes been done. There is no indication that such sacred woods as we have evidence of were used in this way, nor is there any from a small Iron Age shrine at Frilford in Berkshire, nor from the circular wooden building, taken to have been a shrine, at St Margarethen-am-Silberberg in Austria. There is also to be considered the testimony of native-style temples erected under Roman rule where, although some may indeed enhance an ancestral tomb, others can be shown to have had no funerary connections.

Some Celtic shrines

The Frilford site consisted of six large post-holes in two close-set lines of three each. The form of the original enclosure is not known as, at a later date, a roughly horse-shoe-shaped ditch was dug providing an entrance facing the double line of assumed uprights. These latter can hardly have been intended to support a roof, and may therefore be regarded as having been themselves objects of veneration. This theory is strengthened by the fact that at the foot of the central post, in the front row, an iron plough-share was found in such a position that it must have been an intentional deposit. Early in the Romanization of the district, the site was dismantled and levelled, and a circular stone-built wall was erected in its place. It is not clear what kind of structure, if any, this wall supported, but evidence of a conflagration in later Roman times suggests that, by then, at least, a wooden super-structure, perhaps a roof, was in position. It is clear that the sanctity of the Iron Age shrine continued to be held in respect, but the Roman 'rotunda' should possibly be regarded as the culmination of this intent at a moment when the real centre of cult was moved to a newly constructed temple a short distance away. This Romano-British temple is of the simple square-built type that will be described presently.

The site at St Margarethen-am-Silberberg, dating apparently, from the early first century BC, indicated a circular post-built hut some six metres in diameter, probably covered by a conical thatched roof. It cannot be claimed that this was a more archaic house form than the rectangular ones at the same site which were contemporary with it. It would, however, seem to provide a pointer to the nature of the antecedents of the round and polygonal native temples in the Celtic areas of the Roman Empire. It may also have some bearing on those mythological feasting halls (*bruidne*) that play an important part in certain Irish kingship stories, which were wood built, and were possibly, though not certainly, round in plan.

An interesting, and potentially important site in its wider implications, is the earthwork known as the Goloring which lies in the Kobener Wald between Koblenz and Mayen, and which was excavated within recent years. Here a circular area some 190 metres in diameter was enclosed by a bank and inner ditch. In the centre is an elevated area some 88 metres across, and at its centre point was found a hole which had held a wooden post of some considerable height, possibly of the order of 12 metres. Excavation revealed that a long ramp had led down into the hole on one side, and this would have been used for sliding in the foot of the post which would then have been levered and hauled to an upright position. This was the normal method in ancient

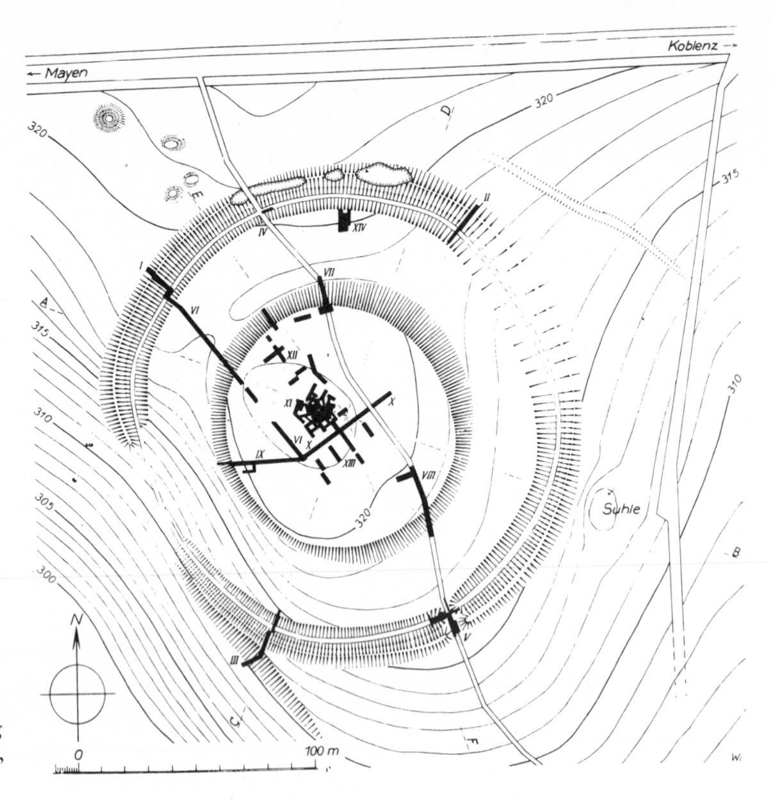

125 Plan of the Goloring earthwork, near Koblenz, Germany.

Europe of stepping large wooden or stone uprights, and the technique was well known, for example, in Neolithic Britain.

There was no evidence for burial or habitation at the Goloring, but stray potsherds in the composition of the central area, and in the ditch silting, indicated construction in Late Hallstatt times, and therefore possibly in the sixth century BC. Although now covered by trees, the Goloring must be envisaged as having stood in open country, and its actual situation was towards the southern side of a low ridge. The standing post would have been a conspicuous landmark for some distance around, and it does not seem unreasonable to interpret the site as a tribal assembly place. Here was adequate space for a concourse with its rites, judgments, deliberations, games and marketing. Furerary associations were not lacking, for in close proximity were two groups of tumuli dating from Urnfield to Hallstatt times.

No other site of this kind has been excavated on the Continent, but there are superficial indications of others, at least in this part of the Rhenish zone. The general nature of the Goloring seems to justify comparison with some of the earthworks at royal assembly places in Ireland as at Tara, at Emain Macha (Navan fort, Armagh), and Knockaulin, County Kildare. At all of these there are earthworks with the ditch inside the rampart, but while this is usually found to be a ritual device, it can be effective for defence if the earthworks are sited on steeply sloping ground. Either, or both, purposes may have been in question at the Goloring and at many apparently similar sites in Ireland. Analogies to the standing post at the Goloring are not as yet known in Ireland, although the use of stone pillars as memorials and gravestones was certainly observed. The possibility that Celtic institutions were brought to Ireland by settlers of Rhenish cultural traditions was mentioned in the first chapter, and if this should be substantiated, the relationship between the Goloring and Irish earthworks will be seen in a clearer light.

In Ireland the juxtaposition, at the principal places of assembly, of various kinds of enclosures with burial mounds stresses the auspiciousness of ancestral tombs. An allusion to the rightness of assembly at funerary monuments is in fact made in the great legal compilation known as *Senchas Már*, dating in its first written form from the eighth century AD. As yet no Irish site has revealed tombs that can be considered as those of founder settlers or immediate ancestors of the Irish Celts, but this must largely be a matter of further excavation. At Tara, the Celtic traditions were only adapted to a hill-top that was already sanctified for centuries by the presence of an Early Bronze Age megalithic tomb, and subsequent burials made in its covering mound. This, after all, should be quite in line with the concept of winning over the pre-existing supernatural powers of the countryside, manifest chiefly in the nature goddess. At Tara, Medb or Étaín might well claim an ancestress in the Early Bronze Age tomb-goddess who was of Mediterranean, not Indo-European, origins.

It seems that no over-all line of development should be sought in considering the holy places of the Celts, but the identification of one type of site clearly incorporating shrine and burial aspects is of particular interest. These sites have been recently identified in the department of the Marne, in North-eastern France. Here, square ditched enclosures formed the burial places for assumed families over a period of some centuries. At the site excavated at Écury-le-Repos, the sides of the square were approximately 10 metres, and at the centre of the enclosed space were found four large post-holes arranged in a rough square with a single large oval post-hole at the centre point. This evidence is very reasonably interpreted as speaking for a roofed shrine covering a free-standing object whether a post or a carved image.

126

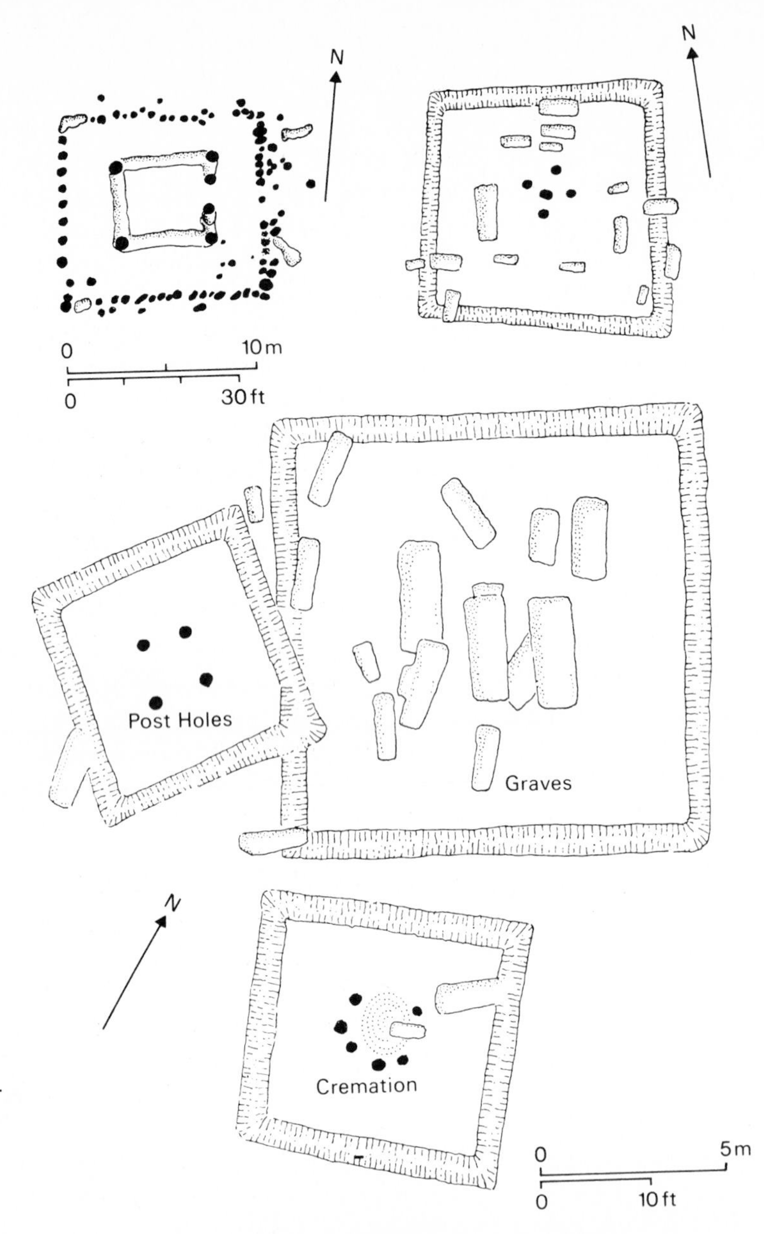

126 Plan of ditched enclosures and post-structures at Écury-le-Repos and Fin d'Écury, Marne, France and of post-structure of temple at Heathrow, England.

The oldest burial within the precinct was by inhumation, and it lay immediately to the west of the shrine. Both it, and another inhumation in a less privileged position, contained brooches of La Tène II style, but the subsequent burials were cremations which, with their pottery, showed continuance of use of the site to Roman times. If the stone figure from Holzgerlingen, already mentioned, did not stand on top of a chieftain's burial mound, as was once suggested, it is not difficult to envisage it within a shrine of the kind discovered at Écury-le-Repos.

Romano-Celtic temples

The squareness in plan of this simple shrine structure, and of the enclosing ditch, may well be thought of as an antecedent to the most common form of native Celtic temple as developed in more durable building material under Roman encouragement. In these the essential features are a small square building, the shrine itself, or *cella*, entered through a single door, and usually surrounded by a portico or veranda. The whole stood, in at least some cases, within a square enclosure. It is clear that the worshippers must have remained outside the building, but the portico provided a place to which the sacred contents, images or symbols, could be brought out for exposure and veneration. The fact that the portico runs round all four sides of the shrine may suggest that its purpose was for processions, and these would doubtless have moved in a sunwise direction about the building. Under the shelter of the portico roof may well have sat the men of sacred knowledge reciting the ritual texts appropriate to each festival. From only one site, and that in Britain, at Heathrow in Middlesex, is an explicit wooden prototype of the Pre-Roman Iron Age known for these square temples which are not at the same time places of burial. This excavation which awaits full publication will clearly be of the greatest interest.

126

It is in Gaul that the Romano-Celtic temple, square, polygonal and round, is found in greatest number. They were erected in towns, at thermal springs, and at many country places including some hill-tops. At some, an original Pre-Roman tomb and sanctuary seems to have been commemorated, and it has been claimed that the special virtue of these temples lay in the presence of a god, or hero, ancestor to whom the local population were as dependants. Without pressing this view, it may be said that the Irish literary evidence all points to tribal god ancestors in the genealogies, and to the tombs of gods and mortal heroes in field monuments recorded in topographical traditions.

Bull and boar sculptures

One further type of visible monument to do with cult must claim a brief notice. In Central Spain and in Northern Portugal, and generally associated with hill-forts of Celtic, or partly Celtic, tribes, there are found large stone sculptures of boars and bulls. The inspiration for these sculptures is probably Mediterranean, but the purpose suited Celtic needs, for these figures seem to

127

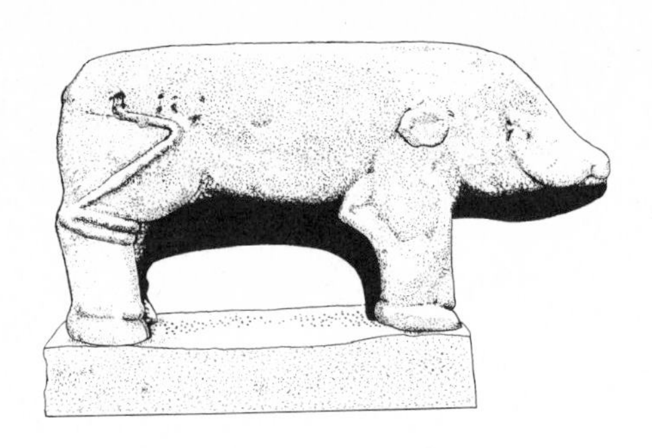

127 Stone sculpture of boar, Central Spain. Somewhat over life-size.

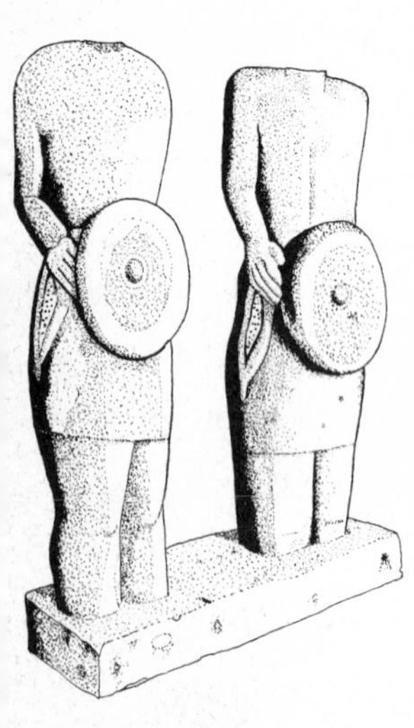

128 Stone sculpture of warriors with round shields. Province of Minho, Northern Portugal. Height 1.7 m.

have had to do with the fertility and prosperity of the herds, and the sculptures are found sited in, or overlooking, cattle enclosures beneath the actual citadels. In Northern Portugal there are also sculptures or armed warriors, and these too would seem to have served as protective forces.

Votive deposits

Perhaps the most spectacular, to contemporary eyes, of Celtic sacred places were those where rested collections of votive offerings exposed to full view in the open. Caesar mentions weapons and other booty heaped on the ground, and these lay unmolested and dedicated to the god of the conquering side in inter-tribal warfare. Poseidonius, who also travelled in Gaul in the first century BC, is quoted by Strabo on the great votive treasure of the Volcae Tectosages which was deposited in sacred enclosures and pools near Tolosa (Toulouse). This treasure was pillaged by the Romans in 106 BC, and it is reported to have been of unworked gold and silver, from which it would appear that ingots of these metals had been made up.

The reference by Poseidonius to sacred pools, which may also imply marshes or swamps, is of particular interest in view of a number of archaeological discoveries that may best be interpreted as votive deposits. Within the Celtic Iron Age may principally be cited the finds from La Tène itself, from Port, another site in Switzerland, from Llyn Cerrig Bach in Anglesey, and from various sites in Scotland. There are also many individual finds from peat bogs and rivers, that may be suspected of having been gifts to the supernatural, and in Northern Europe, beyond the effective settlement of the Celts, there are some very remarkable votive deposits of actual Celtic objects which throw much light on the whole matter.

(*opposite*)
129* Air photograph of the site of La Tène, Lac de Neuchâtel.

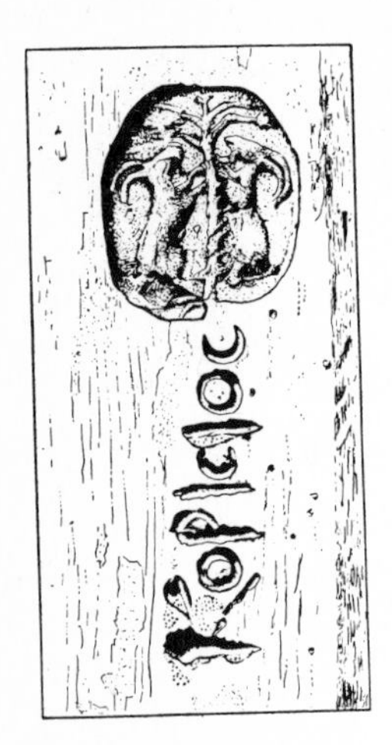

130 Inscription (KORISIOS in Greek letters) and punch-mark on sword blade from Port, Bienne, Switzerland. Slightly under actual size.

131 Portion of slave chain from Llyn Cerrig Bach, Anglesey. Maximum width of ring 18 cm.

At La Tène, the great mass of objects, principally consisting of iron weapons and equipment, but including woodwork and a complete wheel, lay in the peat a little offshore in a small bay which lies at the eastern end of the lake of Neuchâtel. Some human skeletal remains were also found, and the piles of a jetty-like construction which probably provided the platform from which the offerings were made. The discoveries at Port on the Nidau-Büren canal, at the north-eastern end of Lake Biel, came from the bed of an old river. Here, too, the finds have been mainly weapons including spear-heads, and swords, some of the latter displaying punch marks of master swordsmiths, and are of the finest quality. The remains of a wooden structure was also detected at Port.

In Anglesey, the Llyn Cerrig Bach find, made in 1943, has thrown much light on the sources and composition of the objects in a large votive deposit. The site had been an area of standing water, part of a lake, that was close to a rock shelf on the shore. From this vantage point had been thrown numerous weapons, chariot fittings, slave chains, tools, and at least fragments of cauldrons, trumpets, and pieces of fine bronze work decorated in the insular La Tène style. A large quantity of bones, representing ox, horse, sheep, pig and dog, were also found, and these appear to have been sacrificed animals rather than domestic refuse for which there was no other indication.

The dating of the metal objects lies between the mid-second century BC and the mid-first century AD. Although the circumstances of the find prohibited any direct observations, it seems probable that the Llyn Cerrig Bach material represents a series of offerings made over a period of time, but its discontinuation in the mid-first century is almost certainly to be related to the storming of *Mona* by Roman troops in 61 AD. The finer pieces of latest date in the deposit, coming as they did from richer areas in Britain to the south-east, suggest the presence of aristocratic refugees, and their association with final rites to stem the tide of calamity.

Three much smaller collections of votive offerings, from the first and second centuries AD, come from Carlingwark, Blackburn Mill, and Eckford, all in Southern Scotland. In the first two cases the objects had been placed in cauldrons, the ritual significance of which need hardly be stressed again. The objects in all three hoards were mainly tools and equipment of both native and Roman work, and many were broken and worn out when deposited. The offering of defective objects, here and elsewhere, seems to have been quite in order as it was presumably the 'essence' of each piece, rather than its state of completion, that was thought to count with the supernatural. These three deposits are of wide interest, as they were clearly single acts, and made in water at places that were not habitually regarded as especially sacred for such rites.

Of single votive offerings only the splendid bronze shield in late insular La Tène style from the Thames at Battersea, and the somewhat earlier shield and sword from the Lincolnshire Witham, will be cited as objects most unlikely to have been merely lost overboard when crossing the river.

The recovery of votive deposits from water-logged sites must depend to a large extent on geographical factors, changes in water level, and the modern exploitation of peat. The practice of water or marsh depositions is known to remount to the Early Neolithic in Denmark where conditions for preservation have been particularly favourable. The usage seems to have been continuous throughout pagan times in the Teutonic North, but it is not unlikely that elsewhere in trans-Alpine Europe votive deposits were made from as early a beginning.

Sacrifice

Sacred precincts and votive offerings lead on to questions of human and animal sacrifice, and to the persons within the community who were competent to perform the rites.

It is unfortunately impossible to recapture the sequence of ceremonies appropriate for the various seasonal festivals, or for those more sporadic contingencies such as warfare, famine or disease. The Classical notices are too brief and vague, and the Irish literary sources betray only indirect information. In the first case it was too barbarous, and in the second, too heathenish, a custom to merit detailed recollection. With regard to the Irish seasonal festivals, it has been said that cattle were sacrificed at *Bron Trograin*, but there exists a more oblique and interesting reference to human sacrifice at *Samain*. This is contained in a story of how at this season a maiden was wooed at Bri Ele by the men of Ireland, and that for each man that wooed, one of his people were slain, no one knowing who did the deed. Bri Ele was another name for Cruachain, the royal centre of Connacht, and it would appear that the nature goddess's goodwill was secured through the sacrifice of a man from each invoking community. The inference is that the king was amorous of the goddess. The secret dispatch of the victim, presumably by stabbing, recalls some royal deaths, and was doubtless a device in the hands of those in charge of the rites. Somewhat more general and fanciful allusions to the sacrifice of children and beasts at *Samain* are to be found in the manuscripts. That these contain an element of truth is unquestionable, but they do not contribute to any closer understanding of the setting.

One of the most important survivals in Irish mythology is a story concerning sacrifice to redress the misfortunes consequent upon an inauspicious alliance between a king of Tara and a strange woman. The ritual prescribed by the druids is the sacrifice of the son of a sinless couple. The story goes on to relate the fabulous circumstances of his discovery, but once he has been brought to Tara, and at the point of sacrifice, a supernatural woman appears leading a cow which she directs to be offered in substitution. This story has a remarkable parallel in Aryan tradition in India, strongly pointing to a common heritage, but its ritual interest also lies in its demonstration of the kind of myth which justified the substitution of animal for human victims.

The same trend is found in a myth projected into an account of a battle that must have occurred relatively late in Pre-Christian times. In this fray, a people called the Dési overcome the people of Ossory as a result of a druid having allowed himself to be slain in the form of a cow. Here original sacrifice of the most sacred category of human being was undertaken to ensure the outcome of the contest, but the rite had been ameliorated by means of the magician's supposed shape-shifting prowess.

It would be unwise to deduce that human sacrifice had generally been abandoned for animal offerings amongst the Irish Celts. Perhaps it was only so in particular ritual situations, or amongst certain peoples; the evident ritual deaths of kings will not have been forgotten. The Classical evidence for human victims in Gaul and Britain is strong, and to the principal of these attention must now turn.

Caesar understood well the propitiatory nature of sacrifice amongst the Gauls, but of course there was nothing extraordinary in this custom in Gaul, or in the wider Celtic domain; it was only that the Celts had retained archaic practices once also at home in Italy, as in Greece, but now long outmoded. It appears that the most usual method of sacrifice was by a weapon wound, with the sprinkling of blood on sacred objects, as on altars and trees. This much may be inferred from Tacitus and Lucan. There was too, the taking of auspices by consultation of human

132 Scene in which a victim is being ceremonially drowned by being put head downwards into a vessel of liquid, with attendant cavalry and infantry, from a panel of the Gundestrup silver cauldron. Late second-early first century BC.

entrails, but of greater interest are the reports of sacrifice by burning, drowning and hanging.

In the first place, Caesar describes how some Gaulish tribes constructed colossal images of wickerwork, filled them with living victims, and then set the whole thing alight. The victims were said to have been preferably malefactors, and it may be deduced that, whatever the actual crimes, these were persons who had transgressed their ritual integrity. It does not appear that captives taken in battle were offered on these occasions. The sacrifices in this manner appear to have been to ensure tribal welfare, and may therefore be compared to the Irish seasonal festivals and the sacrifices that were conducted at them also. The wickerwork containers, whether or not it can be admitted that they took the form of human figures, recall the various Irish stories, some certainly mythological, of houses burnt down, and the death of people, sometimes kings, within.

These points bear on the well known reference to Teutates, Taranis and Esus, by Lucan in the *Pharsalia*, and the early commentaries that have survived on the text amplifying the information Lucan gives on these three Celtic gods. Here Taranis is stated to have been propitiated by burning, while to Teutates victims were drowned, and to Esus they were hanged. It will be remembered that these three names may have been of general applicability to Gaulish tribal deities, and the rites may therefore have been appropriate to different occasions rather than to different tribes. There is the possibility, too, that these three modes symbolized the elements of earth or vegetation (Esus: hanging), fire (Taranis: burning), and water (Teutates: drowning). The drowning sacrifice is depicted on one of the panels of the great silver basin from Gundestrup in Denmark, itself a votive offering in a peat bog, but in manufacture of Celtic origin, dating probably from the first century BC, and coming from the Celts settled along the middle Danube rather than from the Gauls. The hanging sacrifice to Esus is particularly interesting with its inference for sacred trees, but also because this rite was practised in honour of Othin, the great magician god of the Teutonic barbarian warrior aristocracy, whose cult was centred in Sweden, and who even may have had a Celtic origin.

132

Magicians and sages

The practitioners of magic and ritual must form the subject of the final pages of this chapter, and of these the chief amongst the Celts were the druids. It is perhaps unnecessary to say that despite the romantic fictions of recent centuries, and the mock 'druidic' organizations that still spring up from time to time, there is absolutely no continuity or relation with the druids of antiquity. Nor is there any necessity to evoke wonder, or mystery, in accounting for the ancient druids who, in the light of modern studies in comparative religion, are found to take a natural place in a well-defined socio-religious category common to several, if not at one time all, of the people possessing Indo-European languages and institutions. Of these the most outstanding example are the Brahmins who have continued in existence in Hindu society since the Aryan invasions of Northern India in the mid- or late-second millennium BC. The Brahmins have, of course, for long formed an hereditary caste, but this seems to have been a development subsequent to isolation in India, while, amongst the Celts, the druids preserved the more archaic organization in forming a class recruited from children of the warrior aristocracy. Anterior to the *flamines* and *pontifices* at Rome, there is some evidence for a similar category of sacred person amongst the Italic peoples, but the development of Rome under Mediterranean influence to a great urban state transformed the primitive institutions.

The word druid as used in modern European languages is derived from continental Celtic through Greek and Latin texts. Caesar for instance writes of *druides*, and Cicero of *druidae*. These, of course, are Latinized forms in the plural. In the surviving insular Celtic languages, *druí* (sing.), *druad* (plur.) are forms of the same word from Old Irish texts. *Dryw* is the Welsh equivalent in the singular. Druid, as a word, is considered to derive from roots meaning 'knowledge of the oak', or possibly 'great, or deep, knowledge'. Pliny compared the word to the Greek one for an oak tree, and seems to imply that its connection with oak was intended. The connection between the druids and the oak is indeed explicit in Pliny's account of the cutting of mistletoe from an oak tree by the druids, and the accompanying sacrifice of bulls. It is unfortunately unknown if this rite was connected with a tribal festival and for what purpose it was carried out. The oak groves at Olympia may also have been in Pliny's mind, and these certainly appear to have been a surviving Indo-European element in Greek cult comparable to the Celtic sacred woods, more particularly with the oak sanctuary (*Drunemeton*) of the Galatians. If the oak, principally but not exclusively amongst trees, was the symbol of deity, 'knowledge of the oak' would be apposite for those who mediated with the supernatural.

The essence of druidic knowledge of the supernatural is made clearer by a consideration of the titles of other Celtic learned magicians, although it is impossible to draw any real distinction between their functions. In addition to druids and bards, Strabo mentions *vates*, and this word is cognate with the Irish *fáthi* (sing.: *fáith*). These words spring from a root meaning 'inspired' or 'ecstatic', and thence prophet and poet. Another Irish term, and one that became most prominent in Early Christian times, was that of *fili* (plur.: *filid*). This originally meant 'seer', but became the most usual word for poet in the sense of the learned court eulogist and remembrancer. It was in the ability 'to see' the invisible, to obtain prior knowledge, that the power of the magician was considered mainly to have lain. Knowledge was a matter of seeing, as the philology of the Irish words show, and this again was achieved through trances, frenzies or stimulated inspiration of some kind.

One of the most interesting examples of trance is in an account of the choosing of a new king at Tara when a bull was killed, and a druid gorged on its flesh. The druid then fell in a trance while incantations were recited over him, and on recovery he was able to prognosticate the distinguishing circumstances of the rightful claimant's approach to Tara. This rite was known as *tarbfeis*, 'bull dream'. Frenzy, trance, and shape-shifting, all point to some generic connection between the Celtic magician, of whatever name, and the shaman of the Northern Eurasiatic zone. It is not at all unlikely that this aspect remounts to the early period of contacts over the Pontic steppes.

Although several Classical writers credit the druids with being philosophers, it is difficult to find any evidence that as a body they indulged in any speculative thought, or taught an ethical code beyond anything that could be comprehended in correct ritual behaviour. Divitiacus, the druid friend of Caesar and Cicero, can hardly be taken as other than an exception, and it is only to be expected that such exceptional druids, who were brought into contact with Mediterranean life, and Greek thought, would have developed intellectual realms very different from their up-country cousins. That the druids had views on the nature of an after-life is nothing remarkable in face of the great weight of archaeological evidence, from Celtic graves, showing the solicitude for a continued existence in providing weapons, ornaments and food, for the journey, if not for the feast at the other end.

The pre-eminence of the druids in Celtic society is not in doubt from what Caesar, and others, say about their duties as arbitrators, no less than magicians, and in Ireland their status is best illustrated by the fact that a king might not speak until his druid had first expressed himself. The Irish evidence indicates that druids bore arms and were householders. Caesar suggests otherwise, so far as fighting is concerned, for the Gaulish druids, but these and many other aspects cannot be pursued here. In conclusion something must be said about one of the more instructive and significant features of Celtic learning, the transmission of oral literature.

Oral learning

The modern world is so dependent on written information that it is perhaps difficult for many people to envisage any other means of conserving knowledge, or a national literature. At first it might seem impossible that long texts, whatever the content, could be accurately retained in the memory, and transmitted from one generation to another. This in fact was the ancient practice amongst the Indo-European peoples lying beyond the bounds of the city civilizations where writing first came into use. The survival to modern times of the traditional Brahminical schools in India clearly demonstrates how oral learning is carried on, and, by example, amplifies much that can be learnt of the parallel tradition amongst the Celts.

The mechanism of oral learning is largely that of continuous repetition by chanting simple rhythmical verse or alliterative prose forms. Here again, the rhythm may induce a semi-ecstatic state, and, over years, a great body of received texts can be absorbed. To this may be added the sacred nature of all learning in the ancient world, the widely held concept of merit in accurate recitation, and the magical penalties with which departures from the true tradition were fraught. All these aspects are well seen in both the Indian and Celtic traditions, and they make sense of Caesar's description of the training of the druids' pupils in many verses over many years. Caesar, of course, misunderstood the reason why the druids did not use writing for their learning. It was not just a matter of maintaining secrecy, but because writing had not the necessary ritual acceptance. It was not hallowed by ancient usage.

Oral learning tends also to great conservatism in language so that the everyday spoken language grows farther away from the learned tongue. The most outstanding example of this in the comparative field is the language of the Vedic hymns which is earlier than the Sanskrit in which the commentaries on them came to be taught. Sanskrit in turn became a language only of the learned. These texts were preserved over millennia in India, and did not begin to be written down until the eighteenth century when some Brahmins broke with tradition and dictated them to Europeans. The same general situation existed amongst the Celts, and in Ireland it was only very gradually that oral learning lost its position before the rising prestige of the monastic scriptoria. It is now impossible to tell how archaic the language of the purely pagan oral texts may have been, but the links in ritual terminology, as well as the mythological content, of what survived presumes a similar situation to that developing in India.

Next to sacred literature, the myths, charms and incantations generally that would have been the spoken accompaniment of druidic practice, the most carefully conserved knowledge would have been that of law. It is particularly in this branch that the surviving Irish material is most archaic in language, and abundant in information on early institutions, but here only will be emphasized the normal acceptance of the oral embodiment as in the quotation from the great law compilation *Senchas Már*, 'the joint memory of the ancients, the transmission from one ear to another, the chanting of the poets'. So too, in citing precedents from the oldest sources, the passage is referred to as having been sung or recited. Here the *brithem* comes closest to the *fili*, and it would seem that the former term designates but a specialist growth of the learned poetic order.

There can be little doubt that the oral learning of the continental Celts would have included epic literature and genealogy, as well, naturally, as the eulogistic verse which is vouched for in Classical writers as being the special function of the bards. These categories can, however, now only be found within the insular compass of the surviving Irish and Welsh literatures, although, in form and style, they can be recognized as springing from the common Indo-European heritage.

Notes to Chapter 3

Principally to be consulted are: M. L. Sjoestedt (1940 and 1949), and J. Vendryes (1948). These are important, and contain bibliographies to earlier works, and to texts. See also J. Vendryes (1918) for comparative philology of ritual words, and M. Dillon (1947) for other comparative aspects. A. G. Van Hamel (1934) gives a valuable, if overstated, appreciation. T. F. O'Rahilly (1946) is important for sources, but, as with many authors not here cited, is outmoded, and uncritical, in the interpretation of mythology.

SEASONS: J. Vendryes (1948). On the bronze calendar from Coligny, see: E. MacNeill (1928), and Plate 76.

CERNE ABBAS: Illustrated by J. Hawkes, *Guide to the Prehistoric and Roman Monuments in England and Wales*, Pl. I. London, 1951.

SUCELLOS: For this, and other deities known in Gallo-Roman iconography, see maps and bibl. in P. Lambrechts (1942) and G. Behrens (1944). On Tarves Trigaranos, I follow A. Grenier (1945), 353–54.

MABINOGION: The edition, with introduction, by G. Jones and T. Jones (1949), should be used.

DEIOTAROS: On the Greek funerary inscription of Deiotaros II (ob. *c.* 43 BC) see *Revue Archéologique* (1935), 140–51. On the historical context see F. Stähelin (1907).

EPONA: R. Magnen and E. Thevenot (1953) for recent inventory and map.

ROMANO-BRITISH CULTS: I. A. Richmond (1955), and references therein.

NODENS: R. E. M. and T. V. Wheeler (1932) for excavation at Lydney.

CAESAR: For all Classical texts bearing on the Celtic supernatural consult J. Zwicker (1934–35).

ENTREMONT AND ROQUEPERTUSE: F. Benoit (1955). The seated figures have also been published by P. Jacobsthal (1944), and frequently elsewhere.

PFALZFELD AND RELATED SCULPTURE: P. Jacobsthal (1941) and (1944) for principal discussion.

JUPITER COLUMNS: P. Lambrechts (1942); G. Behrens (1944).

STOCKACH: G. Riek (1941); H. Kirchner (1955).

VAISON: J. Vendryes (1948).

FRILFORD: J. S. P. Bradford and R. G. Goodchild (1939).

ST MARGARETHEN: R. Pittioni (1954), with references.

GOLORING: J. Röder (1948).

IRISH SITES: S. P. Ó Ríordáin (1953). The 'Mound of the Hostages', at Tara, has recently revealed a Passage Grave of the Early Bronze Age.

ÉCURY-LE-REPOS: A. Brisson and J. J. Hatt (1955).

ROMANO-CELTIC TEMPLES: H. Koethe (1933) is the principal study. J. E. A. Bogaers (1955) for recent comment, and I. A. Richmond (1955) for Britain.

HEATHROW: The full report, by W. F. Grimes, is to be published by the Ministry of Works, London.

OTHER SANCTUARIES: K. Schwarz in W. Krämer, edit. (1958), 205–14 for the late La Tène cult sites. A. Grenier (1943) for 'hero-tomb' at Sanxay, Vienne. B. Lacroix (1956) for thermal springs at Fontaines-Salées, Yonne, where there are structures from first to fourth centuries AD.

STONE FIGURES IN SPAIN AND PORTUGAL: P. Bosch-Gimpera (1939); J. Maluquer de Motes (1954b) who also gives list of Celtic deity names in Latin epigraphy from the Peninsula.

LA TÈNE: E. Vouga (1925) for monograph on the site and finds.

PORT: R. Wyss (1955) and (1956) who discusses the votive nature of the finds at Port, La Tène, and elsewhere.

LLYN CERRIG BACH: C. Fox (1946).

CARLINGWARK AND OTHERS: S. Piggott (1953).

DRUIDS: J. Vendryes (1948). T. D. Kendrick (1928) collects the Classical references.

133 Bronze cauldron-mounts in the form of a bull and an owl from Brå, Denmark. Third century BC. Width of owl mask 4.5 cm.

4
The Celtic Survival

The Celts have now been surveyed in general as to their formation as a nation, their mode of life and their attitude to the supernatural. This final chapter must have largely to do with their disappearance, and with their legacy to Post-Roman, and Medieval, Europe through the emergence of those smaller nations, on the north-western periphery, who may be acknowledged as Celtic in their retention of the ancient language and institutions, but to whom the name Celt can no longer be applied in any proper historical sense. These were the peoples of Ireland, and of Northern and Western Britain, and some of the names used of them, such as Gael, Pict, Scot and Welsh, must be considered briefly on account of many popular misconceptions.

Cimbri and Teutones

The virtual political oblivion of the Celts, all but those in Ireland, through the expansion of the Roman Empire, has already been indicated in the first chapter, but the question now primarily concerns the northern and eastern barbarians, neighbours of the continental Celts, who were eventually to overwhelm the Empire, and bring about a complete reorganization of European political geography. For the present purpose a beginning must be made with certain events in the late second century BC which already foreshadowed the disruptions to come. In 113 BC, a Roman army sent to support the Celtic kingdom of Noricum in the Eastern Alps, against northern invaders, suffered defeat. The invaders were known by the name of *Cimbri*, and later evidence suggests that the bearers of this name came from Jutland, although their ranks had probably been considerably augmented on their way southwards. It would seem that they had followed the ancient transcontinental route by way of the Elbe to Bohemia, and thence to the Middle Danube, and the Eastern Alps. In Bohemia they had irrupted upon that long-established Celtic people the Boii, who earlier had contributed to the Gaulish settlement of Northern Italy, and who were now to send migrants seeking security in the west towards, and eventually beyond, the Rhine.

During the following years the Cimbri were engaged in roaming through Celtic lands from Noricum as far as the Seine and the Rhône. They had been joined meanwhile by a people called the *Teutones* who were possibly, but not certainly, of northern origin, and the combined forces, in 108 and 105 BC, inflicted other defeats on Roman arms, but now in Southern Gaul. After further extensive raiding in Gaul, and even beyond the western end of the Pyrenees, the raiders were finally eliminated by Roman forces at Aquae Sextiae (Aix-en-Provence) in 102 BC, and at Vercellae (Vercelli) in 101 BC. It is important to forego any hasty ethnological deductions about the Cimbri on the basis of their geographical starting-point. The personal names of their leaders, such as are known, are all purely Celtic, and passages from Diodorus, Strabo, and Pliny could all be taken as showing that the Cimbri spoke a Celtic language. The name Teutones itself is a Latin form of the Celtic word meaning 'people', as already met in the Irish *túath*, and in the Gaulish deity name Teutates.

The next stage is Caesar's record that in his time, half a century after the defeat of the Cimbri and Teutones, the Belgae, that warlike confederation of tribes in North-eastern Gaul, remembered with pride that they alone of the Gauls had successfully beaten off the invaders; but Caesar also learnt that the Belgae, in earlier times, had themselves come from beyond the Rhine, and that they ascribed their martial superiority to their origins in Germania. The important Celtic tribe centred on the Moselle, the Treveri, were also known to Caesar as having had 'Germanic' origins, but they were not of course part of the Belgic confederation. Modern archaeological research supports tradition in both cases as to the Rhenine, or trans-Rhenine, origins of these peoples.

'Germans'

It is next important, and revealing, to consider the names *Germania* and *Germani*. The latter word, according to Athenaeus, was known to Poseidonius, at the end of the second century BC. An earlier, but less well founded, occurrence might be claimed in the entry for the battle of Clastium, 222 BC, as seen in the fragmentary inscription from the *Acta Triumphalia* at Rome. The existing inscription is, however, much later than the event, and the inclusion of the name Germani, along with the well vouched-for Insubres, is likely to be no more than a learned interpolation of the first century AD. It is along the Rhine that the use of the name Germani is really important, and the archaeological evidence for Celtic settlement east of that river, together with the Celtic topographical names that survive as far east as the Weser, and even the Elbe, combine with the observed characteristics of the Belgae and the Treveri, to suggest that Germani was originally a Celtic tribal name which perhaps, in former days, had achieved a suzerain position. In Caesar's time it is clear that the name was used indiscriminately for any intruders coming into Gaul from across the Rhine, but a source from the end of the first century BC, throws some further light on the matter. Dionysius of Halicarnassus, in his *Roman Antiquities*, describing Celtica, says that the part lying beyond the Rhine, stretching towards Scythia and Thrace, as far as the Hercynian Forest, is called Germania. Though this statement does not agree with the situation in his own time, it does accord well with the other indications already mentioned, and it can be seen how, as viewed by the Gauls, a geographical connotation would have been established so that, by the first century BC, any people coming west across the Rhine, whether refugee Celts, or predatory strangers of still more remote origins, would naturally be dubbed 'Germans'.

In this connection, one further point must be made. Unlike the Celts themselves, whose name had been known from one end of Europe to the other, neither the Cimbri and Teutones, on the one hand, nor the Suevi, and their associates under Ariovistus, on the other, are known to have possessed, or to have claimed any super-tribal, or national name, although *Suevi* did come to have a very wide usage. In calling these people 'Germans' or 'Germanic', a name given by others, not by themselves, is employed. The only alternative, and one which for clarity is preferred in these pages, is to call all the non-Celtic intruders of this period Teutonic. This word in English is of academic origin, but it is at least cognate with the native *deutsch*, itself derived from *thioda*, meaning 'people' within the philological family of 'Teutonic' languages. These words clearly derive from the same Indo-European root as the Celtic examples already cited.

Teutonic peoples

It is with Caesar's encounter with Ariovistus and his horde that the first clear evidence for Teutonic-speaking peoples comes to light, but it is also certain that a large body of this horde consisted of displaced Celtic tribes, more barbaric than their cousins long settled in Gaul, as well as of tribes who can only be described as partly Celtic and partly Teutonic. This is only reasonable when one considers what the nature of rural barbarian Europe is likely to have been. There must have been a shading off of cultural, linguistic and political affiliations from one major natural region to another, and the process must go back to a time when there could be defined neither 'Celt' nor 'Teuton' but only zones of 'Old Europeans'.

It is, therefore, an illusion to think that there can have been any fundamental difference, or antagonism, between the Celtic-speaking, and the Teutonic-speaking peoples of Germania as such. The gradations of interpenetration in all aspects of life, and the tribal politics revealed by Caesar, and later by Tacitus, show how various the combinations of interest could be. Tacitus, indeed, expresses relief that so much internecine barbarian warfare expended energies that would otherwise have been turned against the Roman armies.

The trans-Rhenine aggressors of the first centuries BC and AD represent but an early phase in a movement that involved an ever-increasing element of Teutonic-speaking peoples as they pressed forward from their earlier homelands that had lain eastwards of the Elbe. They had been the hidden cause of the whole series of displacements, but it was not until the overrunning of the Western Empire in the fifth century AD, that they merged into the full view of history. They then appeared as the Vandals, Goths, Franks, Saxons and others, with whom medieval and modern European history is directly linked.

Before going on to consider the Celtic remnants of the fifth century, and of subsequent times, some further note must be taken of the early period of relations between the Celts and their Teutonic-speaking neighbours. The martial and cultural ascendancy of the Celts from the fifth to the second centuries BC, manifest archaeologically in the La Tène culture, exerted a great influence on the remoter barbarians, lying to the north and east. This is shown not only in La Tène imports, but more generally by imitations of La Tène metal and ceramic types. Celtic craftsmen also seem to have continued at work in areas of Central Europe after the decline of Celtic power. There is no way of recognizing the cultural interpenetrations brought about by dynastic alliances, or by military adventures, although these must have played their part, and in this connection it is at least remarkable, in regard to the Cimbri, that some of the finest pieces of Celtic craftsmanship have been found in Denmark.

Celtic finds in Denmark

It is worth mentioning, however briefly, four of these finds. The earliest is that from Hjortspring, on the island of Als, where a large number of wooden shields of the long Celtic type, together with iron spear-heads still mounted on their wooden shafts, and other weapons, were found with the remains of a large wooden boat, and animal bones. The deposit was preserved under peat, and had originally lain in a small pool in the centre of a bog. This seems certainly to have been a votive deposit, and may date to the late third century BC.

92

To about the same date belongs the great bronze cauldron found in recent years at Brå, near Horsens, in Eastern Jutland. It had been placed, in fragments, in a small pit in the ground, and again must be regarded as a votive deposit, being unassociated with any evidence for sepulchral or habitational purposes. This great bronze vessel had a capacity of about one hundred and thirty gallons, but its most remarkable features were the series of ornamental ox heads projecting below the rim, and the owl-mask plastic ornament in the La Tène style which covered the attachments for the pair of ring handles. The Brå cauldron seems most likely to have been a product of Celtic craftsmanship from the Bohemian-Moravian region, and its transport was most likely by way of the Elbe.

133

To the first century BC belong the pair of beautifully made four-wheeled carts found dismantled in a peat deposit at Dejbjerg, in Western Jutland. These had originally been placed on a patch of dry ground in the middle of the bog, and had been surrounded, in at least one case, by a fence. The delicate workmanship of the two carts, and their metal fittings, which include Celtic face masks, proclaim these vehicles as imports from the south, probably from Gaul.

The most curious of all Celtic imports to Denmark is the great silver bowl found at Gundestrup in Himmerland. The vessel had been dismembered into its component plates, and apparently laid on the open surface of a peat bog in which it had eventually become absorbed. The interior of the base, and both inner and outer faces of the walls of the bowl are decorated in high relief with mythological scenes and figures, the majority of which can be compared in subject to Celtic iconography in Gaul, or to

134 Detail from the Gundestrup cauldron. About half actual size.

mythological allusions in Irish literature. Warriors are seen wearing *bracae*, and the Celtic long shield, and the *carnyx*, or trumpet, are in evidence. The basal relief shows the slaying of a bull, and this has recently been interpreted as of Mithraic inspiration. However this may be, there are stylistic aspects of the animals, and exotic creatures, such as griffons, and the elephant, which, together with the unusualness of the metal employed, point to a Middle Danubian origin for the Gundestrup bowl. It may not be irrelevant that a Celtic tribe in that region, the Scordistae, are reported by Athenaeus as valuing silver above gold. All these valuable objects from Denmark were intentionally placed in peat bogs or buried, and so resigned from human use. They do not, however, give the impression of being merely votive trophies from the loot of returning raiders. The Hjortspring deposit might more possibly be so explained, but there are difficulties in view of the northern type of the boat, and some doubt must exist as to whether the shields are of genuine Celtic manufacture, or a local outcome of the prestige of Celtic arms.

132, 134

Teutonic borrowings from the Celts

In spheres other than material culture, the Celtic contribution to a higher barbarism beyond the successive river frontiers, from the Elbe to the Rhine, was doubtless important, but there are considerable difficulties in demonstrating this proposition. The quite numerous Celtic and Teutonic parallels that can be discerned in cult and mythology, in the essentials of social structure, and in a large common vocabulary, are all things that may as reasonably have been derived from a common ancestral source as be borrowings the one from the other. The lands around the Western Baltic had also received strong Urnfield influences, not from the North Alpine zone, but from a more easterly centre, and the cremation rite, with all its possible ritual and social implications, was well established in the north by the opening of the last millennium BC. In due time, too, the presence of Hallstatt iron swords, and bronze horse-gear, has to be accounted for in the Danish islands, in Southern Sweden, and in Northern Germany. These factors, together with the philological uncertainties, suggest that prior to the time of Celtic ascendancy, manifest in the La Tène cultures, at least some elements amongst the Teutonic-speaking peoples were likely to have held a certain shared heritage with the Celts.

Probably one of the most substantial Celtic contributions to affairs of cult amongst the Teutonic peoples was the passing on of the idea of the built temple. Tacitus makes mention of the sacred groves and woods of the Germans, and this is what one would expect of trans-Rhenine dwellers up to his time. It was with the rapid adoption of the Romano-Celtic temple in Roman-held territory, that the way was progressively opened for it to be taken over in wooden form by the unsubdued barbarians; from these beginnings arose the massive structures, as at Uppsala and elsewhere, that became such a feature of northern heathenism down to the Christian conversions.

It is from Tacitus, also, that comes knowledge of Veleda, described as the prophetess and inspiration of the Bructeri, a trans-Rhenine tribe that took part in the Revolt of Civilis (AD 68–69). Veleda is a Celtic word implying the function of seeress, but it seems most likely that the Bructeri were one of the old trans-Rhenine Celtic tribes, Germans in that sense, rather than a Teutonic-speaking people with a borrowed title for their oracle.

In a survey such as this, a discussion of the philology of the few certain loan words from Celtic in Teutonic would be out of place. It must suffice to say that the two most important, of which the modern German *reich*, and *amt* are the descendants, suggest the flow of influence in matters social and political. Finally, it is well always to bear in mind Strabo's comment that the Germans were very like what the Gauls had been before the corrupting influence of Roman urbanism, and to consider his testimony on the very mixed nature of the migrating peoples of Middle Europe, even amongst the Suevi, with their waggon-dwelling element, and occurrence of Celtic personal names.

The Post-Roman Celtic inheritance

A farewell must now be said to the true Celts of antiquity, and attention turned to what may be described as their successor peoples. In the first place, there can be no doubt that the mass of the population in Gaul down to the collapse of the Western Empire, in the fifth century, continued to be the descendants of the Celtic tribesmen. Even the subsequent Teutonic inroads, by Vandals, Visigoths and Franks, were transitory, and did not alter the essential composition of the populace. The Franks certainly gave the country a new name, and a changed political orientation, but if the French people derive in greater part from a Celtic ancestry, their heritage had become that of a civilized Roman province, its strength lying in the continuity of Latin learning and speech, in Christianity, and in concepts of civil government.

It has been, of course, in the peripheral islands of the north-west, in Britain and Ireland, that the archaic heritage of the Celts has remained a direct factor of language and nationality throughout historical times. Apart from the great interest of this legacy from the point of view of knowledge of the past, there have been, and are, political and romantic affiliations with their none too accurate concepts as to what is, or is not Celtic. These latter aspects need not be mentioned again, but it is worth while to consider briefly the general course of events in the islands, especially in Britain, between the first and sixth centuries AD. It was within this span of centuries that emerged the pattern in linguistic and political geography, and of literary heritage, that gives complexion to the modern scene.

Roman Britain

The stages of the Roman conquest of Britain, and the fortunes of the northern frontier, whether between the Forth and Clyde (the Antonine Wall), or between the Tyne and Solway (Hadrian's Wall), are not here directly relevant. What is necessary is to note the areas, and peoples, even dynasties, and personalities, that chiefly contributed to the continuity of the Celtic mode of life, and to shaping the newer, and smaller, nationalities of Post-Roman times. Undoubtedly, for the period of Roman conquest following the Claudian invasion, the most potent influence on the native side was the Belgic dynasty of the Catuvellauni, the house of Cunobelinus. Dispossessed as they were from their southern and eastern territories, it was they, personified in the figure of Caratacus, who carried the will to resist amongst the non-Belgic tribes in the west, even to the Silures and Ordovices, in modern Wales, and who then sought to continue the opposition with the aid of Brigantian tribesmen from near the Pennines. Caratacus was betrayed by Cartimandua, the Brigantian queen, herself perhaps of Belgic stock, but in the western mountain fastnesses, the archaeological evidence for refugee Belgic households is strong, and is witnessed by such objects of fine craftmanship as the Trawsfynydd tankard, the Capel Garmon fire-dog, and the numerous pieces of Belgic metal-work from the Llyn Cerrig peat find. It is not, then, perhaps so surprising that there seems to have survived in Wales, to the Middle Ages, a learned tradition of the genealogy of the Catuvellaunian royal house.

The fate of the tribes in West Britain, lying in mountainous country beyond the river lines of Severn and Dee, was that of close military supervision, unameliorated by the development of towns and civic institutions such as largely came about throughout Lowland Britain. The hill-forts were deserted, in some cases dismantled, and the great legionary fortresses of Chester and Caerleon stood watch on either flank. If Celtic tradition waned through the processes of Romanization in the eastern and southern areas of civil government in Britain, it must also have suffered through the disruption and impoverishment of tribal life amongst the hill people of the west. The aristocracy, and men of learning in particular, could find no abiding place in the adverse conditions of Roman military occupation, and this must be the principal reason why it is that the bulk of the oldest strata of surviving Welsh tradition stems not from the indigenous West British tribes, but from other Celtic sources implanted in geographical Wales on the decline of Roman military strength.

These new Celtic infusions came from Ireland, in the form of settlers, and plunderers, and from Northern Britain in the form of an intentional colonization, probably brought about as a piece of Roman defensive policy. 135

From as early as the late third century, Irish settlements had taken place in South-west Wales, and perhaps as far east as the Severn estuary, as the worship of Nodens at Lydney would suggest. In South-west Wales, these colonists, who in Ireland were known by the name *Dési*, occupied the old British tribal area of the Demetae, and it is from this latter word that the regional name *Dyfed*, still widely used, descends. As archaeology shows slight trace of Roman activity west of the Towy, and of Carmarthen (Maridunum), it may be that the Demetae were a client tribe, hostile to the Silures, and therefore not necessitating Roman military occupation. What the relationships of the Demetae and the Dési can have been is unknown, but the fact that these Irishmen established a dynasty in Dyfed that lasted some five centuries, and that they contributed much to subsequent Welsh literature, suggests that their colonization was not just a plain invasion. Other considerations in this direction will also appear.

In Northern Wales the situation was rather different. Here the Irish plundered, and attempted settlement, in a tract of territory that had remained a military area since the campaigns of Agricola, and here, too, the Irish were of a different stock from those in Dyfed. The philology of the northern regional name *Gwynedd*, together with related evidence, shows that these Irish were of the people known in Ireland as *Féni*, a most powerful and expansionist element in Middle Ireland during the centuries in question. It may not, indeed, be altogether irrelevant that it had been oppression by a dynasty of the Féni that had caused the initial migration of the Dési from the centre to the south of Ireland, and of their subsequent, at least partial, movement overseas. There can have been no love lost between these two peoples, and this may be in some way reflected in the apparent difference of Roman reaction.

By contrast with the course of affairs in Dyfed, the Irish in the north-west were dispossessed; their memorial being little more than the survival of their name in its British form. This dispossession was brought about by the allocation of the disputed territory to a colony from a northern British tribe of dependable fighting qualities. This can best be explained by the known practice, on other Roman frontiers in Europe, where an element of a friendly, but strong, tribe was given land on another frontier in return for its defence from external onslaught. In this case, subsequent Welsh tradition, and the philology of proper names, show that the *Votadini* (Welsh: *Gododdin*) whose homeland lay roughly between the Tyne and the Forth, were induced to send a substantial colony to North-western Wales. The exact date of the movement is disputed, but it must lie about the turn of the fourth and fifth centuries. These were the Sons of Cunedda, and from them descended nearly all the regal houses of Early

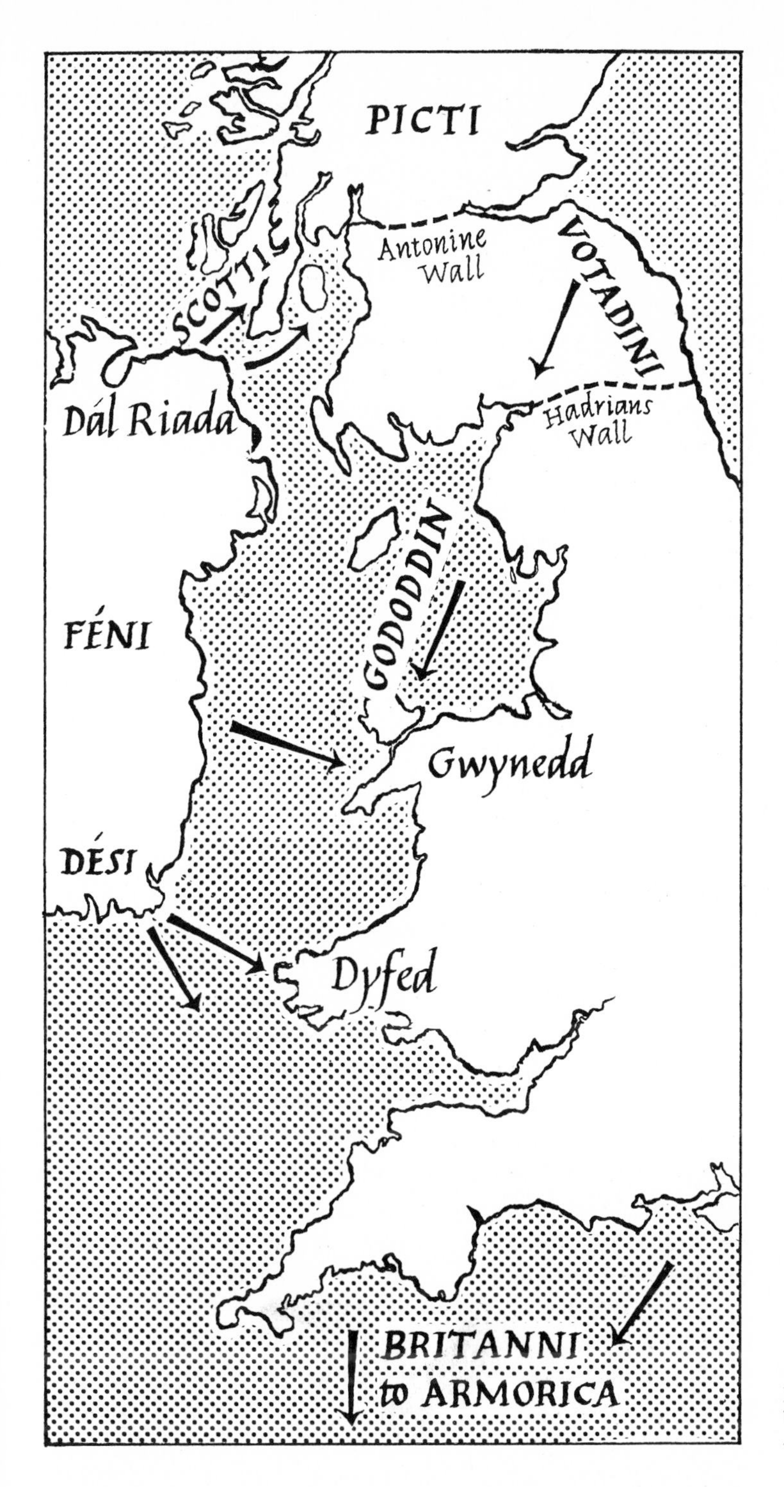

135 The principal Celtic population movements of the fourth-fifth century AD.

Medieval Wales. For the continuity of the British tongue, its forms of literature and traditional learning, the migration of the Sons of Cunedda was of crucial importance. Here was a British people whose Celtic social structure, and inheritance generally, had remained intact, whose politics lay in the Roman interest, but whose outlying northern frontier position had removed them from the seductions of Roman provincialism.

So much for the repeoplement of Wales before the collapse of all Roman rule. But as the name 'Wales' has been used in a geographical context, this is a convenient point at which to explain its derivation. *Welsh*, and *Wales*, are words of Teutonic origin, their root having been brought over by the English in the fifth century. It is a curious chance that the Anglo-Saxon word *Walas*, indicating 'strangers', and then specifically 'Britons', may have derived, long previously, from contact in Middle Europe between the great Celtic tribe, the *Volcae*, and Teutonic-speaking peoples. The Teutonic peoples then seem to have used their version of this Celtic name indiscriminately for strangers, although, as they pressed westwards, these continued to be mainly Celts.

Caledonians and Picts

The Votadini, and other British tribes lying north of Hadrian's Wall, who had become tributaries of Rome, had not done so for love but for expediency. North of them again, in the territory beyond the Forth and Clyde, dwelt hostile peoples against whom they required Roman support. Agricola's campaigns throughout all this region had discovered a hard core of resistance amongst the *Caledonii*. Later, the Antonine defence system had proved untenable against them, and recourse was had to the recognition of autonomous British tribes, as in the case of the Votadini, to provide a buffer zone.

The difference between the British tribes, living south of the Forth and Clyde, and the Caledonians, living to the north, is reflected archaeologically in contrasting types of hill-fort, although very little other material is as yet forthcoming. Tacitus makes an interesting comment that the Caledonians were characterized by reddish hair and large size, and he compares them to the Germans, presumably of the Celtic sort. This may be a factor in determining their origins, but their massive hill-forts, with stone and timber construction, would rather suggest a more immediate

136 Broch at Jarlshof, Shetland of first-second century BC and later wheel-house structures around it of second-third century AD.

western starting-point, farther south along the coastlands of Britain. This, however, much depends on the date of their arrival in Scotland, and the present view tends to a period not earlier than the mid-first century BC.

It may be considered a working hypothesis that in the generally disturbed times of the first centuries BC and AD, the Caledonian tribes had been able to choose the best region of Scotland in which to settle while, at a slightly later date, the British tribes, moving from south of the Cheviot, and the seafaring migrants who built the brochs and wheel-houses, along the north-western and northern coasts and islands, had to be content with second-best. It may be said with some degree of certainty that the Caledonian population included a strong indigenous, as well as an intrusive Celtic, element. The language of the former was almost certainly not Indo-European, and the latter, while of the P-Celtic branch, was probably not identical with the form spoken by the British tribes.

The continuity of identity between the Caledonians, known to Latin writers from the second century AD, and the Picts (*Picti*), who are first mentioned in the late third century, also appears to be now well established. From these Picts derived the historical Pictish Kingdom which was in existence by the seventh century and lasted into the ninth. The Pictish Kingdom, which played its part in the formation of the historical Scotland, must be mentioned again, but some consideration is here due to the name 'Pict' without going over its range of philological connections. The suggestion is that *Picti*, 'the painted people', while being at first used as a descriptive, and rather disparaging, term by the Romans for painted or tattooed barbarians, may well have altered its implication as a name in the course of the four centuries that divide knowledge of its first use in the north and its application to a Christianized native kingdom.

It has been thought that *Picti*, while a descriptive Latin word, also owed something to confusion in Roman ears with the Celtic *Pretani* or *Preteni*, mentioned in the first chapter, and, for these northern people, the latter variant would seem to have been the most likely. On the other hand, it must be remembered that Caesar, who saw only southern British tribes, was the first to mention the practice of blue body colouring, and it would seem probable that this custom was progressively abandoned from south to north, throughout the island, during the Roman occupation. Only amongst the redoubtable folk beyond the Antonine frontier was the practice likely to have continued. In this way the appellation *Picti* would have been directly relevant still in the late third century.

It is certainly not known what the Picts called themselves. *Picti* is only known through Latin written documents, whether late Roman, or Christian Anglian or Irish, but with the withdrawal of Roman arms, and the continued onset of Anglo-Saxon and Irish invaders, the climate of native opinion in Britain seems to have swung towards a new appreciation of the old order, and the prestige of Latin names, and titles, took on a greater value. The name *Picti* may well have become entrenched in this way.

Between the time of Agricola, and the emergence of the historical Pictish Kingdom, this Central Caledonian power had had strength to expand northwards, and to overcome the various communities within the maritime archaeological province of brochs and wheel-houses. These subdued peoples were not important for later history, but the *Orcades* were certainly a Celtic tribe, and their name is still retained by their islands. The Orcadians may have offered their allegiance to Claudius, if Orosius is to be thus understood, and Tacitus reports their submission to the naval forces of Agricola. These amicable moves are just what might be expected of a people hoping to win support against hostile neighbours who, in this case, would have been the Caledonians. The evidence on the language of this maritime province is very scant owing mainly to intense Irish and Norse occupation in later times. Tribal names demonstrate a Celtic element most probably of the British type, but here, again, the tongue of a more anciently settled population may also have been employed at the same time.

Scots

The Irish raiders and settlers in Northern Britain have next to be noticed, and these were the *Scotti*, first recorded in the fourth century, who with the Picts, and a little later, the Saxons, all ravaged the Roman province. The name *Scotti* is almost certainly related to an Irish verb meaning 'to raid' or 'plunder'. It was not, therefore, a tribal name, but a descriptive appellation for bands of adventurers, and, as a result of these incursions, the name *Scotia*, in Latin usage, was first given to Ireland, whence came the raiders. Not until the eleventh century was it transferred to the daughter kingdom set up in Northern Britain.

By the fifth century when the Kingdom of Dalriada was set up in Argyll and the neighbouring islands, settlement had taken the place of raiding. This royal venture was an off-shoot of the house of *Dál Riada* in North-eastern Ireland, and it was from this source, and no earlier than the fourth-fifth centuries, that the implantation of the Gaelic tongue progressively took place in Northern Britain. With the union through marriage of the Scottish (Dalriadic) and Pictish royal houses *c.* AD 843, the Celtic tradition north of the Cheviot was set to become wholly of Irish derivation. This is not to ignore the continued existence of a British-speaking population, and such kingdoms as Strathclyde, and Rheged, which were still potent in the sixth century, and for some time thereafter; but the final outcome was complete oblivion of this Celtic branch in the north, absorbed as it was by the Gaelic-speaking Scots on the one hand, and by the English, who had expanded from Northumbria, on the other. So arose the duality of existing Scots heritage: Highland – Gaelic-speaking, Lowland – English-speaking.

Breton origins

There is one other remarkable transference of a Celtic-speaking population, in this case away from Britain, that must be recorded. These were the migrations from the south and south-west coasts across the sea to the Gallo-Roman province of Armorica, the effect of which was to identify it henceforward with the Britons (cf. Bretagne: Brittany). A recent study of the history and language of these migrants has shown that the movement began in the mid-fifth century, and continued to the early seventh, but it incorporated two peak phases. The first was the beginning of the period, and the second, which was larger, took place in the mid-sixth century. In the earlier phase, the migrants were probably drawn from a wide area along the southern coast, and fled in consequence of the alarm caused by the first extensive Saxon spoliations westwards of the Isle of Wight. In the second, and greater, exodus, the population of Devon and Cornwall were especially involved; for now the men of Wessex were pressing forward in their colonization of land towards the western seas.

From the point of view of Celtic continuity, the British settlement of Armorica is significant only for language history; for these people were of an ancestry long under Roman civil government, and they moved into a territory that had possessed a like administration.

The origin of 'Gael'

The final change in insular Celtic nomenclature that must claim attention has to do with the antecedents of such words as Gael and Gaelic. These are the anglicized forms of words which in their own language have for long been used to denote the Irish people and their language, and it may well be asked how this came about in view of the great antiquity, and lasting use, of *Éire* as the name of the island. It is true that there was an ancient people called *Érainn*, but these, like the *Ulad*, *Connachta*, and *Lagin*, from whom derive the provinces of Ulster, Connaught, and Leinster, were all regarded as people of different origins, locality and status, within the island. It was only when a situation developed that required a general name for the people of Ireland, without discrimination, that one came into being. This was not the outcome of political unification, a concept far from the minds of contesting dynasts when the name *Goídel* first comes into evidence in the late seventh century.

The most reasonable explanation for the origin of *Goídel* is that it is an adaption of *Gwyddel*, the Welsh name for the Irish. It has already been said that in North Wales the regional name *Gwynedd* derives from the name of the Irish settlers, known in their own land as *Féni*. So, too, with the cognate *Gwyddel*, and this name was brought back into Ireland under different circumstances, and taken over as *Goídel*. Why should this have come about at all? The reason is almost certainly the activity of Christian missionaries coming from North Wales in the fifth and sixth centuries. It is in just this area that the use of *Gwyddel* would have been most normal, and it is here, too, that following the pacification under the Sons of Cunedda, the Romano-British Church was at its strongest during these centuries. What more natural than that the Irish should come to think of themselves before the Church as *Goídel*, the name by which they were now exhorted to a new life.

It was long before *Goídel* developed any political or formal national significance; the onset of the Vikings at the end of the eighth century probably did most to bring this about, but in the creation of a synthetic history of Ireland, according to the concepts of Latin learning, a fictitious ancestral figure, Goídel Glas, was brought into being perhaps about the same time. Irish Churchmen were anxious to provide an historical scheme for Ireland, equivalent to that set forth by Orosius for the Hebrews and other ancient peoples. This movement appears to have started already in the seventh century, and the name *Goídel* came in most usefully in the rearrangements, and adaptions, of traditional origin tales, and genealogies, that were extensively undertaken.

The confusion has persisted to the present day, and has been aggravated by scholars who use *Goídel*, in the philological sense of speakers of a form of Q-Celtic, in the same sentence as genuine traditional names such as *Ulad* or *Érainn*, whom they may think did not speak the same language. Again, it must be remembered that *Goídel* as used by Early Irish Churchmen was not the same as *Féni*. *Féni* was, indeed, an old population-group name, and the predominance of these people, at least in Central Ireland, was of the greatest significance in the period immediately preceding the Christian missions. Their name, however, ceased to exist in its original sense, having given way to those of various derived dynastic families, but it was retained in a legal sense to denote the land-owning classes, or men of free status entitled to attend assemblies, and it is thus found in the oldest law tracts.

Goídel and *Féni* should, therefore, never be used as equivalents, but when thought is directed to the historical contexts of the Irish language, the *Féni* remain a prime consideration. This complicated problem cannot be pursued here, nor is it strictly germane to the purpose of the present chapter which is to trace, and clarify, the general line of Celtic continuity; but it provides a reminder that the Irish language, as we know it, Gaelic (*Goídelg: Gaedhilge*), was not the only speech in ancient Ireland. It cannot be here argued whether it was prestige, or quantitive representation, that won for it eventually an exclusive position, and it must suffice to contrast its success in Ireland, and Scotland, with its loss by the Irish colonists in South Wales who, nevertheless, carried into the British tongue much of their own literary tradition.

The thread of continuity

With this summary marshalling of Celtic names, that are still in common use, the historical frontier is approached beyond which a study of the Celts should not go. Thereafter it is the history of the various small kingdoms in their fortunes one with another, and with the English, Norse and Normans. Inevitably, as the centuries passed, new influences took root, and with the disappearance, or transformation, of the patrician grades, the structure of Celtic society was lost. The survival of the languages came to rest on largely peasant populations, amongst whom might be seen the re-emergence of even more ancient ethnic groups overrun by the Celts. Just as all the people who speak English as their first tongue are not necessarily English in any other sense, so too, the total composition of the Celtic-speaking populations included many elements that were of more ancient, or even more recent arrival, than the Celts themselves.

In marking the end of ways of traditional Celtic life, and the kind of literary accomplishment it supported, the chronological line has to be drawn differently in Wales and Ireland. First, however, it should be noted that the Welsh, meaning the British of the north as well as the west, in their struggle against the Angles and Saxons, experienced a new Heroic Age, stimulating a harvest in prose and verse compositions that largely eclipsed their more ancient lore. Of this, the oldest surviving fragments remount to late sixth-century poets, the renowned names of Taliesin and Aneirin, who, in the ancient Celtic manner, eulogized their royal patrons, and the warrior nobles, of Rheged and Gododdin. It is indicative of these stirring times that a new name, *Cymry*, 'compatriots', was now adopted by the resisting British, and it has remained the name by which the Welsh have known themselves ever since. The name also survives in corrupted form in the county name Cumberland, a slight memorial of the northern British territories.

The continuity of Celtic literary tradition was maintained in Wales for many centuries, so long as there was a Welsh nobility

137* Medallion from an Early Christian bronze belt shrine, found at Moylough, Co. Sligo, Ireland. Diameter 3 cm.

to evoke and sustain it, and even at the close of the eighteenth century, the recollection of courtly verse was still in mind so that a country poet celebrated his local squire, and patron, in the manner of his forerunners twelve centuries past.

In Ireland, the freedom from Roman and Saxon intervention had allowed Celtic institutions an uninterrupted flow which was not essentially disturbed either by the Vikings, or by the Anglo-Normans. The part played by the Church, as censor, and adaptor, but also as ultimate preserver in written documents, was indicated in the first chapter, and only a few points can be presented for final consideration.

The advent of new and exotic influences, coming in the train of the Christian missions, drew forth a responsive outburst of native excellence, both in the literary and manual arts, that has assured for Early Christian Ireland a special position in the history of European civilization. If Irishmen looked back to an Heroic Age, in the epics of the aristocratic warriors of Ulster and Connacht, or in the exploits of Fionn mac Cumhaill, and his war bands, the Golden Age has always been that of the saints and scholars, the Gospel books, precious metal-work, and, finally, the great sculptured stone crosses. The legacy in Celtic decorative motifs became but an undercurrent in the new Irish art, but, in the wider affairs of life, the old order flourished. At the great convention of Druim Ceat, held in AD 575, St Columcille (Columba) secured for the *filid* their proper place in Irish life so that for another thousand years oral tradition and poetry were maintained with honour. It was not until the tragedy of the battle of Kinsale, in 1601, that the old Celtic way of life was finally shattered.

Something indeed, might be said of the eulogies and satires – recalling Diodorus' account of the bards – of the Irish sixteenth-century poets, or of the last remnants of oral learning, some of which were extinguished only within living memory. For this book, however, concerned as it has been primarily with remote origins, the most arresting instance of Celtic continuity is neither in literature nor in art, but in a ritual institution. This was the ceremony of kingly inauguration, with its roots wide-spread in Indo-European custom, that continued in Ireland to the end of the sixteenth century. In this manner came, in 1592, Aodh Ruadh Ua Domhnaill to the late Gaelic lordship of Ireland, and such was the relevance of this custom to contemporary Irish life that, even in the dark days that followed, local chieftains continued to assert their inheritance at their stones of inauguration.

The last traditional inauguration of a king of the Scots had taken place in 1249 when Alexander III, having undergone ecclesiastical ceremonies leading up to coronation, within the church, was led outside to the stone of inauguration, and there received the homage of his people, and heard his pedigree recited in Gaelic. In these last ceremonies, the archaic requirements of personal recognition, and the binding of auspicious lordship, through the recitation of illustrious forebears, were duly fulfilled.

Notes to Chapter 4

CIMBRI: Diodorus Siculus, V, 32, 4; Strabo, VII, 2; Pliny, *Nat. Hist.* IV, 27. *Cambridge Ancient History*, IX, *passim*; Grenier (1945) for history. O. Klindt-Jensen (1950) for archaeological background.

GERMANI: Athenaeus, *Deipnosophists*, IV, 153, for reference to use of the name by Poseidonius. A. Degrassi (1954) for *Acta Triumphalia*. H. M. Chadwick (1945) for Celtic origin of the name. T. F. O'Rahilly (1946), and C. A. R. Radford (1955) for comment on Dionysius of Halicarnassus.

CELTIC INFLUENCE IN NORTHERN EUROPE: O. Klindt-Jensen (1950).

HJORTSPRING: G. Rosenberg (1927); J. Brøndsted (1940); O. Klindt-Jensen (1957).

BRA: O. Klindt-Jensen (1953) and (1957).

DEJBJERG AND GUNDESTRUP: J. Brøndsted (1940); O. Klindt-Jensen (1950); S. J. De Laet and P. Lambrechts (1954) make a case for Mithraic allusions in the Gundestrup iconography.

NORTHERN TEMPLES: J. E. A. Bogaers (1955) on Celtic influence. S. Lindquist (1948) for Uppsala; E. Dyggve (1954) on Jelling.

VELEDA: Tacitus, *Germ.* VIII; *Hist.* IV, 61. For discussion of the Veleda inscription at Ardea see: *Rev. des Études Grecque*, LXII (1949), 160.

LINGUISTIC BORROWINGS: M. Dillon (1943).

BRITAIN: For the beginnings and end of the Roman occupation see I. A. Richmond (1955) with bibl.; K. H. Jackson (1953) for rise of Post-Roman kingdoms; W. Rees (1951) provides maps and historical commentary.

PICTS: F. T. Wainwright, edit. (1955) is indispensable on this and related matters.

SCOTS: E. MacNeill (1917); T. F. O'Rahilly (1946).

BRETON MIGRATIONS: K. H. Jackson (1953).

GAEL: E. MacNeill (1933).

FÉNI: D. O'Brien (1932).

WALES: I. Williams (1944) for early literature; V. E. Nash-Williams (1950) for Early Christian monuments; G. E. Daniel (1954) for the history of Welsh studies.

IRELAND: J. F. Kenny (1929) for sources on Irish learning; F. Henry (1940) and (1954) for Christian art. Máire and Liam de Paor (1958) for Early Christian Ireland in general.

DRUIM CEAT: J. Ryan (1946).

LATER IRISH HISTORY: E. Curtis (1950).

ALEXANDER III: M. D. Legge (1946).

Supplementary Notes on the Illustrations

19 Although not amongst the oldest of its kind, the careful excavation demonstrates the essential features of this type of princely burial. The rectangular outline of the decomposed wooden-built burial chamber can be distinguished, as well as the position of the four wheels with iron tyres. The forked object in the centre is the waggon's iron centre-pole, or perch. To its left lie the crushed remains of a large bronze bucket. The body, which had lain on the cart, possessed a small brooch of Early La Tène type, and was supplied with a large iron spear-head. W. Rest, *Bonner Jahrbücher* (1948), 133–189. The material is in the Landesmuseum, Bonn.

20 This important tomb dates from the last phase of the Hallstatt Culture, and is therefore slightly earlier than that at Bell (Ill. 19). The iron tyres of the four wheels are here seen, as well as massive hubs. The sides of the waggon were decorated with embossed strips of sheet bronze. The body with its gold ornaments, as well as iron spear-heads, lay outside (to the right, as viewed here) and the gold cup and two bronze bowls at the farther end of the vehicle.

21 These embossed sheet gold ornaments are amongst the most characteristic of the rich Late Hallstatt Culture chieftain's graves, but their use is undecided. Usually considered to have been head ornaments, a case has more recently been presented for their having been neck rings forming a cylindrical gold covering to a core of perishable material.

22 This exceptional cup formed part of the drinking service supplied in the tomb; such services being an essential feature throughout the tradition of waggon or chariot funerary ritual. The cup is the product of a Middle European goldsmith of the late sixth century BC. The material is in the Landesmuseum, Stuttgart. On the grave as a whole see O. Paret (1935), and generally on the gold work see W. Kimmig and W. Rest (1953).

24,25 The small town of Hallstatt, in the Salzkammergut, gives its name to the first iron-using culture north of the Alps on account of the rich cemetery found, early in the nineteenth century, in the small valley high above the modern town. Ill. 24 shows the town by the lake-side; above it, to the right, the valley containing the prehistoric sites. As viewed in Ill. 25, the prehistoric cemetery lay in the left foregound; the salt-mines, from which the community obtained its wealth, were situated towards the head of the valley.

28 An excellent instance of the counter-attractions of nature and abstraction in Celtic portrayal. The eyes, ears and moustache have been reduced to stylistic elements typical of La Tène art, but the mildness of expression contrasts with the forbiddingly weird faces of the Rhenish group (Ills 110, 118). Note the backward sweep of the hair, and the torc. Middle La Tène period, and probably a cult figure. National Museum, Prague.

30 This bronze figurine, found near Rome, probably dates from the late third century BC. Typifying the Celtic warrior as described in Classical literature, it probably depicts one of the *Gaesatae*, the naked spear-men, who fought at the battle of Telamon in 225 BC. A casting spear is suggested by the figure's pose. The torc and belt are Celtic characteristics, but the horned helmet was something probably acquired south of the Alps. Staatliche Museen zu Berlin.

32 The 'Dying Gaul' is a Roman marble copy of the original in bronze erected by Attalos I (241–197 BC) at Pergamon. The physical characteristics of the Celtic warrior are well exemplified. Note the flowing hair and the torc. The oval wooden shield and the pair of curved trumpets are recognizable Celtic types, but the sword is exotic, doubtless representative of loot. Museo Capitolino, Rome, and casts in numerous museums elsewhere.

33 This bronze appliqué figure of a sleeping (?) Gaul, found at Alesia, is Gallo-Roman, and perhaps a votive object. It is of special interest as an illustration of Celtic trousers (*bracae*). Here they are of long, loose-fitting type in contrast to those seen in Ills 134, 136. St Germain-en-Laye.

35,68,69,70 The Waldalgesheim grave is important for the developed style in La Tène art represented, and for the association therewith of an Italiote *situla* (bronze bucket) which can be dated to the end of the fourth century BC (Ill. 70). The bronze spouted-flagon (Ill. 68) is a native Celtic piece older than the other objects in the grave. Zones of lightly engraved patterns, based chiefly on a lyre motif, encircle the body of the vessel. At the upper end of the handle is a cast ram's head, and at the lower terminal is a human face (Ill. 69) with long curling moustache, pointed beard, and with a pronounced 'leaf-crown' above the forehead. The animal on the lid is indeterminate, but may be intended for a horse. The gold ornaments from the grave (Ill. 35) consist of a neck torc with splendid relief ornament at the extremities of the hoop and on the buffer terminals. The twisted ring bracelet has fine tooling between the ridges, and the pair of penannular bracelets have magnificent relief ornament of the hoops as well as the terminals. These latter are technically close to the neck torc. Landesmuseum, Bonn.

36,37 Gold ornaments from Snettisham, Norfolk. These objects form one of the five groups known collectively as the Snettisham Treasure. The three gold objects of this group were found looped together as shown in Ill. 36. They consist of a large ring terminal torc, seen separately in Ill. 37, a bracelet, and an incomplete buffer terminal torc. The ring terminal torc is an exceptional piece, and, in its plastic relief and chased 'matting' ornament, is characteristic of the eastern school of British art in the second half of the first century BC. This torc contained, in one of the terminals, a small coin of the Gaulish Atrebates. The bracelet, which is hollow, displays closely related decoration, and was probably made by the same craftsman. The fragmentary buffer terminal torc is of a slightly old fashion, and may have been broken up for smelting. It seems that the Treasure as a whole was hidden about the time of the birth of Christ. Norwich Castle Museum. R. R. Clarke (1954).

38,39 The torc has an iron core with thick coating of silver. Its weight is about 6 kg, and it must be regarded as a votive object not meant for human adornment. The confrontation of animal heads on an object of this kind would point to Achaemenid originals, but the mildness of expression of the bulls, and the twisted torcs around their necks, are wholly Celtic and suggest a date within the Middle La Tène Culture. The torc is so far without close parallels, but the use of silver and the stylistic aspects of the bulls' heads suggest a somewhat more eastern origin amongst the Celts than its place of finding. Landesmuseum, Stuttgart. P. Goessler (1929).

44 This head is usually attributed to Rosmerta whose cult was predominant in the Mainz area. It suggests an ideal of Celtic feminine beauty, and the elaborate hair style hides attachments on the top of the head for some ornament or symbol now absent. Altertums Museum, Mainz.

45,46,47,48 The princesses' grave at Reinheim near Saarbrücken is one of the most outstanding of the Early La Tène Culture graves so far found. The burial was in an oak-built chamber, but there was no evidence for a vehicle. Amongst many magnificent pieces were the gold ornaments seen in Ill. 34. These included a neck torc with twisted hoop, a closed-ring bracelet, and a penannular bracelet. There were also a pair of open-work gold finger rings, and other adornments in the same metal. Most remarkable is the terminal ornament of the torc and penannular bracelet of which details are seen in Ills 47, 48. The profusion of human and bird-of-prey masks wrought in great detail with a wealth of other features and ornament is unique, as are the plain bosses at the terminal extremities. A bronze spouted-flagon (Ill. 45) was also present. An entirely mythical animal stood on its lid, and the upper end of the handle displayed the remarkable superimposed human faces seen in Ill. 46. Stylistic considerations indicate that this grave is older than that at Waldalgesheim, probably belonging to the early fourth century BC. Saarlandmuseum, Saarbrücken. J. Keller (1955) for preliminary report.

50 The hill-fort at Old Oswestry is one of the finest of the series along the Welsh Marches. Four stages of development have been distinguished by excavation, the earliest being the two contour ramparts and ditches surrounding the inner area. These were probably erected in the second century BC, and the elaborate entrance defences and outer circumvallations, in the ensuing centuries down to the Roman occupation in the third quarter of the first century AD. The construction of two or more lines of defence was due to the introduction of sling warfare to Britain from the coastlands of Atlantic Europe. W. J. Varley (1950).

51 The hill-fort at Cissbury Rings is one of the largest on the southern chalk-lands, and belongs to a series of widely spaced strongholds in that area, perhaps implying large tribal territories. The site is a classic example of the bivallate

contour hill-fort dating probably from the mid-third century BC. This and the foregoing illustration, with others to follow, introduce aspects of the environment of Celtic tribal life which museum objects cannot provide. E. C. Curwen (1954).

52 The hill-fort at Uffington Castle, on top of the chalk downs, was erected by people of the Iron Age A Culture and displays an interesting arrangement of out-turned ramparts at the entrance forming a 'barbican' gateway, probably having had double gates, and timbered sides and overworks. The site went out of use before the cutting of the white horse on the chalk scarp. On stylistic grounds, the horse is considered to have been made by Belgic settlers in the late first century BC, or soon thereafter. The horse is as likely to have been connected with some kind of sacred site as to have been a mere tribal mark of territorial possession. The over-all length of the horse is about 110 m.

54,55 In the late second century BC, the Celts began to build very large fortified enclosures capable of accommodating much larger communities than previously attempted. These are the *oppida* described by Caesar and others, and they are distributed from Central Gaul, across Southern Germany to Bohemia and beyond. The site here illustrated is that at Otzenhausen near Trier, presumably a stronghold of the Treveri. The photographs are a lesson in field archaeology contrasting with the conditions seen in Ills 50, 51 and 52. The distant view of the hill (Ill. 54) gives no indication of the presence of the *oppidum*, and in Ill. 55 the tumbled stone wall, which must have commanded open ground, is set about by the trees of the modern forest. W. Dehn (1937).

56,57 The Citañia de Sanfins, Paços de Ferreira is one of the numerous hill-forts in Northern Portugal, and excavations have been conducted there within recent years. The culture represented at the site is that of the 'Post-Hallstatt' type of the Celtic overlords mixed with indigenous traits. The mixture of house types, of which the foundations and lower courses of masonry were well preserved (Ill. 56), show the circular, indigenous type preponderating over the intrusive, rectangular form. Apart from a large hoard of Roman coins, there is no evidence of Roman influence, and the inhabitants remained in sturdy independence into the first century BC. The air photograph (Ill. 57) shows the encircling walls and the clusters of house sites excavated to date. The lower and outer enclosures were evidently used for cattle, not inhabitation. A. do Paço (1953).

58 The Castro de Monte Bernorio is one of the great hill-forts of the north Spanish Iron Age province of the Celts. The main fortification consists of a massive stone wall, now much ruined, but which is estimated to have stood to a height of about 3 m. This wall represents a final phase in the fortification of the site, of which there are other traces. Excavations have also revealed hut foundations of rectangular plan, and a cemetery. The stronghold was abandoned in the second century BC. J. Maluquer de Motes (1954b).

59 The Citañia de Briteiros is the largest of the numerous hill-forts overlooking the fertile basin of the Rio Ave. The site is some 15 km north of Guimarães. It was surrounded by two massive stone walls, and was occupied from probably the third century BC to the beginning of the fourth century AD. Much Roman influence is therefore evident, but the old forms of house construction continued, and there are important native funerary and cult monuments. M. Cardozo (1948).

65 The rich chieftain's grave found at Klein Aspergle, Ludwigsburg, Württemberg, is one of the earliest and most important within the La Tène Culture. Particularly significant for chronology and trade relations is the painted Attic cup here illustrated. It can be dated closely to the year 450 BC. Another Attic cup, unpainted, was also present, but both had undergone lavish embellishments in gold leaf by Celtic craftsmen after their arrival north of the Alps. The motive seems to have been to hide breakages, but a complete scheme of decoration was arranged for both surfaces of each cup employing a larger number of gold pieces than now affixed.

66 The sheep heads of this pair of drinking horns from the Klein Aspergle grave differ in size, and may be intended to represent ram and ewe, but the mounts differ in other details on the parts not included in this photograph. This is Celtic work inspired by Greek prototypes.

67 The flagon is of Celtic workmanship copying very closely an Etruscan original. The stamnos is an actual Etruscan import. It may be assumed that the Attic cups go with these two vessels as a wine-drinking service, while the gold-mounted drinking horns were for the native beer. The objects are in the Landesmuseum, Stuttgart. P. Jacobsthal (1944) for material from the Klein Aspergle grave.

72,73 Excavations in recent years have revealed that the great fortified site of Heuneburg, overlooking the Danube, was the seat of a wealthy community in trade relations with the Massiliote Greeks during the sixth century BC. Not only were fine drinking vessels (Black Figure Ware) and wine amphorae imported, but, for a period, the fortifications were adapted to a Mediterranean style. This was in the second of five building periods distinguished at the site, and it involved the erection of mud-brick walls, with forward projecting bastions overlooking the steeper slopes of the plateau. An immense earthern rampart with timber lacing, and stone facings, in the native style, protected the site along the easiest approach. Ill. 72 shows the north and west faces of the fortifications. The Danube can be seen in the left foreground. The stone foundations for one of the mud-brick bastions, after excavation, are shown in Ill. 73. W. Dehn (1957), and other references in Chapter 2 notes.

76 These coins give, amongst other things, further illustrations of the Celts as seen by Roman and native coin engravers.

(a) Denarius of L. Hostilius Saserna (*c.* 48 BC). The Obverse shows a Gaulish head, sometimes wrongly attributed to Vercingetorix. It is of interest in showing the stiff, backswept hair style. Behind the head is a long Celtic shield in miniature. The Reverse might well be an illustration from one of the early Irish epics. The naked and long-haired warrior hurls a spear whilst in retreat from the enemy. In his left hand is a shield. His charioteer, crouching well forward on the pole, urges the paired horses. The open front-, and curved side-screens of the chariot are of particular interest. The scene may be deliberately archaic, but the use of chariots in some parts of Gaul in Caesar's time cannot be quite excluded. E. A. Sydenham (1952), no. 952.

(b) Denarius of Julius Caesar, *c.* 54–44 BC. Reverse. Above the inscription, CAESAR, is a trophy of arms flanked by a Celtic shield, and by a *carnyx*, or long trumpet with animal-head opening. Below is the seated figure of a Gaulish captive with head turned and looking upwards, and hands tied behind. Note the torc and belt. E. A. Sydenham (1952), no. 1011.

(c) Obverse of silver coin of the Carnutes. This tribe was situated between the middle courses of the Seine and the Loire, and in their territory, according to Caesar, the druids held an annual convocation. The head, which is derived from an ultimate Greek prototype, is more naturalistic than often in Celtic coinage. The hair has been reduced, however, to form a pattern based on the bulbous-leaf motif of La Tène art, and the moustache is directly comparable to that seen in Ill. 28. A torc encircles the neck. L. Lengyel (1954), no. 129.

(d) Obverse of a silver coin of the Baiocasses, a tribe that was located near Bayeux. The ecstatic facial expression is a widespread characteristic. In this example, three other mythological attributes are the boar, the horn-like dotted lines which may be connected with the 'leaf-crown' (cf. Ill. 110), and the hair gathered into three locks ending in roundels. L. Lengyel (1954), no. 160.

(e) Obverse of gold coin of the Arverni, showing head and inscription of VERCINGETORIX. The degree of Roman influence amongst tribes bordering the *Provincia Narbonensis* is illustrated by the style of portraiture and the inclusion of an inscription. L. Lengyel (1954), no. 85.

77 These coins are shown principally for their illustration of particular objects, but two have important historical connections.

(a) Tetredrachm of Aetolia. Reverse. The figure represents Aetolia seated victoriously on a pile of Celtic and Macedonian shields. At her feet lies a Celtic trumpet, *carnyx*, with its head pointing upwards just behind her staff. This, with related coins, falls within the years 279–168 BC, but the trophies would be appropriate to the Aetolian success in 279, so that the coin provides a useful chronological indication for the archaeology of the shield and trumpet types. British Museum, *Principal Coins of the Greeks*, Plate 36, 14.

(b) Bronze coin of the Remi, one of the most important of the Belgic tribes in their relations with Julius Caesar. Their name, seen on both faces of the coin, is continued in that of Reims which became their cantonal centre under Roman administration. The Obverse shows three heads, doubtless an allusion to the triad symbolism of Celtic deities. The Reverse shows a chariot scene of which the general composition with winged figure derives from Greek originals, but the chariot itself is of Celtic type with open front, and curved side screens. L. Lengyel (1954), no. 433.

(c) Denarius of L. Cosconius. Reverse. A warrior standing in the chariot hurls a spear, and holds in the other hand a long shield and *carnyx*. The scene is interesting for the heroic figure and his arms, but unrealistic in the absence of a charioteer, and in the schematic treatment of the chariot. The structure beneath the warrior's feet is a perfunctory copy of a Greek original that was also imitated on coins of the Arverni and Turones. The date of this coin is generally given as 112–109 BC, but 118 BC has more recently been suggested, thus connecting it with the foundation of the *colonia Narbo*. The Gaulish figure depicted is thought to represent Bituitus, king of the Arverni, who was made captive in 121 BC. E. A. Sydenham (1952), no. 521. S. Piggott (1952).

(d) Denarius of the Revolt of the Civilis (AD 69–70). This coin belongs to one of the groups of independent coinages struck during the Civil Wars. Although not reverting in style to the ancient types of Gaul, it is emblematic of resurgent nationalism. The Obverse shows Gallia wearing a torc, and accompanied by a trumpet.

The Reverse depicts the time-honoured boar symbol, together with clasped hands, two ears of corn, and the reassuring, but unavailing inscription FIDES. British Museum, *Catalogue* (*Empire*) I, p. 308 (c).

79 The great iron sword employed by warriors of the Early Hallstatt Culture, in the seventh century BC, may be taken as symbolic of the political and economic events that preceded the emergence of the Celts in the following century. Landesmuseum, Stuttgart.

81 The chalk-cut pit grave of La Gorge Meillet, probably once with a wooden roof, replaces, in the region of the Marne, the older, Hallstatt, tradition of a wood-built burial chamber. The chieftain was laid out on his chariot, the wheels having been let into special holes. He was equipped with a gold armlet, an iron sword in its scabbard, iron spear-heads, and a tall bronze helmet which lay between his feet. An Etruscan beaked-flagon, and fine pottery vessels of native production, as well as a large flesh knife, iron cooking-spits, and joints of beef and pork, made provision for the feasts. At a position corresponding to the end of the chariot pole, there lay, on a shelf in the chalk, a pair of bronze three-link bits, and other trappings for harness horses. Above the chieftain lay the skeleton of another man armed with an iron sword. He was presumably the charioteer and personal attendant.

82 This is one of the finest of the surviving Celtic helmets which must have been rarities at all times. The embossed discs had coral settings, and the finely composed pattern, executed in tremolo lines on the sheet bronze surface, is based on a swastika motif.

83,84 Pottery vessel and bronze beaked-flagon from the grave at La Gorge Meillet. The pottery vessel with its pedestal foot, and finely curved body with red, burnished surface is representative of the high standards of native potters in this region during the Early La Tène Culture, a tradition which exerted its influence long and widely, manifest finally in Belgic pottery in Gaul and Britain. The beaked-flagon is an Etruscan import, and it was from ornamental detail, especially in plant motifs, of exemplars such as this, that some elements in La Tène art had been drawn in the initial period.

85 This bronze helmet has two open-work hoops, and the whole was covered with gold-foil. Numerous enamel studs were mounted around its lower edge. A large lyre-shaped ornament has been lost from either side, but otherwise the helmet provides an excellent example of Early La Tène artistry, and of the principal motifs employed. Original in the Louvre. Facsimile at St Germain-en-Laye.

87 These bronze snaffle bits are excellent examples of insular Celtic craftsmanship, and of the British school of La Tène art. The bits are of the three-link type, made of solid bronze, the cheek rings are of iron coated with bronze. The decoration differs at either end of each bit, but matches from one to the other; thus they were clearly intended for a pair of chariot horses in the same harness. They have been dated on stylistic grounds to the middle of the first century BC. Norwich Castle Museum. R. R. Clarke (1951).

88,89 These illustrations show Celtic trophies carved on the balustrade of the Temple of Athene Nikephoros at Pergamon. They were executed during the reign of Eumenes II (197–159 BC), the son of Attalos I of Pergamon who overcame the *Galatae*. Accuracy was observed in the carving of the balustrade frieze, of which there were numerous panels, the actual trophies having doubtless been available to the sculptors. In Ill. 88 the bull-headed object, probably a *carnyx*, should in particular be noted, while in Ill. 89 the most interesting object is the chariot yoke clearly copied from the wooden original, and comparing closely with the remains of actual yokes from La Tène itself, and from a find in Ireland. The long shield with pronounced umbo and midrib, typical of the Celts, is well in evidence, but in the coat of mail, the humped shield with running animal, and the helmets, may be seen that mixture of Mediterranean armour to be expected amongst the *Galatae* by the end of the third century BC. R. Bohn (1885) for only detailed study.

90,91 The early history and commemorative purposes of the Orange arch are complex, but conquest of the Gauls is one theme not in doubt. While relying for the general idea on the trophy friezes at Pergamon, the Orange sculpture is not a copy of the Greek, and types of Roman and Gaulish arms proper to the first century BC can be identified. In Ill. 90, long shield and *carnyx* are much in evidence, and Celtic proper names can be seen on some of the shields. Decapitated heads, such as the Gauls prized, are also shown. The battle scene in Ill. 91 is a good illustration of Classical literary descriptions, and the difference in stature between Gaul and Roman should be noted. P. Coussin (1924). I. A. Richmond (1933).

93 Recent investigation has shown that these objects were not part of a horse trapping as previously accepted. The terminals are of hollow sheet bronze, one of them still retaining a solid cast bird-head finial. Otherwise the decoration,

different on each horn, is executed in the same engraved technique, and demonstrates motifs of the early phase of the British La Tène art style. The terminals, which were clearly meant to be used as a pair, probably date from the second half of the third century BC. The size and curve of the terminals suggest their use on the horns of *bos primigenius* (aurochs), and a reconstruction of this sort is shown. National Museum of Antiquities, Edinburgh. R. J. C. Atkinson and S. Piggott (1955).

94 The somewhat stiff and symmetrical arrangement of the plastic ornament on the roundel is representative of Irish bronzes derived from the eastern British tradition of La Tène art. The trumpet probably dates from the first century AD. The trumpet itself consists of a tapering bronze tube, almost semicircular in its curve, and derives from the same tradition as those seen in Ill. 93, stemming originally from ox horns. National Museum, Dublin. R. J. C. Atkinson and S. Piggott (1955) for stylistic comments. C. Fox (1946) Plate XIIa, for whole trumpet.

97 These coins exhibit points of interest on cult. The Celtic coins further witness to the geographical range of this currency in Europe, and, of these, the British coin is important for its historical and linguistic connections.
(a) Gold coin from Pannonia. This belongs to the currency of the east Celtic tribes, the Boii and others who extended from Bohemia to the Lower Danube. The Obverse shows a Janus head, already noted as a symbol of deity. The Reverse shows a horse with a female rider, and this must be another manifestation of Epona, or whatever the nature-goddess may have been called in that region. K. Pink (1939), Plate XI, 235.
(b) Gold coin of the Aulerci Cenomani, a tribe settled in the area of Le Mans. The Reverse composition is ultimately derived from the stater of Philip II of Macedon, but coming through the medium of coins of the Treveri. Here the subject has been entirely adapted to Celtic mythological symbolism with emphasis on the single horse, the streamers and emblems which are conspicuous on many related Gaulish coins, and on the conducting figure holding a Celtic torc in its hand. The chariot has become unimportant and vestigial. Cf. La Tour (1892), no. 6493.
(c) Gold coin of Tasciovanus, probably the son of Cassivellaunus the Belgic king who opposed Caesar in Britain, but certainly his successor. The Obverse of this coin shows an abbreviation of his name with the word RICON which is recognizable as a version of a Celtic word meaning 'kingship'. Tasciovanus was the first of the kings of the Catuvellauni to place his name on coins, and RICON is thought to have been a riposte to the client kinglets of Rome, amongst the Atrebates on the south coast, who enjoyed the title REX. On the Reverse, the horse continues to be an auspicious emblem. Tasciovanus died about AD 15 and was succeeded by his son Cunobelinus. R. P. Mack (1953), no. 184.
(d) Denarius of Augustus, from a mint in Asia Minor. The Reverse face of this coin illustrates a building that is of no normal Classical type, but which exhibits many of the features deduced for Romano-Celtic temples. No direct association can be claimed although some allusion to Celtic territory might not be inappropriate on coins of Augustus, or in reference to Julius Caesar if the building should be connected with him, as has sometimes been suggested. Allowing for the limitations of the coin engraver, one may note the relatively tall *cella*, with window over the door, and the colonnade which does not support the pediment, but indicates a covered way along each wall. The architrave bears an inscription IMP CAESAR, and a winged figure of Victory supported by two warriors stands on the pediment. British Museum, *Catalogue* (*Empire*) I, p. 103, no. 631.

98 This fragmentary bronze calendar, of which the left-hand portion is here seen, is the oldest extensive example of writing in a Celtic language. A late-first-century BC date, or one at least within the reign of Augustus, seems probable on philological and historical grounds. Despite its Roman appearance in lettering and entablature, the composition is wholly Gaulish, and must have been the work of the native learned order, the druids, at a point before their final suppression. Enough of the tablet survives to show that it measured some 1.5 × 1 m, and that it was divided into sixteen vertical columns providing a table of sixty-two consecutive lunar months, with two intercalary months. It is possible that this sequence formed part of a nineteen-year system which was completed on other tablets. Each month is divided into a bright half and a dark half, the division being marked by the conspicuous word ATENOUX 'returning night'. The days are numbered I–XV in the light halves, and I–XIV or XV in the dark halves. Special abbreviations mark certain days, and the months are marked with the abbreviations MAT or ANM, 'good' and 'not good' signifying auspicious or otherwise. The names of the months are thought to have been learned inventions of the calendar makers, there being no need for such under more barbaric conditions. Festivals are not named, but there are calendar indications for ones corresponding to Beltine and Lugnasad although none to Samain which was the important autumnal division between the years in Ireland. The first column begins with one of the intercalary months, and is followed by the months SAMON and DUMANN; the other columns contain four months in proper

sequence, except in col. 9, not here included, which contains the other intercalary month with two ordinary ones. The public nature of the calendar, and the frequency of abbreviations, suggests a wide familiarity with reading. The peg holes opposite each diurnal date, and other features, suggest that the Gaulish calendar owed its origin to Greek originals at a somewhat earlier period.

The original is in the Palais des Arts at Lyons. E. MacNeill (1928).

99 This inscription, found in the Gallo-Roman settlement at Alise-Sainte-Reine, Côte d'Or, is important as an example of the Gaulish language, set in Roman epigraphy, but also because of the inclusion therein of the name Alesia, thus identifying the site, apart from other kinds of evidence, with the Alesia where Vercingetorix made his last stand against the Romans. The first word in the inscription is the dedicator's Latin name, but thereafter the words are Gaulish. GOBEDBI, in the last line but three, means 'smiths' and is cognate with words in Irish and Welsh. The place-name is seen in the last line. The terms of the dedication are somewhat obscure, but it is made to a god Cuetis.

The original is in the Musée Alesia. A convenient commentary on the inscription is given in A. Grenier (1945), 309–311.

100 In this bronze votive plaque with engraved subject and inscription the drawing of the two-wheeled vehicle and the horse is clumsy; they are too obscure to be informative for the type of harness. The inscription shows a simple dedication by Satigenus son of Solemnis to the goddess Epona. This, and other evidence, shows Alesia to have been an important centre of the cult of Epona whose attribute is the mare, and whose name is derived from a Celtic word for horse. St Germain-en-Laye. R. Magnen and E. Thevenot (1953).

101 In the foreground is the village of Alise-Sainte-Reine, and north of it the steep-sided hill on which was the Gaulish *oppidum*. The settlement extended along this elevated plateau to the east, and fortifications blocked the easier slopes of ascent. Caesar's main siege-works lay around the hill, especially on the low ground to the left, as seen in this photograph, and towards the railway at Les Laumes in the background. The Gallo-Roman town that grew up after the defeat of Vercingetorix in 52 BC, was situated immediately to the east of the Gaulish stronghold. As compared with other Gaulish *oppida* of the period, Alesia was neither large nor strongly defended. Its especial sanctity to Epona, 'the holy queen', must have been a determining factor in its choice for a last stand by the Gaulish leader.

102 In this relief there is no inscription but the attributes are sufficiently clear. In the upper register, Epona is seated in the centre and flanked by three horses on either side. In the lower register, a four-wheeled vehicle with driver is drawn by three horses, and the sacrifice of a pig is also being undertaken. The mythological allusions in the triple arrangement of the horses will be noted. Landesmuseum, Stuttgart.

103 This inscription is one of a number of epigraphic witnesses of Roman times for a Celtic god with a name related to, or identical with, that of Taranis who is mentioned by Lucan. Derived from a Celtic word for thunder, the name might be of very general application amongst the Celtic deities. Landesmuseum, Stuttgart.

110 The Pfalzfeld pillar is the most remarkable example of surviving Celtic stone-work which, unlike the sculpture in the Provençal sanctuaries of Entremont and Roquepertuse, was far removed from direct Mediterranean inspiration and technique. The monument was originally about 2 m high, and was surmounted by a head which was destroyed in the seventeenth century (see Ill. 109). Individual details such as the rope-pattern edges, and the column-like base, are of Etruscan derivation, but the composition as a whole is Celtic, and the pear-shaped face, surmounted by a massive 'leaf-crown', is the same on all four sides as is the rest of the stylized floral carving. The foreheads are marked with a trefoil (compare Ill. 91). The inverted 'fleur de lys' below the chin invites comparison with the arrangement of three tassels below the face on the Reinheim torc (Ill. 34). The monument presumably dates to the turn of the fifth and fourth centuries BC. Landesmuseum, Bonn.

111 This piece of iconography identifies the anthropomorphic deity with the boar, itself the most conspicuous emblem of the Gauls in the last phase of independence. The attribution might be appropriate to any tribal god, and a few Gallo-Roman dedications incorporate Celtic 'boar' or 'pig' words. The treatment of the boar suggests a date in the first century BC. St Germain-en-Laye.

112 This figure is made of sheet bronze with details in *repoussé*. The face and head were cast, not beaten, and the six separate pieces forming the whole were fastened together. One eye, of blue and white glass, is still in position. A torc encircles the neck, and the legs are arranged in the 'yogi' squatting position which may have been the normal sitting posture amongst the Celts. Generally considered to have been the work of a bronzesmith accustomed to making cauldrons, and to be of early Gallo-Roman times, a third-century BC date has recently been

proposed. St Germain-en-Laye. The original study is by R. Lantier, *Monuments Piot* XXXIV (1934).

115 The two faces of the Holzgerlingen stone statue are identical, but the one shown here is better preserved. Ill. 116 shows them in profile (right), as well as the broken horns reconstructed. Note also the single arm extended across the body, and the belt, or girdle. The Janus motif, of Etruscan origin, seems to have been propagated northwards by the Rhône route, and the treatment of the Holzgerlingen face has some affinity with the more sophisticated work at Roquepertuse. Landesmuseum, Stuttgart.

117 This figure is a unique piece, though there is no information about the destroyed upper portion. The presence of a naturalistic single arm placed across the figure suggests a ritual pose, seen also in Ill. 115, and known from carvings in Ireland. The geometric ornament is in the style of the native art in the Waldalgesheim grave, and indicates a late-fourth-century date. It is possible that the curvilinear design on the lower part of the stone, may represent the folds of a garment while the upper, rectilinear, ornament may owe something to the square-cut cape worn by the Roquepertuse figures. Alternatively, if the stone figure was sufficiently tall, the band of rectilinear ornament may represent a belt, with or without metal mounts, and this view is supported by the continuation of the curvilinear design above the arm. Landesmuseum, Stuttgart.

118 This head, of which both faces and a side view are illustrated, is a much rougher production than any of the foregoing pieces of Celtic stonework. It is a northern outlier of the Rhenish group, but the wedge-shaped nose links it with Ill. 115. The up-turned mouth, rounded eyes, and the presence of ears, so that the head has a genuine lateral aspect, are points of merit. The moulded flange at the base of the neck suggests that the head formed the finial of some kind of pillar. Landesmuseum, Bonn. P. Jacobsthal (1944) treats of all the pieces in Ills. 110, 115, 117 and 118. Leichlingen he miscalls Solingen.

122 Emain Macha is the traditional royal centre of the Ulaid, a people on whom centres the Ulster Cycle of early Irish epic literature. The earthworks give the impression of having been for sacred or funerary ends rather than for human habitation. Macha was an Irish equivalent of Epona with marked horse attributes and associations.

124 The Hill of Tara is the most important of royal centres in traditional literature, and its geographical setting, a limestone ridge with extensive views over rich pasture land, made it particularly suitable for early settlement. A chambered tumulus of the Early Bronze Age is the oldest monument on the hill so far recognized, but the circular earthworks would appear to date mainly to the traditional period of occupation in the centuries immediately preceding, and following, the opening of the Christian era. One site recently excavated has produced Roman pottery of the first to third centuries AD, but the general aspect of the monuments, seen in the photograph, is ritual or funerary rather than habitational. Further excavations will go far to elucidate important questions in Irish archaeology and early history. S. P. Ó Ríordáin (1954) for general description.

129 La Tène gives its name to the Iron Age culture, and art style, succeeding that of Hallstatt. In the photograph, the retaining walls of the Canal de la Thièle are seen projecting into the lake and at the point where the short oblique wall touches land was the area of the great deposit of weapons, with other equipment, and wooden piles. Prior to drainage operations, the lake had stood at a higher level, but the photograph also shows that the ostensible votive deposit was made at the mouth of the old river Thièle whose former ramifications can be seen as dark bands. La Tène is situated near Préfargier at the north-eastern end of the lake. The alignment of the canal is approximately NE–SW.

137 This medallion is of the early eighth century AD. In the centre is an open-work triskele design in silver. This is surrounded by a bronze border with champlevé enamel and millifiore glass settings, and the terminals of an equal-armed cross project beyond. This piece is included here as a reminder of that final contribution of Celtic tradition to the life of Europe recreated in the Irish Church. National Museum, Dublin. M. and L. de Paor (1958).

List of Museums

containing important collections bearing on the archaeology of the Celts

Austria
- Graz, Steirisches Landesmuseum Joanneum.
- Hallstatt, Museum.
- Klagenfurt, Kärntner Landesmuseum.
- Vienna, Naturhistorisches Museum.

Belgium
- Brussels, Musée Royale d'Art et d'Histoire.

Czechoslovakia
- Prague, National Museum.

Denmark
- Copenhagen, National Museum.

France
- Aix-en-Provence, Musée Granet.
- Bourges, Musée de.
- Châtillon-sur-Seine, Musée de.
- Epernay, Musée.
- Lyons, Musée des Beaux Arts.
- Marseilles, Musée Borély.
- Paris, Musée des Antiquités Nationales, St Germain-en-Laye.
- Rheims, Musée de la Société Champagnoise.
- Strasbourg, Musée archéologique.

Germany
- Berlin, Staatliche Museen.
- Bonn, Rheinisches Landesmuseum.
- Koblenz, Mittelrheinisches Museum.
- Mainz, Römisch-Germanisches Zentralmuseum.
- Munich, Vor- und Frühgeschichtliche Staatssammlung.
- Saarbrücken, Saarlandmuseum.
- Speyer, Historisches Museum der Pfalz.
- Stuttgart, Württembergisches Landesmuseum.
- Trier, Rheinisches Landesmuseum.

Great Britain
- Cardiff, National Museum of Wales.
- Edinburgh, National Museum of Antiquities.
- London, British Museum.

Hungary
- Budapest, National Museum.

Ireland
- Belfast, Municipal Museum.
- Dublin, National Museum.

Italy
- Bologna, Museo Civico.
- Rome, Museo Nazionale.

Portugal
- Guimarães, Museu de Martins Sarmento.

Spain
- Barcelona, Museo Arqueológico.
- Madrid, Museo Nacional.

Switzerland
- Bern, Historisches Museum.
- Neuchâtel, Musée d'Art et d'Histoire.
- Zürich, Schweizerisches Landesmuseum.

Select Bibliography

Note: The majority of works cited refer to the chapter notes, and the supplementary notes on the illustrations but some additional titles are included.

ÅBERG, N., 1931. *Bronzezeitliche und Früheisenzeitliche Chronologie*, Teil II, Hallstattzeit, Stockholm.

ALLEN, D., 1944. 'The Belgic Dynasties of Britain and their coins', *Archaeologia* XC, 1–46. London.

ALTHIN, C. A., 1945. *Felszeichnungen von Skåne*, 2 vols, Lund.

AMSCHLER, J. W., 1949. 'Ur- und Frühgeschichtliche Haustierfunde aus Österreich', *Archaeologia Austriaca* III, 1–100.

APPLEBAUM, S., 1954. 'The Agriculture of the British Early Iron Age as exemplified at Figheldean Down, Wiltshire', *Proc. Prehistoric Society* XX, 103–114. Cambridge.

ATKINSON, R. J. C. and PIGGOTT, S., 1955. 'The Torrs Chamfrein', *Archaeologia* XCVI, 197–235. London.

BEHN, F., 1954. *Musikleben in Altertum und Frühen Mittelalter.* Stuttgart.

BEHRENS, G., 1944. *Germanische und Gallische Götter in Römischem Gewand*, Römisch-Germanisches Zentralmuseum. Mainz. 1950. 'Kelten-Münzen im Rheingebiet', *Prähistorische Zeitschrift* XXXIV/V, 336–354. Berlin.

BELOCH, K. J., 1926. *Römische Geschichte.* Berlin.

BENOIT, F., 1955. *L'Art Primitif Mediterranéen de la Vallée du Rhône.* Paris. 1956. 'Relations de Marseille Grecque avec le Monde Occidental', *Revista di Studi Liguri* XXII, 1–32. Bordighera.

BERSU, G., 1940. 'Excavations at Little Woodbury, Wiltshire, Part I', *Proc. Prehistoric Society* VI, 30–111. Cambridge.

BIEŃKOWSKI, P., 1908. *Die Darstellung der Gallier in der hellenistichen Kunst.* Vienna.
1928. *Les Celtes dans les arts mineurs gréco-romains.* Cracow.

BINCHY, D. A. ed., 1936. *Studies in Early Irish Law*, Roy. Irish Acad. Dublin.
1941. *Críth Gablach*, Stationery Office. Dublin.
1943. 'The Linguistic and Historical Value of the Irish Law Tracts', Rhŷs Lecture, *Proc. British Acad.* XXIX, 195–227. London.

BITTEL, K., 1934. *Die Kelten in Württemberg.* Berlin-Leipzig.

BITTEL, K. and RIETH, A., 1951. *Die Heuneburg an der oberen Donau.* Stuttgart.

BLANCHET, A., 1905. *Traité des Monnaies Gauloises.* Paris.

BOGAERS, J. E. A., 1955. *De Gallo-Romeinse Tempels Te Elst...*, (English Summary). 'S-Gravenhage.

BOHN, R., 1885. 'Das Heiligtum der Athena Polias Nikephoros' *Altertümer von Pergamon* II. Berlin.

BOSCH-GIMPERA, P., 1940. 'Two Celtic Waves in Spain', Rhŷs Lecture, *Proc. British Acad.* XXVI, 25–148. London.

BRADFORD, J. S. P. and GOODCHILD, R. G., 1939. 'Excavations at Frilford, Berkshire, 1937–8', *Oxoniensia* IV, 1–70. Oxford.

BRISSON, A. and HATT, J. J., 1955. 'Cimetières gaulois et gallo-romains à enclos en Champagne', *Revue Archéologique de l'Est et du Centre-Est* VI, 313–333. Dijon.

BRØNDSTED, J., 1940. *Danmarks Oltid* III, Jernalderen. Copenhagen.

CARDOZO, M., 1948. *Citaña e Sabroso.* Guimarães.

CHADWICK, H. M., 1913. 'Some German River Names', *Essays and Studies presented to William Ridgeway*, 315–322. Cambridge.
1945. *The Nationalities of Europe.* Cambridge.

CHILDE, V. G., 1929. *The Danube in Prehistory.* Oxford.
1948. 'The Final Bronze Age in the Near East and in Temperate Europe', *Proc. Prehistoric Society* XIV, 177–195. Cambridge.
1950. *Prehistoric Migrations in Europe.* Oslo.
1957. *The Dawn of European Civilisation* (6th edit.). London

CHILVER, G. E. F., 1941. *Cisalpine Gaul.* Oxford.

CLARK, J. G. D., 1952. *Prehistoric Europe: The Economic Basis*. London.

CLARKE, R. R. and HAWKES, C. F. C., 1955. 'An Iron Anthropoid Sword from Shouldham, Norfolk, with related Continental and British Weapons', *Proc. Prehistoric Society* XXI, 198–227. Cambridge.

CLARKE, R. R., 1951. 'A Hoard of Metalwork of the Early Iron Age from Ringstead, Norfolk', *Proc. Prehistoric Society* XVII, 214–225. Cambridge.
1954. 'The Early Iron Age Treasure from Snettisham, Norfolk', *Proc. Prehistoric Society* XX, 27–86.

COON, C. S., 1939. *The Races of Europe*. London.

COUSSIN, P., 1926. 'Les Frises de l'Arc d'Orange', *Revue Archéologique* XIX, 29–54. Paris.
1927. 'Les Armes Gaulois sur les Monuments Grecs', *Revue Archéologique* XXV, 142–176, 301–325; XXVI, 43–79.

CROSS, T. P. and SLOVER, C. H., 1936. *Ancient Irish Tales*. London.

CURTIS, E., 1950. *A History of Ireland*. London.

CURWEN, E. C., 1954. *The Archaeology of Sussex*. London.

DANIEL, G. E., 1954. 'Who are the Welsh?' Rhŷs Lecture, *Proc. British Acad.* XL (1954), 145–167.

DÉCHELETTE, J., 1913–14. *Manuel d'Archéologie* II, 2e et 3e parties. Paris.

DEGRASSI, A., 1954. *Fasti Capitolini*. Turin.

DEHN, W., 1937. 'Der Ring von Otzenhausen ...', *Germania* XXI, 78–82, 229–232. Römisch-Germanische Kommission, Berlin.
1957. 'Die Heuneburg beim Talhof ...', *Fundbericht aus Schwaben* XIV, 78–99. Stuttgart.

DILLON, M., 1943. 'Germanic and Celtic', *Journ. English and Germanic Philology* XLII, 492–498. Illinois.
1947. 'The Archaism of Irish Tradition', Rhŷs Lecture, *Proc. British Acad.* XXXIII, 245–264.
Ed. transl., 1949. See: Sjoestedt, M. L. (1949).
Ed., 1954. *Early Irish Society*. Dublin.

DINSMOOR, W. B., 1950. *The Architecture of Ancient Greece*. London.

DIXON, P., 1940. *The Iberians of Spain*. Oxford.

DOBBS, M. E., 1913. 'A Burial Custom of the Iron Age ...', *Journ. Roy. Soc. Antiq. Ireland* XLIII, 129–132. Dublin.

DUIGNAN, M., 1944. 'Irish Agriculture in Early Historic Times', *Journ. Roy. Soc. Antiq. Ireland* LXXIV, 124–145. Dublin.

DYGGVE, E., 1954. 'Gorm's temple and Harald's slave-church at Jelling', *Acta Archaeologica* XXV, 221–239. Copenhagen.

FILIP, J., 1956. *Keltové Ve Střední Europě* (Die Kelten in Mitte Europa). Prague.

FOX, C., 1946. *A Find of the Early Iron Age from Llyn Cerrig Bach, Anglesey*. Cardiff.

GIMBUTAS, M., 1956. *The Prehistory of Eastern Europe* I. Harvard.

GOESSLER, P., 1929. *Der Silberring von Trichtingen*. Berlin-Leipzig.

GRENIER, A., 1943. 'Sanctuaires celtiques et tombe du héros', *Comptes Rendus d'Acad. des Inscriptions et Belles Lettres*, 1943, 360–371. Paris.
1945. *Les Gaulois*. Paris.

GRIFFITH, G. T., 1935. *The Mercenaries of the Hellenistic World*. Cambridge.

VAN HAMEL, A. G., 1934. 'Aspects of Celtic Mythology', Rhŷs Lecture, *Proc. British Acad.* XX, 207–242.

HANČAR, F., 1956. *Das Pferd in prähistorischer und früher historischer Zeit*. Vienna.

HATT, G., 1949. *Oldtidsagre* (with English Summary). Copenhagen.

HATT, J. J., 1955. 'Commence grec du VIe et commerce italo-grec du Ve siècle', *Revue Archéologique de l'Est et du Centre-Est* VI, 150–152. Dijon.

HAWKES, C. F. C., 1948. 'From Bronze to Iron Age: Middle Europe, Italy, and the North and West', *Proc. Prehistoric Society* XIV, 196–218.
1952. 'Las Relaciones en el bronce final entre le Peninsula Iberica y las Islas Britanicas', *Ampurias* XIV, 81–118. Barcelona.
1956. 'The British Iron Age: Cultures, Chronology, and Peoples', *Actas de las IV Sesion, Madrid*, 1954, Congreses Internacionales ... Prehistoricas ... Zaragoza.

HAWKES, C. F. C. and DUNNING, G. C., 1930. 'The Belgae of Gaul and Britain', *Archaeological Journal* LXXXVII, 150–335. London.

HAWKES, C. F. C. and HULL, M. R., 1947. *Camulodunum*, Soc. Antiq. London.

HENCKEN, H. O'N., 1932. *The Archaeology of Cornwall and Scilly*. London.

HENCKEN, H., 1955. *Indo-European Languages and Archaeology*, American Anthropological Assoc. Memoir No. 84. Wisconsin.

HENRY, F., 1940. *Irish Art in the Early Christian Period*. London.
1954. *Early Christian Irish Art*. Dublin.

HOLDER, A., 1896–1904. *Alt-Celtischer Sprachschatz*. Leipzig.

HULL, E., 1907. 'Observations of Classical Writers on the Habits of the Celtic Nations, as illustrated from Irish Records', *The Celtic Review* III, 62–76; 138–154. Edinburgh.

HUXLEY, J. S. and HADDON, A. C., 1935. *We Europeans*. London.

JACKSON, K. H., 1953. *Language and History in Early Britain*. Edinburgh.
1954. 'Two Early Scottish Names', *Scottish Historical Review* XXXIII, 14–18. Edinburgh.
1955. 'The Pictish Language' being Chapter IV in: F. T. Wainwright, ed. (1955), *infra*.

JACOBY, F., 1923. *Fragmente der griechischen Historiker* I. Berlin.

JACOBSTHAL, P., 1941. 'Imagery in Early Celtic Art', Rhŷs Lecture, *Proc. British Acad.* XXVII, 301–320.
1944. *Early Celtic Art*. Oxford.

JOFFROY, R., 1954. *Le Trésor de Vix*. Paris.

JONES, G. and JONES, T., 1949. *The Mabinogion*. London.

KELLER, J., 1955. 'Das Fürstengrab von Rheinheim...', *Germania* XXXIII, 33–44. Römisch-Germanische Kommission, Frankfurt a.M.

KENDRICK, T. D., 1928. *The Druids*. London.

KENNY, J. F., 1929. *The Sources for the Early History of Ireland*. New York.

KIMMIG, W., 1940a. *Die Urnenfelderkultur in Baden*. Berlin.
1940b. 'Ein Keltenschild aus Ägypten', *Germania* XXIV, 106–111. Römisch-Germanische Kommission, Frankfurt a.M.
1952–54. 'Où en est l'étude de la civilisation des Champs d'urnes en France', *Revue Archéologique de l'Est et du Centre-Est* III, 137–172; V, 7–28, 209–232. Dijon.
1954. 'Zur Urnenfelderkultur in Südwesteuropa', *Festschrift für Peter Goessler*. Stuttgart.

KIMMIG, W. and REST, W., 1953. 'Ein Fürstengrab der Späten Hallstattzeit von Kappel-am-Rhein', *Jahrbuch des Römisch-Germanischen Zentralmuseums Mainz* I, 179–216.

KIRCHNER, H., 1955. *Die Menhire in Mitteleuropa und der Menhirgedanke*. Mainz.

KLINDT-JENSEN, O., 1950. *Foreign Influences in Denmark's Early Iron Age*. Copenhagen.
1953. *Bronzekedelen fra Brå* (English Summary). Aarhus.
1957. *Denmark before the Vikings*. London.

KOETHE, H., 1933. 'Die Keltischen Rund- und Vierecktempel der Kaiserzeit', *23 Bericht der Römische-Germanischen Kommission*, 10–108. Berlin.

KOSSACK, G., 1953. 'Pferdegeschirr aus Gräbern der älteren Hallstattzeit Bayerns', *Jahrbuch des Römisch-Germanischen Zentralmuseums Mainz* I, 111–178.
1954a. 'Zur Hallstattzeit in Bayern', *Bayerische Vorgeschichtsblätter* XX, 1–42. Munich.
1954b. *Studien zum Symbolgut der Urnenfelder- und Hallstattzeit Mitteleuropas*. Frankfurt a.M.

KRÄMER, W., ed. 1958. *Neue Ausgrabungen in Deutschland*. Berlin.

LACROIX, B., 1956. 'Un sanctuaire de source du IV siècle aux Fontaines-Salées', *Revue Archéologique de l'Est et du Centre-Est* VII, 245–264.

LAET, S. DE and LAMBRECHTS, P., 1954. 'Traces du culte de Mithras sur le chaudron de Gundestrup?' *Actes III Session, Zürich, 1950*, 304–306. Congrès International des sciences préhistoriques... Zürich.

LAMBRECHTS, P., 1942. *Contributions à l'Étude des Divinités Celtiques*. Bruges.

LEGGE, M. D., 1946. 'The Inauguration of Alexander III', *Proc. Society of Antiquaries of Scotland*, LXXX, 73–82.

LENGYEL, L., 1954. *L'Art Gaulois dans les Médailles*. Paris.

LINDQUIST, S., 1927. 'Uppsala Hednatempel', *Ord. och Bild*, 641 ff. Stockholm.

LIPPOLD, G., 1950. *Griechische Plastik*. Munich.

LOUIS, M. and TAFFANEL, O. and J., 1955. *Le Premier Âge du Fer Languedocien*, 1ère partie: *Les Habitats*. Bordighera-Montpellier.

MACK, R. P., 1953. *The Coinage of Ancient Britain*. London.

MALUQUER DE MOTES, J., 1954a. *El Yacimiento Hallstattico de Cortes de Navarra* I. Pamplona.
1954b. 'Pueblas Celtas', *Historia de España* I, iii, 5–194. ed. R. M. Pidal. Madrid.

MAGNEN, R. and THEVENOT, E., 1953. *Épona, déesse gauloise ...* Bordeaux.

MARIËN, M. E., 1952. *Oud-België*. Antwerp.

MILNE, J. G., 1940. 'The "Philippus" at Rome', *Journal of Roman Studies* XXX, 11–15. London.

MITCHELL, G. F., 1946. 'Evidence of Early Agriculture', *Journ. Roy. Soc. Antiq. Ireland* LXXVI, 16–18.

MORTON, F., 1953. *Hallstatt und die Hallstattzeit*. Hallstatt.

MOZSOLICS, A., 1952. 'Die Ausgrabungen in Tószeg im Jahre 1948', *Acta Archaeologica Hungarica* II, 35–69. Budapest.
1956. 'Spätbronzezeitliche Durchbrochenene Wagenbeschläge', *Acta Archaeologica Hungarica* VII, 1–16. Budapest.

MÜLLER-KARPE, H., 1955. 'Das urnenfelderzeitliche Wagengrab von Hart a.d. Alz', *Bayerische Vorgeschichtsblätter* XXI, 46–75. Munich.

MURPHY, G., 1955a. *Saga and Myth in Ancient Ireland*. Dublin.
1955b. *The Ossianic Lore and Romantic Tales of Medieval Ireland*. Dublin.

MYRES, J. L., 1907. 'The Sigynnae of Herodotus', in *Anthropological Essays Presented to Edward Burnett Tylor*, 225–276. Oxford.

MacNeill, E., 1919. *Phases of Irish History*. Dublin.
1923. 'On the Calendar of Coligny', *Eriu* X, 1–67.
1933. 'The Pretannic Background', *Journ. Roy. Soc. Antiq. Ireland* LXIII, 1–28. Dublin.

McClintock, H. F., 1948. 'Cuchullain's Hair', *Journ. Roy. Soc. Antiq. Ireland* LXXVIII, 184–185.
1950. *Old Irish and Highland Dress*. Dundalk.

Nash-Williams, V. E., 1950. *The Early Christian Monuments of Wales*. Cardiff.

de Navarro, J. M., 1928. 'The Coming of the Celts', *Cambridge Ancient History* VII, 41–74. Cambridge.
1936. 'A Survey of Research on an Early Phase of Celtic Culture', *Proc. British Acad.* XXII, 297–341.
1952. 'The Celts in Britain and their Art' in *The Heritage of Early Britain* (ed. M. D. Knowles), 56–82. London.

O'Brien, D., 1932. 'The Féni', *Eriu* XI, 182–183. Dublin.

Ó Danachair, C., 1955. 'The Flail and other Threshing Methods', *Journ. Cork Hist. and Arch. Soc.* LX, 6–14. Cork.

Ó Duigeannaín, M., 1940. 'On the Medieval Sources for the Legend of Cenn (Crom) Croích of Magh Slécht', *Féil-Sgríbhinn Eóin Mhic Néill*, 296–306. Dublin.

O'Rahilly, T. F., 1946. *Early Irish History and Mythology*. Dublin.

ÓRíordáin, S. P., 1946. 'Prehistory in Ireland 1937–46', *Proc. Prehistoric Society* XII, 142–171. Cambridge.
1953. *Antiquities of the Irish Countryside*. London.
1954. *Tara: The Monuments on the Hill*. Dundalk.

do Paço, A., 1953. 'Citânia de Sanfins, II, Muralhas', *Zephyrus* IV, 489–494. Salamanca.

de Paor, M. and L., 1958. *Early Christian Ireland*. London.

Paret, O., 1935. 'Das Fürstengrab der Hallstattzeit von Bad Cannstatt', Anhang I der *Fundberichte aus Schwaben* N.F. VIII. Stuttgart.

Piggott, S., 1941. 'The Sources of Geoffrey of Monmouth', *Antiquity* XV, 269–286, 305–319. Southampton.
1949. *British Prehistory*. Oxford.
1952. 'Celtic Chariots on Roman Coins', *Antiquity* XXVI, 87–88.
1953. 'Three Metal-Work Hoards of the Roman Period from Southern Scotland', *Proc. Soc. Antiq. Scotland* LXXXVII, 1–50. Edinburgh.
1958 ed. *The Prehistoric Peoples of Scotland*. Edinburgh.

Piggott, S. and Daniel, G. E., 1951. *A Picture Book of Ancient British Art*. Cambridge.

Pink, K., 1939. *Die Münzprägung der Ostkelten und ihrer Nachbaren*. Budapest.

Pittioni, R., 1954. *Urgeschichte des Österreichischen Raumes*. Vienna.

Popescu, D., 1956. 'Einige Bermerkungen zur Bronzezeit Siebenbürgens', *Acta Archaeologica Hungarica* VII, 301–320.

Powell, T. G. E., 1948. 'Celtic Origins: A Stage in the Enquiry', *Journ. Roy. Anthropological Inst.* LXXVIII, 71–79. London.
1950. 'The Celtic Settlement of Ireland', *H. M. Chadwick Memorial Studies*, 171–196. Cambridge.

Radford, C. A. R., 1954. 'The Tribes of Southern Britain', *Proc. Prehistoric Soc.* XX, 1–26. Cambridge.
1955. 'Contributions to a Study of the Belgae', *Proc. Prehistoric Soc.* XXI, 249–256. Cambridge.

Rees, W., 1951. *An Historical Atlas of Wales*. Cardiff.

Rice, T. Talbot, 1957. *The Scythians*. London.

Richmond, I. A., 1933. 'Commemorative Arches and City Gates in the Augustan Age', *Journ. of Roman Studies* XXIII, 149–174.
1955. *Roman Britain*. London.

Riegl, A., 1893. *Stilfragen, Grundlegungen zu einer Geschichte der Ornamentik*. Berlin.

Riek, G., 1941. 'Ein hallstättischer Grabhügel mit Menschendarstellung bei Stokach bei Reutlingen', *Germania* XXV, 85–89. Römisch-Germanische Kommission, Frankfurt a.M.

Rix, H., 1954. 'Zur Verbreitung und Chronologie einiger Keltischer Ortsnamentypen', *Festschrift für Peter Goessler*, 99–107. Stuttgart.

Röder, J., 1948. 'Der Goloring', *Bonner Jahrbücher* CXLVIII, 81–132. Bonn.

Rosenberg, G., 1927. *Hjortspringfundet*. Copenhagen.

Rostovtzeff, M., 1922. *Iranians and Greeks*. Oxford.

Ryan, J., 1946. 'The Convention of Druim Ceat', *Journ. Roy. Soc. Antiq. Ireland* LXXVI, 33–55.

von Sacken, E., 1868. *Das Grabfeld von Hallstatt*. Vienna.

Sandars, N. K., 1957. *Bronze Age Cultures in France*. Cambridge.

Schiek, S., 1954. 'Das Hallstattgrab von Vilsingen', *Festschrift für Peter Goessler*, 150–167. Stuttgart.

Sjoestedt, M. L., 1940. *Dieux et Héros des Celtes*. Paris.
1949. *Gods and Heroes of the Celts*, transl. with additional notes by Myles Dillon. London.

Smith, M. A., 1957. A study on Urnfield Interpretations in Middle Europe', *Zephyrus* VIII, 195–239. Salamanca.

Stähelin, F., 1907. *Geschichte der kleinasiatischen Galater*. Berlin.

Sydenham, E. A., 1952. *The Coinage of the Roman Republic*. London.

TACKENBERG, K., 1954. *Fundkarten zur Vorgeschichte der Rheinprovinz.* Bonn.

THURNEYSEN, R., 1946. *A Grammar of Old Irish*, transl. from the German by D. A. Binchy and Osborn Bergin. Dublin.

VARLEY, W. J., 1950. 'The Hill Forts of the Welsh Marches', *Archaeological Journal* CV, 41–66. London.

VENDRYES, J., 1918. 'Les Correspondances de Vocabulaire entre l'Indo-Iranien et l'Italo-Celtique', *Mem. Soc. Linguistic* XX, 265–285. Paris.
1937. 'La Position Linguistique du Celtique', Rhŷs Lecture, *Proc. British Acad.* XXIII, 333–371.
1948. 'La Religion des Celtes', in *Les Religions de l'Europe Ancienne* III, 239–320. Paris.

VOUGA, E., 1925. *La Tène.* Leipzig.

WAINWRIGHT, F. T., ed. 1955. *The Problem of the Picts.* Edinburgh.

WEIERSHAUSEN, P., 1939. *Vorgeschichtliche Eisenhütten Deutschlands*, Mannus bd. 65. Leipzig.

WHEELER, R. E. M. and T. V., 1932. *Report on the excavation . . . in Lydney Park, Gloucestershire.* Soc. Antiq. London.

WILLIAMS, I., 1944. *Lectures on Early Welsh Poetry.* Dublin.

WYSS, R., 1955. 'Das Schwert des Korisios', *Archaeologia Helvetica* 5. Frauenfeld.
1956. 'The Sword of Korisios', *Antiquity* XXX, 27–28.

ZWICKER, J., 1934–5. *Fontes Historiae Religionis Celticae.* Bonn.

List of Illustrations

Castle, Dorset. Photo Ordnance Survey, crown copyright reserved.

50 Hill-fort at Old Oswestry. Cambridge University Collection, copyright reserved.

51 Hill-fort at Cissbury. Photo Cambridge University Collection, copyright reserved.

52 Hill-fort at Uffington Castle. Photo Cambridge University Collection, copyright reserved.

53 Hill-fort on Crickley Hill: Stone-walled entrance defences, traced by Rosalind Bignell from a drawing by Philip Dixon; entrance and long houses, drawn by Patricia Borne.

54 Iron Age hill-fort of Otzenhausen. Photo Landesmuseum, Trier.

55 Ruined stone wall of the Otzenhausen hill-fort. Photo Landesmuseum, Trier.

56 Stone-built houses in the Citañia de Sanfins. Photo Col. A. do Paço.

57 The hill-fort of Citañia de Sanfins. Photo Col. A. do Paço.

58 Air photograph of the Castro de Monte Bernorio, Palencia. Photo Servicio Geografico del Ejercito.

59 Air photograph of the Citañia de Briteiros. Photo Col. M. Cardozo.

60 Post-holes of a circular timber-framed house at Pimperne. Photo National Monuments Record Airphotographs.

61 Plan of settlement of Hallstatt date on the Goldberg. Drawn by Mrs D. D. A. Simpson.

62 Storage pits and other features within the hill-fort of Danebury. Photo Mike Rouillard.

63 Greek 'griffon cauldron' with tripod found at Ste-Colombe-sur-Seine. Drawn by Mrs Margaret Scott.

64 Fragment of Rhodian bronze flagon found at Vilsingen. Drawn by Mrs Margaret Scott.

65 Fifth-century Greek cup with Celtic gold appliqué ornament from the grave of Klein Aspergle. Württembergisches Landesmuseum, Stuttgart.

66 Gold terminals of drinking horns from the Klein Aspergle grave. Württembergisches Landesmuseum, Stuttgart.

67 Flagon and wine jar from the Klein Aspergle grave. Württembergisches Landesmuseum, Stuttgart.

68 Bronze spouted-flagon from the Waldalgesheim chariot grave. Rheinisches Landesmuseum, Bonn.

69 Detail of handle of the flagon from the Waldalgesheim chariot grave. Rheinisches Landesmuseum, Bonn.

70 Bronze Italiote situla, Waldalgesheim grave. Rheinisches Landesmuseum, Bonn.

71 Map showing Greek wine trade with the Celts. Drawn by Mrs Margaret Scott.

72 The Heuneburg hill-fort. Photo courtesy Professor Dr W. Kimmig.

73 The Heuneburg hill-fort: foundations of the defensive bastion. Photo courtesy Professor Dr W. Kimmig.

74 Map showing the expansion of the Celts between the late fifth and mid third century BC. Drawn by Mrs Margaret Scott.

75 Black graphite dish from Eschenfelden. Drawn by Mrs Margaret Scott.

76 Roman and Celtic coins: (a) Denarius *c.* 48 BC; (b) Denarius *c.* 55–54 BC; (c) Coin of the Carnutes; (d) Coin of the Baiocasses; (e) Coin of the Arverni. (a)–(c) British Museum, London, (b) and (e) Bibliothèque Nationale, Paris.

77 Coins illustrating the Celtic world: (a) Tetradrachm of Aetolia *c.* 279 BC; (b) Coin of the Remi; (c) Denarius of 118 BC; (d) Denarius of AD 69–70. (a)–(c) British Museum, London, (d) Ashmolean Museum, Oxford.

78 Iron 'currency bar' from Llyn Cerrig Bach. Drawn by Mrs Margaret Scott.

79 Hallstatt iron sword with gold-mounted hilt from Sternberg and detail of the sword hilt. Württembergisches Landesmuseum, Stuttgart.

80 Spoke-wheeled chariot on tomb wall at Kivik. Drawn by Mrs Margaret Scott.

81 Reconstruction of the Early La Tène chariot burial at La Gorge Meillet. Musée des Antiquités Nationales, St-Germain-en-Laye. Photo Lauros-Giraudon.

82 Bronze helmet from the chariot burial at La Gorge Meillet. Musée des Antiquités Nationales, St-Germain-en-Laye. Photo Giraudon.

83 Pottery vessel from the La Gorge Meillet chariot grave. Musée des Antiquités Nationales, St-Germain-en-Laye.

Index

Page numbers in italics refer to illustrations.